Praise for *Tiny Altars*

"*Tiny Altars: A Midlife Revival* is courageous. Birthed from a place of goodness, Minnesota Nice, and the women in her family, Amy Hallberg walks us through vignettes of memories on her path of self-discovery. Amy is masterful at blending life's simplicities with thought-provoking questions on race and individual truths. In the end, *Tiny Altars* gives us permission to examine the origin of our stories, lean into discomfort, and use our voices, so we may create change within ourselves and our communities. I highly recommend this book!"
— Lisa Harris, storyteller, narrative coach, CEO/founder of Lisa Harris & Company, and author of *Unveiled Beauty: Handwritten Stories from a Poetic Heart*

"How do we grow up and into our own true selves, different from who our family and our society has told us we are supposed to be? With crisp, frank writing, Amy Hallberg in *Tiny Altars: A Midlife Revival* shares her own journey of becoming—some moments a love letter to tender memories and lost relatives, other times defying and rebelling against them, but always with a steady reckoning for fuller context. Along the way, Hallberg finds herself witnessing a series of inflection points of the United States in real time, giving her a depth of perspective that allows her to see patterns and problems that most Americans miss, or choose to ignore. For Hallberg, the reckoning of her family stories parallels confronting the selective history popularized in the United States—indeed, why are there never peasants or outlaws on our family trees, never slaves and immigrants, or authoritarians, centered in America's building of democracy?"
— Ray DePaola, master coach and wayfinder doing men's work at Sunrise Journeys Life Coaching

"In *Tiny Altars*, Amy Hallberg has clearly shown up. Her book hits on so many marks and yet still reads like butter. She unpacks Minnesota's particular brand of racial injustice, the comforts and confines of religion, what it is to be a woman in America today, and alternative paths to healing. I love Amy's easy, engaging writing and had a hard time putting it down."

—Katherine Quie, PhD, LP, clinical psychologist, founder of ADHD&U, and author of *Raising Will: Surviving the Brilliance and Blues of ADHD*

"It's no coincidence that Amy calls herself a Courageous Wordsmith, because courage is what rings through this story—to wade bravely into one's own past, peer into what is murky, and come out with something gold. Amy has given us a gift by walking us through her own story and asking us to walk through ours with similar courage."

—Katherine North, author of *Holy Heathen: A Spiritual Memoir*

"What an amazing read! A perfect companion to *German Awakening*. The author's struggle is palpable, from being molded into 'the good Lutheran woman' to becoming 'the dangerous woman.' This is a story that will resonate with many. The courage in *Tiny Altars* is contagious and inspirational. A bold and relevant write for these times. So much truth and so much heart."

—Bradley L. Bodeker, author of *Bar Napkin Rants*

"With *Tiny Altars*, Amy Hallberg has masterfully brought us into her journey of self-discovery and self-love through beautifully crafted stories and insights. This book is a must read for anyone reflecting on how their past has shaped them as well as anyone inspired by creative expression as a means of resolving past traumas."

—Roseanne Cheng, co-founder of Evergreen Authors and author of *Portable Magic: How to Write and Publish a Great Book*

Praise for *Tiny Altars*

"Dazzled by Amy's vivid, heart-on-the-sleeve sharing while traversing midlife intersections of lineage, liberation, and leaving one's own legacy."
—Demetrius Bagley, nationally-recognized events producer and award-winning movie producer of *Vegucated*

"Amy Hallberg offers us stories of family and self. With a willingness to wade through the messy parts, she explores how from the ashes of one dream, another is born. This book asks us to consider the forces that shape us—and how we can shape ourselves."
—Emily P.G. Erickson, journalist and essayist

"*Who are you when you are no longer the person you thought you were destined to be?* This is not only a question that Amy introduces for herself, but one she invites readers to ponder for themselves. *Tiny Altars* is steeped in the realness of her own journey, yet also allowing a reflection of what we have all experienced—feeling like we don't belong and the struggle of finding ourselves."
—Rebecca Shisler Marshall, PhD, shamanic life and wellness coach, author of *Whole Body Upgrade*

"*Tiny Altars* is one woman's story of choosing to stay in discomfort and uncertainty while navigating the universal questions of identity, faith, and responsibility with self-awareness. Courageous."
—Keri Mangis, author of *Embodying Soul: A Return to Wholeness—A Memoir of New Beginnings*

"*Tiny Altars* is a beautiful example of what happens when we courageously dive deep into our souls and reveal the stories that need to be told. Hallberg is vulnerable, authentic, and honest. She generously shares her fears and insights, and invites us to join in on her journey of discovery and self-growth."
—Kelly D. Holstine, owner of WordHaven BookHouse and Minnesota Teacher of the Year

Praise for *Tiny Altars*

"Amy Hallberg gives us permission to find sanctuary in an increasingly bewildering world. Those seeking to live with integrity, when so much in life is shifting, will find both hope and heart in this book and in its author's compassionate, engaging perspective."
— Reverend Susan P. Thomas, ELCA

"Being surrounded by dangerous women all her life, Amy Hallberg sets out determined to not be one of them. At midlife, she leaves her traditional job to pursue writing and, inadvertently, steps onto the hero's journey to dismantle the societal conditioning inside herself. She begins to release all the stories that have held her back from being the beautiful hummingbird child that she is at heart."
— Sarah Bamford Seidelmann, author of *How Good Are You Willing to Let It Get?*

"Reading *Tiny Altars* feels like sitting around a campfire or kitchen table swapping stories with a dear friend. Amy Hallberg's experiences echo many of my own, but even if they didn't, she brings the reader right into the past with her by giving us rich sensory detail, poignant phrases, and quick wit. Scenes are so expertly painted and compelling you can't wait to flip to the next page! A book well worth reading!"
— Michelle Wolff, MEd, author of *Confetti: Unruly Bits of Poetry, Prose, and Essays*

Tiny Altars

Tiny
Altars

A Midlife Revival

Amy Hallberg

Tiny Altars: A Midlife Revival

ISBN: 979-8-9879215-0-0 (print), 979-8-9879215-1-7 (eBook)
Library of Congress Control Number: 2023903916

Book design by Paul Nylander | Illustrada Design

Published by Courageous Wordsmith
Minneapolis, Minnesota

www.AmyHallberg.com

For Grandma.
And for my aunt.

Contents

Contents

Contents

Foreword–Please read

In October 2018, I threw a party to launch my first book, a true-life novel called *German Awakening: Tales from an American Life*. One evening soon after that, I attended a Minneapolis forum for creative entrepreneurs hosted by Minnesota Public Radio.

The featured married couple spoke on stage with a local reporter about the pillars of their business, a performance company run by—and for—artists of color, and how their framework supports the mission of educating, empowering, and connecting people, extending to the wider community.

Enraptured, I sat several rows back in the dimmed auditorium, taking notes at a furious pace, wondering how I might translate that community vision to Courageous Wordsmith, my fledgling life-coach-meets-writing business. I appreciated that here in the Twin Cities, where people who look like me usually stand front and center, they'd created sanctuary space. It was tiring work, I knew, but important.

Somehow, while I was getting up from my chair and making my way to the exit so that I could bypass the reception, a young woman stopped me in the aisle. "I saw you taking notes," she said. "Do you know the speakers?"

I found myself talking with one person and then the next, nibbling a banh-mi sandwich, until suddenly I stood face-to-face with the woman I so admired, who had performed on stages all over the world. I fumbled in my purse and handed her a bookmark with the finches from my *German Awakening* book cover. "I'm an author," I said. "I've written a memoir about Germany."

She smiled brightly and held my gaze. "I've worked in Germany too."

Emboldened, I started to spell out what I really wanted to do. "I'm writing a second book about parallels between twentieth-century Germany and what's happening in America now. Sins that were always here, but I just didn't see them because of how I was raised." As I heard myself say it, I looked away. "Except who am I as a white woman, really, to be telling this story?"

And then she hit me. I mean, she actually hit me.

Not hard, to be sure, with her open palm, and I had on a down jacket to soften the blow. But she definitely hit me. This slender Black woman with a powerful presence looked me straight in the eyes.

"Please tell your story," she said. "Please. Tell it to YOUR people. Because we're tired. You have to start telling the truth." And then she turned away to greet a friend, and I was dismissed. It was a sentiment that—once I started listening—many women of color would echo. *Don't co-opt our stories, but maybe you should take on your own.*

I knew it would take me a while to integrate the message. I was meant to be in that lag and feel the discomfort. More invitations would surface later and—I now understood—they wouldn't stop. I would require new language for this clarified calling. My mind was spinning all the way back home to the suburbs.

Mentor

Origin

I could start by telling you who said and did what, and all the countless ways I tried to fix things. And how in the end, I failed anyway. But that's for later.

I want to start with another story.

When I turned six, with my grandparents and great-grandparents gathered in our living room, my mother handed me a small package as if she were bestowing a great treasure. I eagerly unwrapped it to find a plain wooden block. I held it in my palm, speechless.

"It's a chimney," Mom exclaimed. "For a dollhouse like your cousins have."

Then I heard my dad's footsteps on the stairs from the basement. He emerged, carrying the rectangular shell of a two-story, six-roomed structure.

"We'll fix it up fancy, like theirs," Mom said. I would have smiled brightly and thanked them profusely. They had it all planned out.

All my other presents went with the dollhouse. Using the smallest of hooks, my paternal Grandma Doris crocheted a tablecloth to grace a dining room table. Mom's oldest sister, Betty, went to town painting needlepoint canvases: Cushions! Rugs! An American flag! We'd hang Betty's miniature framed oil paintings on pins. Mom's middle sister, Vivian, embellished a four-poster bed and upholstered wooden chair with dainty acrylic flowers. My aunts were the daughters of a commercial artist, and it showed.

In the coming months, my parents added a roof to shelter an attic and hidden bathroom. In the new front wall that swung open from hinges and latched shut in the middle, they installed window frames, divided as if for panes of glass, plus a big bay window and a working front door with a tiny doorknob and keyhole.

Mom and I sought diminutive plaid and floral wallpaper prints. At that first wallpaper store, I gleefully danced from pattern to pattern. That's where I first learned that you can provide too much information.

"Yes, this one's wonderful," Mom nodded at one tiny wall square. "The others don't match the color scheme." Our palette was primary: red, yellow, blue. But then I must have told the sales clerk we wanted the samples for my dollhouse because Mom gave me a pointedly wide-eyed look, paired with a tight, toothy smile. We suddenly had to go someplace else.

Mom explained in the parking lot, while my eyes adjusted to the bright midday sun: "You have to be careful what you say to people." She walked to our car at a fast clip, forcing me to keep up. "They only give out samples because they expect you to buy something more."

I would have done my earnest best to comply with her, my earliest mentor. I was a curious, hummingbird child, observing everything, seeking the sweetness of reaching perfection, and with it, my family's love.

Mom carpeted the whole dollhouse with gold velveteen and slipped in a thin sheet of wood veneer as a dining room floor. It was all perfect, all to scale, and I understood from the start that I needed to handle this dollhouse with absolute care.

From then on, for a few years, my aunts and cousins gave me boxes each Christmas and birthday, filled with tiny replicas of life's necessities. I amassed ornate chairs and beds, stately desks and lamps, brown teddy bears and a magazine rack, half-inch cartons of food, a tiny muffin pan, and quarter-inch crystal salt and pepper shakers. Each time a miniature relic appeared, I'd deflate a little, before I atoned with my big smile and overeager declarations of how much I loved it. Because despite its dainty perfection, I didn't exactly. And I felt disloyal. But they loved their gifts. And they loved me. I had no reason to complain.

Here's how I interpret this story, looking back: All gifts—especially truly good ones—were conscripted to a higher purpose for the living of an idealized life. I was raised for this. Grandma Doris managed City Hall and her family like clockwork. She tasked me early on to maintain her family tree and traditions. She was my second mentor, though she and I tussled over our narratives. Who gets to decide whose stories get told, and in what way?

Mom's middle sister, Vivian, taught me how to step out of the stories. *Let people be people but tune people out*, meaning anyone who misunderstood me. She was my third—and most subversive—mentor. Vivian's latent powers fully emerged after she walked through the valley of the shadow of death (she lost an infant) and quit giving a damn about what people said.

Women who challenge traditions are dangerous. Vivian left her marriage after she couldn't forget what she lost, moved to Florida when I was nine, and went into business for herself. Her crazy tales of everyday magic—including wild dreams and eerily spot-on psychics—were fodder for family lore.

Growing up, I vowed not to be like those dangerous women, nor teach high school like my math-loving mom. Not surprisingly, I would live to see myself play out all the same roles. (Read: *Never say never.*) I became a straight-laced high school teacher, guardian of the status quo but less wed to tradition, and later I became a dangerous woman.

She's gone now, my former teacher self.

By the time you read this, I will have lived into another version of myself, the curator of these tales replaced by other future editions, and so on. But the me who's present, here and now, offers you a blessing: May the journey that breaks you open also open you to compassionate love.

Shiny Objects

Let's back up a moment and look at my family culture. We call it *Minnesota Nice*, the mainstream Protestant version. You may recognize it as doing things *right*, being *good*. We don't share uncomfortable feelings—at least not with the people involved.

The thing is, if you don't acknowledge your feelings, they come out sideways, since the energy's there. In other words, we smile politely while we think, say, or do shitty things. Thus the correlating phenomenon: *Minnesota Passive Aggressive*.

If you're like me, and you're hypersensitive to other people's emotions, and your brain can't help spotting patterns, you can't ignore the moods around you. And so you read into everything. If someone acts strangely, you wonder if you should take it personally. We do not love such questions, we nice Minnesotans—we might not like the answers.

We're not supposed to ask for what we want, and God forbid we impose. Our Lutheran Confession, which I spent my teen years reciting, absolves us of the resulting chaos, but barely: *I have sinned against*

God in thought, word, and deed, by what I have done, and by what I have left undone. I have not loved God with my whole heart, nor loved my neighbor as myself. Lord have mercy on us.

With such standards, there's no possible way I could measure up, ever. I'm a truth-teller, born with a clear voice. And I'm also an obliger, trying to do what's expected of me, in a way in which I can still maintain self-respect. Mercifully, I was confirmed into what would become the Evangelical Lutheran Church of America (ELCA), the most liberal of all Lutheran denominations, where women purportedly enjoy equal rights. Except that, in the Bible, women don't have fair representation, and nobody claims that they do. How then could the ELCA bestow equal rights upon women? With careful wording and only partial success, in my teenaged estimation.

Even though I liked to narrate real-life stories in my head in real time, I also knew that I had to parse out exactly what I could say, and what I had permission to write, especially regarding myself. Do I really want to tell you that I walked oddly, a long-limbed, too-skinny, knock-kneed smart girl who leaned forward bouncing up on my toes? That I spoke vibrantly with precise words and made friends very quickly but couldn't keep them? Of course not, but it's true.

I lacked social graces and said wrong things, which I knew all too well—both too good at school and too naïve for my own good, simultaneously hiding while trying to fit in. And possibly even shine.

At sixteen, I met my German exchange sister, Eva. She came to live with my family in Minnesota for three months and promptly identified that nasty Minnesota Nice I'd steeped in for my whole life. "People here greet me by asking 'How are you?'" she once said. "But they don't want to hear the answer. I should say that I'm fine. In German, we call that *oberflächlich*." She gestured with her hand as if skimming a surface.

"Superficial?" I asked.

She nodded. "Yes, I think so."

"That makes sense." Candor was a virtue with Eva.

At seventeen, I spent three months in West Germany living with Eva's family in what turned out to be the end of the Cold War. Eva helped me to make sense of her divided homeland, as I processed my visit to both sides of the Berlin Wall with American teens I didn't much like. It was, in some ways, the perfect metaphor for my sense of disconnection with home. I found more belonging as an outsider, as an American, living with West German peers.

I am different now primarily thanks to Eva, who as my first friend outside of my culture, showed me *how* I acted inside it. Because I didn't have strong enough language fluency to assimilate, Eva's West Germany gave me a time-out to focus on being myself. That felt like freedom.

Returning to my hometown in that context was painful. But I learned how to survive, find true friends, and make sense of division by way of the Berlin Wall. That was a book that I thought I could write. How the Wall must come down, and walls like it. Walls outside us, and walls within. America loved—and still does—the horror show that is twentieth-century Germany, and I was not immune.

I was studying German at college when the Berlin Wall that we all thought would never fall suddenly fell, and I no longer had anything to write about. Germany was reunified. End of story. Clearly, I declared, I would never write a book! Ah, but never say never.

First I successfully taught German, even after becoming a mom of twin daughters. The year I turned forty, everything changed. By then, I'd taught for fourteen years, six as a mom, and adapted to every added responsibility. But a whole new level of awful was looming: new principals, new textbooks, and a whole new schedule of classes—some ninety minutes, some less than an hour, two levels of German per class, four levels of German all day, daily, while traveling between two high schools. This was a shit ton of work that pushed me to my limits, when added to all the preparation, communication with parents, correcting, and grade reporting that is a teacher's baseline.

But a part of me—let's call it my soul—understood that if school was going to eat up all of my free time, I might as well spend some of that time doing something I loved. My soul required it.

When my church choir friend Christi suggested out of the blue that we take a writing class, a shiver ran up my legs.

To be blunt, I was not doing well in my vocation. I struggled every day: mentally, emotionally, physically, spiritually, my attention torn between people and places. With no end in sight for the foreseeable future, I needed the singing *and* writing to stay afloat. And, dare I say it?

I hungered to write a book, even more than I hungered for sanity. So Christi and I enrolled in an eight-week class at the Loft Literary Center in Minneapolis over the summer. In October, I received an invitation to apply for a writing apprenticeship there. Not that I had time for such things. It's just that getting the invitation felt like walking into the sunshine, out of a dark and dreary haze.

The day that I submitted my writing samples for the Loft Foreword program, I borrowed time from an active exchange program. Twenty-one German teens and their two teachers were in town, dispersed among community families I'd recruited. I carved out time from arranging logistics while I made last-minute edits to my application. I never expected the writing to pan out.

Nonetheless, the depth of my grief surprised me when the Foreword mentors didn't accept me. They didn't even interview me. I sensed—deep within me—that this was something big. Maybe I was becoming a writer despite my protests, in the sense that writing could become my vocation instead of a pastime. I loved it that much. Those stories of West and East Germany called to me, how I saw the Berlin Wall from both sides before the wall fell—and how many people can speak to that kind of historic experience?

And then there was my beloved Aunt Vivian. She'd recently died after years of an illness that silenced her. I needed to write about her, to capture her magnificent spirit.

Your writing's pretty, said each writing instructor, no matter the topic. *But what's at stake in this story for you?* I had no idea.

Still, when something calls you this loudly, it matters.

And you heed the call.

Legacy

Enter my paternal Grandma Doris. I never planned to write about her, though I've told copious Grandma stories to anyone who would listen over the years.

During her life, we shared a relationship best described as complex. She took care of me a lot as a child and micromanaged me as I grew older. Although she loved me endlessly, she had a fierce (sometimes quite arbitrary) agenda for me, and for all of her descendants. I just *knew* that she'd live long and die fast, and regardless of timing, her end would come too soon and I'd struggle for resolution.

I'd also thought that she'd last longer than ninety-four, and maybe not die my first week of the new school year. But then, why wouldn't she? When my now-husband and I announced our engagement, I'd just hung up from telling her the good news from my cell phone in my parents' living room, when *their* landline rang. It was Grandma, attempting a stealthy campaign to move my wedding from June to September. Because clearly teachers have nothing better to do in September.

13

She might die, she said. Plus September was the month she'd married Grandpa, her first husband and father of her two children, who'd left her a widow at sixty.

Beyond that, she'd mocked my sensible bridal shoes, insisted that my wedding dress had too few beads, and pressured us to honeymoon in the same Florida condo where she'd honeymooned with her second husband, Hubert (her treat).

"No, thank you," I said. "I spent vacations there as a kid."

"You poor child." Her voice dripped with sarcasm. Grandma never was one to hide her opinions. Except for the month when she finally died.

She and I left so much unsaid.

For example, that Florida condo she'd bought with my parents was Vivian's dream long before it was hers. They weren't even related except by marriage and happenstance. Twenty-three years separated Grandma and Vivian. Nobody could have predicted that both would depart in the span of two years. My two most significant elders.

I returned from Grandma's funeral to a darkened house, with a headache. Despairing of life with her gone, I found an email that invited me to introduce myself to my fellow writers on the first day of the first online writing class I'd ever signed up for. So I announced myself by writing where I'd just been.

And just like that, I put my grief into a box wrapped in wallpaper remnants. Writing training commenced.

I got up at 5:00 a.m. and wrote every day. That's how I started excavating family tales, gathering artifacts, threading them in. A charm, a poster, a seashell. A lovely turn of phrase. I believed—and still do—that my spirit guides were pointing me toward writing. The number 123 often cropped up, in countless signs related to writing, as if the Universe wanted to reward my magical thinking.

In the absence of other direction, I hung my hopes on these sightings. It was, to put it bluntly, a matter of survival. I promised myself that after I finished my book, I'd quit my job in an orderly fashion. Everyone knew that I was writing a book, and everyone knew that my career was living on borrowed time. I couldn't write fast enough.

Here's the hidden story that started to emerge:

As a beginning teacher in my twenties, administrators lauded me as a golden child, fated to become a master teacher. They nurtured me until my voice was strong. In a cruel twist of fate, my strong voice recast me as a nuisance in my forties. Though I did the right things— old methods that had always worked, and new strategies that certain people admired—things overall were completely chaotic for me.

New administrators came in from Minneapolis and changed all the rules. They wanted to make their mark on education, so they decided to eliminate German as soon as possible in a school district rich with German heritage.

Worse yet, for the first time ever, neither Vivian nor Grandma Doris was there to console me. In their gaping absence, I suddenly realized that both women had turned a page in their forties. Grandma had taken over City Hall. Vivian had moved out of town in the prime of her very confining marriage and constructed a whole second life. And me? I was permanently reassigned to teach introductory Spanish, when Spanish was my backup plan, in case of emergency only. This was that just-in-case moment.

I desperately clung to a fragment of advice I'd transcribed onto steno paper at age twenty-seven, from a tape-recorded handwriting analysis by my aunt's preferred psychic. This mysterious Florida woman predicted my difficult passage with eerie precision. It would start by age thirty-nine, lasting up to nine years. Its shadow loomed over my thirties, but—make no mistake—the reading prepared me for trouble ahead.

Specifically, she said that a burden would arise to teach me a lesson and create wonderful new foundations—and it would be very emotional, due to its nature. I would do twelve things at once and the work of three people. But as a result of what I would learn then, I'd be ready to take on leadership roles around creativity later, around forty-seven or eight. I was to stay positive. And I'd need confidence.

"People will take you at your word," my aunt's psychic said. "Opportunities will fall into your lap. Take advantage." It was as if she'd handed me a personal fortune cookie, one I savored until it grew stale.

And so I followed her advice. I reapplied to the Foreword writing apprenticeship *and was accepted*, taking personal time off from school to attend the two sessions a month. I flew to Chicago for nine weekend seminars, earning concurrent certificates in Editing (Chicago style) and German-to-English translation. The only remaining items on my self-styled curriculum were life coach training and a finished book. But so far, no real opportunities had materialized, career-wise.

Simultaneously, I'd piloted every promising new technology that my school district adopted in pursuit of a more perfect learning system. For example, lecture notes written directly onto a laptop and posted online. Except that now, I couldn't stay caught up because moderating online content exponentially increased my workload. Also, new grading systems and new grading software to go with a new grading philosophy. "Personalized, Standards-Based Learning," they called it. I was determined to show people that it could work.

You can be sure that this didn't endear me to people who liked the status quo.

One time, a colleague's *husband* reviewed class enrollment numbers and determined that there was no possible room for me to teach Spanish Three. But my fellow teachers didn't allow me to look at those numbers, to see if I could suggest something else. Why should he— a non-employee—be allowed to see and not me? Because my colleagues didn't pretend that they wanted me to teach Spanish at all, let alone Spanish Three. And I was counting on my book for an exit.

My chaos came to a head at a summer island writing retreat, where

I conjured up portals to my family's collective past. All day I staged my private room like that miniature dollhouse, dresser and table and armoire laden with the treasures and toys that I'd brought there myself: Fairy-tale dolls. Birdhouses. Colorful notes to self. I cut up jig-saw pieces of text and taped them back together, creeping ever closer to manic.

I stared out the window, imagining what had passed between my elders and me. I wrote with abandon. Secrets emerged in that self-padded cell. Above the sink, I saw my other grandmother's ghost. She was pictured and framed on the wall, an old lady transported back to her childhood farm.

I knew—even then I understood—that I was driving myself to the edge. Luckily, another part of me stood watch.

That side, the witness, looked over my shoulder when I poured blood-red herbal tea down the drain, saw the vibrant color and said, "Well, this doesn't look good! But keep going anyway."

That part of me knew what was at stake, knew that despite all of my magical thinking and efforts, I'd reached a dead end at school.

On the final evening of the writing retreat, I found myself sobbing, holding three fellow writers emotionally hostage while I read rambling stories. We all clearly knew that I was at my breaking point.

I'd tapped into something profound, but didn't know what it could mean.

The next morning, more lost than ever, I drove to a beach at the far end of the island and parked my minivan in the gravel lot. Stones crunched under my feet. Green branches shielded me from dappled sunlight while I read a sign explaining the ecosystem. Everything—and I mean everything—was connected. That's when a realization hit me:

Chaos and fractals! The idea lit up for me like a lightbulb.

Fractals are geometric patterns that repeat themselves at every scale, as found in a seashell's mathematically precise ratios. Ever the math teacher, Mom had explained it so many times because this concept was *her* creative passion at midlife. It may look like you're surrounded by chaos, but in fact there are patterns, called fractals, rippling out. If you zoom back a great distance, you'll see them. Zoom way in under a microscope, and those same patterns appear. But specific patterns aren't a given, I told myself. Because patterns can be interrupted. Patterns can change.

Even after my island revelations, with no alternative plans for supporting my family and myself, I returned to teach in September. I might've talked myself into staying the full year, if only I could have ignored the searing pain of my suddenly frozen right shoulder. It froze right after my return home from the island. Plus my hip went out for no reason, requiring a cortisone shot to keep me limping along. And I had nosebleeds. And a breast cancer scare (benign, but still).

We'd have to live off of retirement savings for me to quit working and heal. Or I could keep my savings, continue teaching, and hope that I survived. Mercifully, we wouldn't lose our house, thanks to my inheritance from Grandma Doris. That made me feel guilty too.

What did that say about me? And what if that money ran out? My meddling inner trolls kept me teaching far longer than I should have. In the end, my body overruled my fearful mind. When at last I couldn't lift my arm high enough to write on the board, I picked up a metaphorical piece of chalk, drew a door in the wall, and showed myself the way out.

Pose Questions

I had a postcard taped to my desk, four river stones etched with four German words. They shaped themselves in my mind like a poem or a prayer:

> *Liebe, Glück, Vertrauen, Mut.*
> *Alles kommt und es ist gut.*
> *Diese Sachen hier für mich,*
> *Und das ist nicht willkürlich . . .*

I composed an English version as well:

> *Love and Luck, Courage and Trust.*
> *Everything happens as it must.*
> *These things that are here for me*
> *Did not show up randomly.*

19

In theory, my found-object invocation meant that everything laid before me had arrived as it was meant to arrive. Even the tiny mystery dollhouse dresser drawer on my bookshelf. Even—*maybe especially even*—a giant spiraling shell that I chose at a shell shop to remind me of my Aunt Vivian.

My beloved Rainer Maria Rilke's famous instructions from *Letters to a Young Poet* echoed in my brain:

> *Have patience with all that is unresolved in your heart, and try to love the questions themselves, like closed-off rooms, like books written in a very foreign language. Don't research the answers now, which cannot be given to you . . . Live the questions. Maybe then one distant day, without even noticing, you'll live into the answer.*

I prayed for dear life that I would live into the answer. Because three and a half years after I was reassigned to teach introductory high school Spanish full-time, the same two basic classes in endless iterations, I walked away from a secure twenty-and-a-half-year tenured teaching career that first formed the core of my grown-up identity, then devoured it.

I used to be Frau Hallberg, quirky high school German teacher. My failure to thrive socially in my youth was a festering wound that I needed to heal in my own way, and I did it through teaching for over two decades. Teaching (German in particular) was healing. And teaching (first German and later Spanish), the thing I thought I was meant to do, and the thing I loved best, broke my heart.

It wasn't the Spanish language that caused me to surrender. I'm good at navigating grammar and words. Reinventing myself while still in the classroom—in a breakneck era of hyperaccountability, bare-boned budgets, and shifting educational landscapes—had been brutal. I never knew where I stood.

There's not one person I can blame, though I could point fingers in many directions. Call it an ecosystem that worked in my favor until fortunes turned. The same power dynamic that set me up as a winner was the exact reason I was fated to lose. It was a painful lesson that I needed to learn.

Before I left my former school district, people I'd never considered close would ask me if I was OK. People I used to consider close averted their eyes when we passed. People talked about me in my absence; word of course filtered back. Teachers are nothing if not communicative. And parents spread gossip, as do their kids.

Even in hiding afterward, I couldn't escape contact with schools. I was a mom in a family of teachers, surrounded by constant reminders that nothing had turned out as I'd planned. So here I was back home, ostensibly to finish writing my memoir, but all evidence showed that everyone—and I mean everyone—knew the truth. I was a hollow shell of my former self. Maybe the best part of me had already died.

And I was living into my question: Who are you when you're no longer the person you thought you were destined to be?

Innocent Child

Clarity

Who was I now that I was no longer the person I thought I was destined to be?

My only purpose that I could see was the manuscript that I'd been chipping away at for six years. Writing a book was hardly a reliable safety net, but it was all I had. All the extras I'd taken on before I quit teaching were meant to create a bridge to becoming an author before I left my career. So much for a bridge. It was more a leap of faith, or leaping with a sliver of faith. So I guess I was now a writer. A writer needing to write a whole book. After I'd already run out the clock.

I remember a morning after I quit—like too many others—when I awoke to an empty house, hours after I'd shuffled the girls out the door to their bus, and gone back to sleep. The silence rang too loud.

I got up, passed through the bedroom and hallway, and into my writing studio in the spare bedroom. There I sat on the carpet, stared at the blank page, and set the notebook and pen back down. How could I possibly tell my story while drowning in shame? Part of me believed that I deserved to lose my career. After all, I'd hollered at children. Everyone had heard me lose control, more than once. And yet I was a victim too—of agendas beyond my control. As often as I revisited the stories of my downfall, they still held sufficient power to suffocate me. Recent stories. Ancient ones. Unspoken tales I couldn't place my finger on yet, though the shame was so pervasive that it was frozen deep in my body.

So I sat down on my grandma's velvet chair, sheltered in the walk-in closet where no one could hear me, planted my feet on the floor, and let the emotions wash over me. I took several deep breaths and tapped on my body at specific pressure points.

Toward the end of my career, I'd come to rely on Emotional Freedom Technique (EFT tapping) to talk myself out of the parking lot and into school. It's not hyperbole to say that it may have saved my sanity and my life, by bringing up the painful energy so that I could release it, enough to hold on a little while longer, until my reprieve.

Here's how it works: Tap with two fingers, gently, on the side of your left hand as you talk. "Even though I have no clue what I'll do now, I deeply love myself." It's a setup statement, in which you verbalize your focus, and repeat it three times before the rounds of tapping begin.

You start with a variation on this script every time: *Even though (insert the most painful thing on your mind here), I deeply and completely love and accept myself, and I honor how I feel.* It's meant to state where you're starting. From there you keep tapping and talking, saying whatever feels true at that time, and the story meanders. Sometimes I haven't managed to say that I completely accepted myself. Or even that I honored how I might feel. Such thoughts weighed too heavily on me.

Yet I've always known I was beloved. And that day, sitting on the closeted velvet chair a fragment arose. "That's what your name means," my mother said. "Beloved." In my mind's eye, I picture Mom behind the wheel, with ten-year-old me beside her. "A heart is your logo," she concluded, as she had countless times throughout my youth.

We always had our best conversations on the go. Mom smiled with assurance, flipping on blinkers, as if it were divinely arranged that her day-after-Valentine's baby ended up with a heart-themed name, though she hadn't figured out the synchronicity until afterward. Yes, I'm beloved, but now the story shifts.

Slippery details chime in: Unpredictable. Talkative. Saying things I wasn't supposed to? All the time. The tapping brings it all to the surface. I feel undeserving. I want to crawl out of my skin. I know that I just said I was ten in that story, but suddenly inside, I'm four years old. And thus doomed to misunderstand the instructions.

I move to tap on meridian points, to purge these painful emotions. Inside my eyebrow (it doesn't matter which one): "I'm struggling." Side of eye: "And I don't know what I'm gonna do." Under my eye: "Seriously struggling." Under my nose: "So deeply ashamed." Collarbone: "How will I ever move forward?" Under my arm: Anxiety rises in my brain. "I'm not courageous." Top of my head: The energy is palpable. "Please God! I'm a good person!" Where did this thought come from? It feels preverbal, if four-year-old me weren't so verbal, so young.

Tapping brings these stories out into the open. They're there anyway. Buried memories flood me, of an innocent child, long redirected and shushed, albeit beloved.

I learned to read from children's television but seldom stayed in the room sitting upright, staying still. Instead, I flitted in and out, babbling happy sounds. Part of me remembers. But also, I have physical proof.

Squirreled away in a cedar chest at the back of my closet, a cassette tape documents my earliest memory of my paternal Grandma Doris's house. Darkness had filled all the corners, but we sat squarely under the lamplight on her living room sofa. My parents had dropped me off on their way to somewhere else. And Grandma had made a recording. On the cassette tape, she says my full name—first, middle, last—and announces that I am turning five tomorrow. She asks in her perky voice what day it is today.

"Vathedad Dad," says my own much younger yet articulate voice.

"Amy! Don't be silly," Grandma Doris chides, suddenly stern. She is recording this for posterity, after all.

"No really, it's Vathedad Dad," I repeat. "That's Valentine's Day in Spanish."

With that, I begin the story she actually wants to hear, *Big Farmer Big*, reading each word with precision. Inside the book's hardcover, a ripped paper pocket had once contained its companion book, *Little Farmer Little*, but that had gone missing ages before. And so I know this for sure: As a child I loved Spanish so much that I used to invent my own words for it.

I also learned to be compliant, to first push things just far enough, then step into line and say the right words for the record. All of this was somehow connected to love.

Artifacts

I often stayed with Grandma Doris on weekends, especially when Dad lived in Texas for work, when I was seven and eight.

Mom had stayed behind, trying to sell our house on her own. She'd painted and planted a lawn sign that read For Sale by Owner. Then she waited around every weekend for someone—anyone really—to drop by, while she steeped in worry. Those were the days before answering machines.

On the first bite, I'd insisted on showing our newfound friend (read: *potential homebuyer*) the special place under the stairs where lilies of the valley grew wild. That's when Mom dispatched me off to see Grandma Doris, in the house she shared with my grandpa.

Grandma brought me to City Hall on Saturdays while she prepared the agenda for city council meetings. Nobody else worked weekends, except a policeman or two. She knew them all. I perched on the carpet in front of her desk, filling in card-stock forms, writing in the boxes marked For Office Use Only.

Grandma's fingers flew, clickety tapetty tap. Afterward, if I'd been very patient, we stopped off at the room with the giant Xerox machine. As my reward, she gave me sheets of copy paper: blue, green, pink, canary, salmon, and gold. Funny how much I loved colorful papers and would to the edges of my career.

When she could manage it, Grandma had all four of us over, bracing herself for the chaos: my older cousin Ellen and her younger brother, my brother and me. Even in the summertime, we barely ever played in her fenced-in back yard because the acorns pricked our feet. But she gave us the run of the house, encouraging us to explore all of her beautiful things.

In the basement that smelled of dusty cedar, we played her ancient children's records on the turntable: *A tisket, a tasket, a green and yellow basket, I wrote a letter to my love, and on the way I dropped it.*

On the main level, we kept time to a porcelain clock that Grandma Doris wound every day. Above the fireplace, goddesses danced at the base of two gilded candelabra.

Upstairs, portraits of long-dead aunts and grandmothers watched over us, we girls draping ourselves in faded taffeta dresses while the boys plastered their arms and legs with expired license stickers from City Hall.

Grandma Doris, an only child, framed all of her stories within the much larger landscape of family heritage. Even when she wasn't in the room, I felt the ancestral spirits watching over me, listening to everything I did.

She had married into a family of Swedes, but she belonged to the Daughters of the American Revolution, like her mother before her, tracing her lineage back through soldiers in the Civil War to before the Mayflower. She traced her family tree back to Sir Guy Carleton, first lieutenant governor of Canada. "Like a Canadian George Washington," Grandma Doris said with a knowing nod.

She claimed Thomas Hooker, founder of Connecticut and the Congregational Church (our family church before we all became Lutherans or Catholics). I stood tall beside Grandma Doris during Sunday hymns, singing out melodies, while she proclaimed the text on a single random note that she called harmony.

Someday, Grandma reminded us, her treasures would be ours to divide amongst ourselves: her collections of spoons, thimbles, blue china plates, bracelet charms. I only wanted one thing.

Two precious Hummel figurines resided in the back bedroom. Ellen and I cradled them in our hands, a blond boy behind a fence and a girl who wore a red scarf on her head, also behind a fence, finger raised to address a yellow bird. W. Germany, read the blue ink stamped on their bases. Grandma had patiently explained that Germany was divided into two countries following the Second World War. W stood for West, the *good* Germany. I had my heart set on that bird girl.

At night, the boys slept in that back bedroom, one-time home to Grandma's long-dead parents, the bed draped in an heirloom floral quilt. By day, the boys commandeered the room over the garage, where Grandma stored genealogical research and office supplies.

But we girls occupied a room all our own: twin beds in the front bedroom next to hers at the end of the hall. In the middle of the night, while Ellen lay sound asleep, I frequently awoke to the sound of creaking footsteps, traveling up the stairway and toward our room, always coming and never arriving. Grandma told me that it was just the furnace, but I could never be sure.

My grandfather, still half alive, was like one more ghost in that house. His body had just about given out, but his spirit was not leaving without a fight. I cringed to hear his voice thunder from his bedroom beside ours, above the crackle and beep of the police scanner that kept him company. "Turn down the voicebox," he shouted from bed, where he lay all day eating sticky danishes and giant pills, smoke billowing from bittersweet cigars between courses on his breathing machine. He had a shop of power tools I never saw him use. I remember his TV blaring detective shows into the night. I especially remember how his rants landed squarely on me, the girl most likely to talk just to hear herself think.

He didn't scare me as much as he might have if Grandma hadn't run interference. "Good bye," she said to him, all sweetness and light. "We're off to Burger King and the movies." Then she grabbed a handful of cash from her dresser, and we trundled down the stairs and piled into the backseat of her giant sedan for an evening with Disney. Grandpa always looked happy to see us go.

When we returned, full of popcorn and Dr. Pepper, we had to be extra quiet because Grandpa was already asleep. We had to go to bed too, so that Grandma could start typing up the minutes from city council meetings. She played recordings over and over to capture every word.

One Saturday evening, Mom came to get me, and I wasn't ready to leave. But Grandma had another meeting, so they gave me a choice: I could stay with Grandpa, or I could go home. I'd never stayed with Grandpa alone—the thought made my insides quiver. But I knew that in the morning, Grandma would make the three of us breakfast: Wheaties, bacon, orange juice for me, and prune juice for Grandpa. Then we'd hurry into the car for church, just Grandma and me. So I stayed.

Grandma knelt beside the bed, helped me to say my prayers, tucked me in, and turned off the lights. I heard her footsteps move down the stairs and the garage door close behind her.

As soon as she left, I knew that I'd made a big mistake. Alone in one twin bed, in the darkness, I began to cry, feeling tiny. Long moments passed. Finally, I heard a stirring outside. The doorknob turned, and light streamed in from the doorway. There stood my grandfather, frail in his apricot bathrobe, looking in through horn-rimmed glasses. He didn't come in, just stood there, the first and only time that I felt he really saw me.

"Don't cry," he said finally. I stammered some sounds. His raspy voice continued. "It's good you stayed. It'll be fine. So . . . you should go to sleep now."

He closed the door and left me in astonished silence.

I drifted off to sleep.

Hidden Agendas

The following year, 1977, while we were in Texas for Thanksgiving, visiting Dad in his little rental apartment, Grandpa died before we could get home to say goodbye. That time, Dad stayed in Minnesota for two full weeks.

While he was home, a math teacher quit at the local junior high. The principal—our nosy backyard neighbor who liked to peek through the lilacs when we were outside—offered Mom the job. That teaching position turned out to be our family's salvation.

My parents finally hired a realtor, and Mom returned to work. She arranged for a neighborhood girl to watch us in the mornings, a surly teen who yelled at us to brush our teeth even after we'd already done it, never getting up from the television until she and my older brother, Ben, had to catch their bus.

The first time she let me oversleep, Ben helped me to cross the highway and I walked the rest of the way alone. After that, Mom decided that we could get ourselves to school.

At Easter, Grandma flew down to Texas with us for one final road trip. Without Grandpa to take care of, she could finally travel, and Dad was coming home soon. His company had gone out of business just as we'd finally landed a buyer for our house. Mom stitched up a Texas flag to fly—red, white, and blue with a single star. It flew for one day. Then she took it back down.

Perhaps if we'd moved to Texas, I'd have grown up bilingual. In 1978, I was eight, that sweet spot where kids mimic sounds without even trying, and grammar starts to makes sense. But Spanish would elude me till later.

I remember how Grandma and my family crossed over into Mexico for one day. She joyfully bartered in English with street vendors who gesticulated over turquoise and silver jewelry, using catch phrases to get their point across. Watching them tangle, I dreamed of speaking fluent Spanish one day.

Instead, I'd have to wait until high school, where I'd take Spanish for seven trimesters, all told, before dropping out. My time in West Germany, where I'd fill my brain with German, miss a term of Spanish, and skip the remedial work, would derail me.

Growing up Texan, I wouldn't likely have chosen German. Nor would Grandma Doris have had such an outsized influence on me, but that isn't how this story goes. We all returned to Minnesota.

After Grandpa's passing, Grandma took liberties. She redid all the wallpaper, recovered the sofa with flowery fabric, and filled her house with plush pink carpet. She wrapped our birthday and Christmas presents in surplus wallpaper samples.

With Mom working, we spent more weekends than ever keeping Grandma company, watching lamps we weren't allowed to touch go on and off, magically controlled by automatic timers. The house felt dimmer with Grandpa gone.

One fall afternoon, from the passenger seat of Grandma's Oldsmobile, I snapped at a traffic light frozen on red. "Goddamn it, change, will you?"

Grandma's head swiveled, eyebrows pinched, voice controlled. "Amy Kathryn Hallberg! I am shocked and ashamed of you. Nice young ladies don't say words like that."

At nine, I had never used those words myself, but out they came, as if I were testing them, and maybe Grandma. "Ellen would never say such a thing," she assured me. "I wish I could take the best qualities from each of you. All four of you. I'd mix them together and divide them into four equal parts."

I winced, remembering matching taffeta Christmas dresses she'd bought us girls, which didn't endear me to Ellen. I'd long since grown tired of opening Christmas Day presents identical to ones my older cousin had opened the previous night, that surprised nobody but me.

"Grandma, don't you like me as I am?"

"Well, sure I do, Amy. But Ellen is so nice and polite. She never fights with her brother."

Grandma and I had tangled many times (and would continue to for years) about who actually started said fights. She never had a brother *or* a sister and vocally wished that she had, so how would she know? I took another tack.

"You know I'm smart, Grandma, right? In the top reading group."

Grandma pursed her lips. "It's nice to be important. But it's more important to be nice."

That winter, Mom and I stopped off at a dollhouse store on our way to Grandma's house. We wanted to see if they had nicer dolls than my original wiry family, but we left without buying anything new. Now running late, we passed the cash register, where I saw a stack of pocket calendars on the counter, the kind Hallmark shops gave away for free, with yellow cartoon ducks on the covers. Remembering Grandma's instructions to be nice, I grabbed two on the way out the door—one for me, one for Ellen.

Rushing into the slushy, gray parking lot behind Mom, I flipped through the pages to see that these calendars had no pictures inside, just boring white grids. On the backs, I found small, white stickers. My breath caught. The stickers said $2.00. I'd stolen the calendars.

At this point in the story, my grown-up self wants to ask that younger Amy, why couldn't she ask her mother for help? Confess her sin and return the calendars to the store unharmed? Ask for forgiveness? Be done with it, even if we were running a little bit late? I certainly knew better.

Instead, I panicked. In the backseat of our station wagon, I stuffed the booklets into my purse, desperate to get rid of the evidence. Once we reached Grandma's house, I raced upstairs to our bedroom and wadded up both calendars as best I could, hands shaking, fighting against rigid card stock. From the cupboard in the wall, I grabbed several sheets of salmon paper to crumple around them, wrapped the outsides in gold paper, and placed the bundle into the wastepaper basket. I threw a few blue sheets on top for good measure.

That evening, Grandma took Ellen and me to a band concert at the high school where my father had once played the flute. In the darkened auditorium, I slumped in my seat, mind burning with shame, replaying the day's events. I prayed for forgiveness. I prayed that nobody would look in our room. Most of all, I prayed for the music to end so that I could do a better job of covering my tracks. I thought of my dollhouse back home, and how I stashed things in the attic space when they didn't fit elsewhere. I needed a similar place at Grandma's house.

While Ellen brushed her teeth, I grabbed the calendar bundles and snuck into the garage, feeling short-winded all the way down the stairs. I buried the wad under a stack of newspapers in a bitterly cold metal garbage can. Someone might easily have found those two calendars, though I don't believe they ever did. Only after garbage day passed did I breathe freely again.

Observe Clues

We knew so much and so little about each other, Grandma Doris and I. For example, how had she come to own those Hummels, since we weren't German and she hadn't visited *any* Germany? Decades after Ellen let me claim the bird girl, and only because I made a fuss, I realized that her parents must've bought them. My uncle was stationed in West Germany during the nineteen-sixties. By all rights, both Hummels should have been hers.

And it never occurred to me why Grandma felt so entitled to lay her heavy claim on what I thought, said, and did, or why she wanted me around so often, or how I brought lightness to her life. Her father had died of larynx cancer before I was born. Her mother died in a nursing home when I was five. The Hallberg Pattern Shop, a family foundry, had gone out of business and its heir—her husband—lost his career and his health, while she performed endless city clerical duties. That was her backstory. That and her family tree. But what then was rightfully mine?

At twelve, it had never occurred to me to question Grandma's family tree per se, her careful delineation of who family was and was not. She introduced that disruption herself. The Sunday it happened, I expected Grandma Doris to drive me home after an overnight visit. My bags were already packed and waiting by the front door, when she made the announcement.

"A nice gentleman I know is coming over." Her words felt rehearsed.

"You have a boyfriend, Grandma?" I asked, feeling the tightness in my face. The thrill and terror of it set my pulse racing.

A blush spread across her cheeks. "His name is Hubert. He's a widower. He wants to drive us to your house."

I pictured the tangled web of highways across the river, with no direct route. "That's forty-five minutes away."

"It's OK. He offered."

My mind ran wild. She was my grandmother, not *sexy*. She was hearty and boisterous—a genuine force of nature—and she'd been on her own for five years. I hadn't considered that she might date again.

She'd met him when he volunteered to set up voting machines. He carried them for her, to lighten the load. She'd just barely told me when her doorbell rang, and I opened the door. On the step stood a large man with a serious face, squarish glasses, and a ring of gray hair around the crown of his head. Hubert stepped into the cramped entry and took my hand. "You must be Amy."

His deep voice resounded in the small space. Grandma stepped into the back hallway, purportedly to dab on lipstick and blot it with tissue, leaving us alone.

"I hear you went to the Shrine Circus," he said. "What did you like best?"

"I liked it when the lions jumped through rings of fire." The words felt like something he might like to hear. I wanted to get this answer right, and hopefully, to impress Grandma's friend.

Hubert trained his blue eyes on me. "I hear that lions fear fire more than anything." He inhaled. "So I suppose it's cruel to make them jump through those rings."

"Oh." I fidgeted with my fingers, words now extinguished, heart beating faster. I'd never considered what the lions wanted, or that they should have a choice in the matter, but his words intrigued me. Nobody in my family thought to talk about animal rights.

Mercifully, Grandma's keys jingled on a brass ring, interrupting. "Here I am, ready to go!" she announced. We got into Hubert's car, me up front, she in the back.

I watched Hubert drive, gentle but assured, softly clearing his throat, eyes on the road. This man wasn't what we were used to, Grandma Doris or I. But maybe he was what we needed.

At Christmastime, he and his son's family came to celebrate at our house, where Hubert would surprise me with a simple pair of gold hoop earrings. He got my cousin Ellen a ski cap, meaning that he'd thought only of me when he bought my present.

Within a year, Grandma made plans to retire. She and Hubert put their houses on the market. They were getting married and moving into a condo together, in that order. Hired ladies dispatched most of Grandma's belongings in an estate sale. She kept a fraction of her heirloom treasures. Most of the rest she wanted us to take, splitting up collections of etched crystal between her two offspring and their descendants.

One Sunday afternoon, Mom found my stoic grandma in front of the basement fireplace, sobbing over her yellowing ivory wedding gown, a rare display of emotions that she held at arm's length. Was she mourning happy times or dashed expectations?

We took the gown home and stored it in a cedar chest at the foot of my bed. Later on, in high school, I would try it on for a play and reject it. The rigid fabric would constrain me so much that I could barely breathe, let alone squeeze myself out, even as skinny as I was. Either the dress had shrunk, or my buxom grandmother had been a slip of a girl at twenty-three.

Grandma and Hubert would be at my play, bursting with pride. Grandma was my harshest critic—and staunchest patron. She attended every dance recital, every choir and band concert, every play from elementary through high school, and sometimes even college.

She never mentioned my edgy delight in the twelfth grade when I delivered several of Thornton Wilder's thornier lines as the (usually male, but not this time) Stage Manager in *Our Town*. During a cemetery tour, the character says that "genealogists come up from Boston— get paid by city people for looking up their ancestors. They want to make sure they're Daughters of the American Revolution and of the Mayflower . . . Wherever you come near the human race, there's layers and layers of nonsense . . ."

Those lines—like all the happy endings and dramas—were scripted, but I leaned into them heavily. We'd studied the play in English class and I'd longed to play Emily, the ingenue who dies too young. Instead our teacher, who was the director, cast me as the narrator because, she said, I was the only person who could learn the part, more than an hour of speaking all told. In retrospect, my facility with words was the same reason Grandma hoped that eventually I'd take over her genealogical mission that I so gleefully mocked in that play.

I memorized the role over spring break, wading in the Florida surf, and delivered the lines in a sweet gray dress that I bought at my Aunt Vivian's shop. As with every performance that she and Hubert attended, Grandma kept both programs for me, regardless of my wishes.

Until her remarriage, Grandma Doris saved everything, a true child of the Depression. One particular Sunday, we waded through cigar boxes and paper clips, decades of National Geographics with cheery gold covers touting tales of New Guineans, and dried-up old pens. I refused most of those relics, especially at fourteen.

The afternoon when Mom found her crying over her wedding dress, Grandma foisted my own ditto-paper magazine on me—a copy of a juvenile first draft that I made in the fifth grade. Its green cover and faint purple ink made me cringe. On a page inside, I'd drawn a woman in profile with ginormous breasts, the kind that I wished for, the kind that I never developed. I didn't need the reminder.

"I don't want this," I said point-blank.

"Someday you'll want it," Grandma insisted. But, and I mean this sincerely, I don't. These were the unfiltered musings of a girl who published embarrassing things in a gifted enrichment class, with minimal guidance from her male teacher. I'd long since destroyed all the copies but hers.

When Grandma left her office, I dumped the manuscript in the trash can and returned to testing pens on steno pads. An hour later, she returned, saw its green cover amongst the dead ballpoints, and fished it out. "I saved this for you."

"It's stupid," I said. "I don't want it, Grandma." She stared me down. Cheeks burning, I finally took it.

Once home, I marched to my room and ripped it into small pieces, savoring the angry rush in my body, my furiously triumphant act of rebellion against her nostalgia.

I did receive the Hummel girl addressing a bird on a fence—that German artifact not meant for me, but my cousin Ellen. I insisted on having that bird girl. Ellen got the Hummel boy and the floral patchwork quilt. She was the agreeable one.

For Grandma Doris, I was that lion that wouldn't jump through her flaming hoops. And yet. Before Grandma introduced Hubert to any other family member, she introduced him to me. Her decision spoke volumes.

Wild
Woman

Peace

I remember the first time Mom broached the subject. We were waiting to turn right out of Grandma Doris's neighborhood. While she watched oncoming traffic from the left, I studied the cemetery on the other side of the road. Mom said, "Do you ever wonder why peasants and outlaws never show up on your grandma's family tree?"

"What do you mean?" I spoke in a hush, as if conspiring against something sacred, though nobody could hear us.

"Why does she only name dignitaries? People who prospered? The right groups? She chooses the details that suit her."

I leaned toward my mother. "Why do you say that?"

Mom didn't lower her voice. "What are the odds?" She smirked knowingly. "What are the odds that everyone in her family was perfect?" Her lips twisted into a wicked smile. "As for me, I'm descended from Vikings."

Mom's parents, children of immigrants, resembled those wild ancestors who wouldn't be tamed. Indeed there were stories. My

49

artist grandpa, Oscar, had left his Swedish mother, a widow named Amelia, on the Minnesota Iron Range the day before he turned eighteen. He'd refused her pleas to stay even one more day for a birthday cake. He'd already dropped out of school after the ninth grade to work in lumber camps and the like.

He returned for Grandma Lillie, an orphaned schoolteacher he'd met in the lobby of a Duluth movie theater, where she was working when he dropped off some signs. By then, he was a self-taught sign-painter. He'd given her a ride home, two blocks away from the theater, and she'd given him a kiss.

They bought a small house on a triple lot in a new Minneapolis suburb, with a garage to work in. They could afford to live in that town, albeit the poor side, because it wasn't redlined to keep Jewish people out. That worked in their favor, even though they were Christian Scandinavians like so many Minnesotans. They cobbled together a life. He painted. She kept their home and made sure their daughters received educations. He told stories about his past all the time. She frequently shushed him.

We consigned ourselves to Grandpa's wildness. Within reason.

Every Christmas Eve at dusk, we passed through the arbor gate of the white picket fence Grandpa Oscar built and painted himself. Just inside the house where Mom and her sisters grew up, a cacophony of voices greeted us, mingled with the aroma of Grandma Lillie's legendary Swedish meatballs.

She made them every year without fail, mixing pork sausage with ground beef, black pepper and chopped onion, just enough salt, an egg, and some breadcrumbs. She added cinnamon last, her secret ingredient.

One time I helped her, squashing the icy pink meat against the big glass bowl, rolling a few misshapen lumps between my chilled palms. "Here, I'll do the rest," Grandma Lillie said, hands moving swiftly, filling the spare bowl with perfect little spheres, exactly one inch across.

"They all have to be the same size," she said, almost as an afterthought, "or some will burn."

First she boiled them to make broth for the gravy we poured over mashed potatoes. Then she scooped them into a frying pan, sizzling them in butter to a golden brown. Finally she tucked them into the oven to achieve a crispy finish, quiet satisfaction written across her face as she pulled them out. She may have been the orphaned daughter of immigrants, and Grandpa may have been fatherless, but these immigrant orphans still had traditions and pride.

I never touched the pickled herring that swam in vinegar with slivers of onions. I always partook of Grandma's special Peter Rabbit salad with cabbage, carrots, and radish. We'd have buttery spritz cookies to take home afterward, pressed in the shape of Christmas trees.

But we never, ever, had leftover meatballs, no matter how many pans Grandma Lillie made, and didn't she know it.

At a certain point, Aunt Vivian would call, and we'd pass around the phone in the kitchen, tangling up the cord. We talked fast to counter long-distance prices.

"Hello, Sweetie! Merry Christmas! Did my presents arrive?"

"Yes," I said. "I saw the boxes under the tree."

"Very good." Her voice rang out. "Now I'll see you in Florida next summer. Put your mommy on, OK?" I'd long since stopped calling my mother Mommy.

Vivian always seemed to have misplaced the recipe for the meatballs. Mom would read it melodramatically over the phone. Vivian would call several more times to hear the instructions again. "Her meatballs never turn out right," Aunt Betty said, after Mom hung up the phone. "And she serves them over rice." I chalked it up to one more thing—such as divorce—that nobody but Vivian would do.

"She'll probably just serve shrimp," said Mom. "Vivian loves shrimp." Her voice conveyed a mix of admiration and worry. What does one do with a sister who walks away from a good life? Who reminds you that cherished traditions never were quite what they seemed? And you still want to believe, so what do you do? For example, that treasured family recipe? Grandma got it from a cook at a resort in Northern Minnesota. When you ask my Aunt Betty for her copy, she'll have added white pepper. So I really don't know.

Was our problem that Vivian went too far—both figuratively and literally—or that we couldn't "fix" her? There's nothing more foreign to established people than those of us whose lives haven't worked out in the conventional ways.

Little did I know how fully I would someday become that wild woman, the one who could barely keep up pretenses, no matter how hard she honestly tried.

Exactly one month after I quit my job, we went to a family wedding. Normally, I don't drink. Not even a little. A slender woman like me? I've lived long enough to know that I drink fast, the effects hit me hard and, afterward, I can get mean and my head hurts—a lot. But that day, I decided to drink, enough to get noticeably drunk.

It was worth the hangover to look happy in pictures. I look ecstatic in the three-shot photo booth series: Dave with our twelve-year-old daughters and me, made up in festive attire. We three females wear berry-red lipstick, toothy grins, and flowing brown hair. Hints of silk dresses peek out: sapphire, ruby, aquamarine. Dave, in his suit coat, wears a gray-and-pink tie.

It didn't take much. Three glasses rimmed with my berry kisses: one champaign toast, one glass of white over dinner, a Moscow mule heavy on the vodka. My girls laughed at me for being a lightweight. They'd say we had fun.

My girls know how I freaked out—and I freaked them out—while buying those dresses I wasn't sure we could afford. We bought them anyway, but we felt sad driving home because shopping was rough. So maybe they preferred drunk to freaked out.

What did I have to talk about while celebrating this joyful event? That three and a half years earlier, before I left teaching altogether, I'd lost my German program and soldiered on? And I still wasn't over it yet? Maybe I'd never get over it? I'd lost my purpose. Possibly indefinitely.

What was it my artist grandpa always said? *Laugh and the world laughs with you. Cry and you cry alone.* I managed to make it through the celebration and save my disintegration for private, where no one would see.

I learned that from Vivian, who suffered far worse than me, but was her father's daughter, and left her painful past behind to start a new life.

My aunt had escaped winter holidays in Minnesota, but she called and made meatballs, though she served them on rice. We saw her each summer, when tradition didn't matter as much. December was tough, and would always be.

Vivian had lost her first son one month after his birth—seven years before she left Minnesota. Every year while decorating our artificial tree, Mom mentioned my too-soon deceased cousin. She tenderly unwrapped her Joshua bubble, a slightly imperfect glass sphere. Mom found the ornament after he passed, and made a tradition of hanging it every year to honor his brief life. His little heart couldn't survive the surgery he would have needed to live.

Boundaries

Whenever Dave and I met up with sympathetic people who reached out from my past, I found myself explaining how my life was—anticipating questions, fishing expeditions for answers that hadn't yet come, and wouldn't for the foreseeable future. I anticipated their curiosity at the specimen I felt I'd become: *former German teacher, unintentional stay-at-home mom, the last person you would ever expect to drop out—except when she did in spectacular fashion, wild woman adrift.*

I didn't want friends guessing at stories. I feared they would view me as delicate. Or us: Dave and me. These meetings were both welcome and fraught. Everyone else's lives were still in progress, and we had limited time to catch up. Any opening meant to be social could lead me to talk obsessively, then lose myself in awkward, enveloping silence, fixating on how much I should tell them, and what I could say. I sensed, for all of our sakes, that they didn't need to hear the whole thing. I tried to sum it up anyway. My explanations only drew our vast distinctions in deeper relief.

Afterward the emotional riptides came, unannounced. Uninvited. Brought on by well-meaning people who only meant to support me. *Being Misunderstood.* There's the painful thought, the one that sent me rearing up and afterward skittering down, ashamed of trying to beat back forces for which I was never a match. Also—because it's complex—I felt ashamed of feeling ashamed. At the same time, I did understand that everyone else wasn't thinking of me.

I pushed against that energy—a forty-six-year-old woman immobilized by fear, locked shoulder both frozen and searing. I prayed that I could actually write my way out of the trap. I wanted to reassure my readers that I'd be OK. I wanted to know that you'll get it when at last you read this page. It was awkward, though. And explaining what had happened exhausted me. Mostly I kept writing. And remembering—hope against fear—that Vivian made a new life.

Maybe she would have remained a specimen for me: *flamboyant wild woman, mysterious tradition breaker, epic, flawed, larger than life, subject of stories.* Except after my brother's wedding, Vivian called me all the time.

At the historic (said-to-be-haunted) inn near the Catskills, we'd roomed together. At twenty-five, I was on the verge of landing the only open German teacher position in the Twin Cities; she'd long since sold her deli to focus on dress shops. Each of us single, tucked into matching quilts, Vivian and I spent those few evenings comparing mutual tales of single women by lamplight.

She'd clearly wanted to set the record straight. When we switched off the overhead light, she began at the start and leveled with me, as if confessing to a near stranger. She knew that we talked about her.

"You know that?" I asked, relieved that we didn't have to pretend.

"Of course I know. My family thinks I'm crazy. Amy, it hurts."

"I'm sorry."

I looked across the space between us to her shadowy face. My aunt told me about losing her second child, the baby boy that we mourned with a Christmas ornament.

"Joshua had Down syndrome. And I loved him. I wanted to bring my baby home. The nurses didn't tell me he was dying, but they knew. *They let me go to Target.* I was standing in the checkout line at Target while my baby was dying."

I offered mostly watchful silence. Reverence, really. Someone in my family was telling the truth about herself for a change. What, besides *I hear you*, can you say to a story like hers?

I focused on her voice—so like my mother's and so like my own that you might mistake any one of us on a phone call. "You know, Joshua visits me. I feel his touch on my cheek. Right here. It's like a little tickle. He's with me now."

That was the first time I knew—really trusted—that the veil was real. I'm talking about that membrane between the realms of the living and the dead, the in-between place where we touch. I'd sensed it before— felt my hairs raise and energy rush through my veins—but you don't, in our family, talk of such things. Not directly.

Sure, there were hints in stories. But still. Those stories were twisted. They left out certain, uncomfortable truths. Such as, our carefully curated stories won't ward off misfortune.

"It changed me," Vivian said. "I tried to carry on as a good wife. But I couldn't pretend my son had never lived. I made up my mind that I didn't want to be sad all the time. I wanted to laugh, not to defend myself to family members. Your mom tries hard to understand." Vivian sounded so quiet. "But she's my baby sister."

It was true. Until motherhood, Mom had followed Vivian, Kindergarten through college sorority, straight into marriage. But not divorce. And certainly not the death of a child. Mom flew to Florida sometimes to wallpaper Vivian's dressing rooms in floral prints that they both adored. My grandpa flew down and hand painted signs for the walkways. Even that evening, I understood that I was a stand-in. If she could have poured out every word to my mother or her father, Vivian would have.

But Vivian was willing to drop the pretenses and level with me. Because I listened, she listened to me. We acknowledged the hidden trauma behind our family's stories because we both knew it and felt it. Because it was already there. We both required much more interior space than family sometimes provided.

"Do you know how I chose my German major?" I asked that evening. "I mean the final decision?"

"Tell me." Vivian gazed intently at me.

"Remember that Easter when you came to Minnesota? You, Nick, and Sam celebrated with us at my parents' house?"

"Yes?" Eight of us had gathered at the dining room table, including Betty and her husband.

"We were having a conversation and I said that the pizza we eat in America wasn't authentic Italian. Nick agreed, and I added that Minnesota chow mein wasn't really Chinese."

Vivian cut in, anticipating the punch line. "What did my big sister do?"

"After I returned to college, she mailed me a manila envelope full of pages photocopied from Betty Crocker cookbooks, where she'd highlighted sentences that said pizza was from Italy and chow mein was Chinese. In their typed letter, she and her husband wrote that I should be careful about revealing my ignorance."

"Of course they did." Vivian's laughter filled the air. "So you majored in a language she can't speak and they left you alone. Smart girl."

I think we were all relieved when Vivian and I became confidants, first that night and from then on, over countless phone calls, until she lost all her words. Even then she would find a way to get her point across. After she died, the Joshua bubble disappeared, never to be seen again.

That evening in the said-to-be haunted hotel, she leaned into the circle of lamplight. "Let me show you something. Do you see this charm?" Pinching her gold chain between two fingers, she held it aloft.

"Yes." I propped myself up on my elbow.

"It's a tiny cockle shell. When I moved to Florida, I had next to nothing. I lost everything in my divorce. I couldn't afford this charm, but I bought it as a reminder: I came to the ocean, and I live my own dreams."

I returned from my brother's wedding to find my dream German teaching job waiting for me. In time I would come to realize that although Vivian never much liked Germans—whom she found demanding as tourists—I'd still taken a page from her book. Because nobody in my family—not even my semi-fluent brother, Ben—was capable of disputing my expertise, I could relax. They'd never have the skills for cross-examination. They came to respect my language skills. I learned to cultivate playful authority. Those were boundaries no one could cross.

Likewise, nobody was a Florida expert before Vivian went there. Afterward, didn't we all want to go? Extended family and friends. We all came. Us tourists, buying Vivian's jewelry and dresses. Florida was Vivian's home. She was the ultimate authority. Shrimp was best cooked in pickling spices. And did you know that fresh shrimp were always frozen on the boat, just as crab legs were always steamed?

True story. Vivian told me.

Breakdown

In truth, no tradition is sacrosanct, no two situations entirely equal, nor life fair, no matter the promises made, nor their magical sheen. No matter how hard my elders might try to avoid that reality, even though we shared common roots and family traditions, we each had troubles and joys all our own. The dollhouses would have brought that into focus, had I paid attention.

Ellen's dad worked for the power company. Her dollhouse was wired with working electrical lights. I remember it was kept in the basement. My dollhouse was stalked by our butter-yellow tomcat. No matter how many times I set the pieces in place, he'd reach into the exposed back windows and bat things around, leaving me to straighten them. That's mostly what I remember. At least Yankee derived joy from the place.

Aunt Vivian's daughter, my cousin Samantha, had the most elaborate dollhouse. Her dad was an architect, and as I recall, her Victorian dollhouse with turrets was an architectural wonder. I don't know where it went when her toys were sold. Or what happened to the husky who lived in the stylish doghouse outside.

There were whispered stories and strong innuendo, enough to help us children suss out the situation, even as the grown-ups worked out their official stances. So even back then I knew that there were steep costs to my aunt for her freedom.

That's the summer I learned an important truth: If you can't come to a resolution, then you decide what you're willing to live with. That's how, before they left Minnesota, my aunt and two cousins came to stay at our house one summer. We gathered around the table every night.

"Pour the milk," Mom called brightly, breaking spaghetti noodles into boiling water. Red sauce bubbled on the stove.

"Set the table," Vivian chimed in, chipper, washing the iceberg lettuce. "Somebody get salad dressing and parmesan."

We couldn't get between them, my mom and her sister, waltzing around the kitchen like manic clockwork. The best we could do was hurl a few words into the swirl of conversation and hope that some made it in.

Likewise, Sam was a sister to me. We hunted the cat in the backyard and dressed him in doll clothes. At night, my cousin woke me from the flip bed on my floor, teasing me when I nodded off midsentence. "Amy! Wake up. Tell me who you like."

I yawned and named my favorite heartthrob. "Shaun Cassidy."

She laughed. "It's so funny how you said that. You just sighed." Her lilting tone echoed mine. "Shauuun Cassidy." Like a teasing big sister, Sam played on my embarrassment and genuine adoration. We talked for hours nightly, in an extended slumber party that I hoped would never end.

Down in the basement where Sam's mom and little brother slept, it always looked as if a bomb had exploded, their clothing and papers strewn everywhere. And every day the house grew chillier, Mom's voice more clipped, doors shutting ever more forcefully as sisters retreated.

The evening before they left town, the four of us kids fled to the backyard, sitting atop the monkey bars, pondering reasons for the stormy kitchen exchange.

I hadn't noticed, in the midst of the turmoil, how often our fluffy yellow cat disappeared into the backyard. He also took longer to emerge from the darkness when Ben called him back home every night.

The morning that Vivian and my two cousins left for Florida, my parents and I gathered in the driveway to hug them goodbye. Ben had spent the night at a friend's house, so there were only three of us. Once Vivian's car rolled out of sight, my parents turned to face me.

"Yankee didn't return last night," Mom said. "Ben wasn't here to call him home."

I studied her face, unable to grasp what she meant.

"One of the neighbors saw him lying by the highway," Dad continued. "There wasn't a mark on him. We think he was thrown by a truck. We buried him this morning."

I felt my face crumple up.

Mom put her arm around my shoulder. "I didn't want to spoil the last morning."

"Does Vivian know?" I snuffled, holding back sobs.

Mom walked me back into the house. "Yeah, she knows."

Sam mailed me a sweet note. She'd heard about Yankee and she was sorry. Eventually we got a black poodle.

There was so much more to that story than I saw from my sheltered perspective. I can't remember what anyone looked like that summer. The only picture I have is of me, surrounded by puppets and dolls lined up against my bed so that I could teach them lessons. Even a magenta, googly-eyed, six-foot tall stuffed rabbit we called Big Dumb Bunny. And behind us that dollhouse. I barely had places to put all those toys.

What was it like for Vivian? Her kids were ten and four. They'd had to give up all of their toys.

My kids are twelve in the drunken wedding photo. They get to stay in their house. We'll have to count pennies, but they'll keep their cats and belongings. That's something.

I remember standing with Vivian in the Target checkout line. She bought Nick a white turtleneck and a plastic Stormtrooper mask so that he could dress up for Halloween. She pointed out that she couldn't afford it.

I didn't know that, prior to leaving her marriage, my aunt nearly bled to death of an ulcer. Mom told me much later.

When I quit teaching, I always knew that Mom thought of my daughters when she looked out for me. And though I was still married to their dad, I had to wonder: What would my children remember about our family now?

The toll on our marriage remained to be seen.

Play Freely

I recall the first time I looked out across the Atlantic Ocean. Along the shore, green waves crested, broke open, and washed over silt. Out at the horizon, crystalline sky wed impossibly turquoise sea. We stood further back, on jagged sand, tossing crumbs from bread bags to seagulls. They swooped down, their insistent squawks punctuating the crash of the surf. A few loners strode down the beach on their little stick legs, away from the flock.

My bronzed, blond cousin Samantha bent to pick up a shell. "Look. A cat's paw." She held out her cupped hand. "The name tells you what it's like. Do you see it?"

"Oh, yes I do." I stood close to admire the tiny peach paw print.

She picked up another. "This one's a turkey wing. See the markings?" I peered at the long, flat shell, rippled with brown-and-white stripes. She pressed it into my hand and turned toward the shore. "Come over here."

She squatted down and swiped away the top layer of sand, just smoothed over by the pulsing waves, to reveal a whole bed of tiny mollusks in every shade. "These are coquinas. My favorites."

Would I have loved them so well if she hadn't pointed them out? I'd long since learned to calibrate my tastes to hers. I wore Sam's hand-me-down clothes and retained custody of her best toys. Now she'd revealed a beach full of gems. I enjoyed her favor while it lasted.

By late afternoons, my cousins, my brother, and I hid away from white-hot Florida sun in my parents' air-conditioned, shaded condo. I picture us, four sweaty kids draped across the living room sofa. We stared through sliding glass doors to the well-groomed lawn and palm-shaded path. Geckos darted past, here and gone. I smelled sulfur outside and the blend of salt and chlorine in our hair.

I mentioned something or other. Was it that open swim hour—for grown-ups only—was over, and we could go back in the pool? Maybe Marco Polo. Or coquinas. It doesn't matter.

My thespian cousin never missed an entrance. "OHHHHH," Sam said, pointing. "Listen to your Minne-sOOOOHHH-ta accent."

"You're from Minnesota too," I protested.

She waved it off. "You have an accent. I don't."

There was no time to think. "I don't have an accent."

"Hear that?" She rounded her lips. "I dohhhhhn't have an accent."

"No, but I don't have an accent." I laughed despite myself. "I mean it."

Her little brother chimed in. "Minn-EE-SOOOOHHHH-TA."

They laughed. My brother laughed. "Minn-EEE-SOOOH-ta!"

It didn't matter that he spoke the same way. I tried to stop laughing, gasping in that painful way we do when the joke's on us, and really we're drowning and very much not amused. I was ready to pee my pants and they knew it, making it funnier still to them, which mortified me. They'd never let me live that down.

Finally I caught my breath and shouted, "It isn't funny!" My raised voice still hovered in the air as the front door opened.

My Aunt Vivian entered, suffused with a glow, formidable in her forties, tall, thin, gorgeous. Her straw-blond hair and sea-blue eyes matched the island landscape. I tried in vain to explain the gravity of the situation. The other kids watched with suppressed smirks.

Vivian, impervious, cut me off. "You do have an accent, Amy. Quit whining." I stormed away to the bedroom that Ben and I were sharing. Eventually, I returned to eat dinner.

Another day, Sam and I biked out to Vivian's deli. We parked our bikes out back and went inside for some water. Earlier that week, I'd eaten lunch out front with my family, sandwiches and sundaes that we ordered from oversized gilt-framed chalkboard menus. My aunt had smiled, animated as she placed the china plates and tulip glasses before us.

"Your hair looks so pretty like that," she'd said when she served me. "I love your ponytail."

This time, Sam and I found her slicing tomatoes in the kitchen with a sharp paring knife. She handed us two paper cups and sent us outside for ice from the chest.

My cousin slid the door open and grabbed the silver scoop. Feeling the rising cool merge with sweltering heat, I realized something and went back inside. "Do you know that anyone could reach inside the chest," I reported, "and touch the ice?"

Vivian turned to size me up, knife still in hand. "You can assume that any food you encounter has had something bad happen to it," she said. "Best not to think about it or you'll never eat." That was her naked truth, disguised as a culinary directive. Horrible things can happen. Things don't turn out as you plan, but the world spins on. So you make do.

For example: If you couldn't—under the terms of your nasty divorce—own any portion of the vacation condo you'd found yourself, you saved up your pennies and bought the decommissioned Post Office and turned it into a deli, quaint like your mother's kitchen, but much sweeter still. You stocked the shelves with charming food-themed keepsakes, nostalgic so that tourists would flock to your carefully curated semblance of home. And when your labor paid off, you bought the dress shop next door—the oldest house on the island, and probably haunted.

When one dream fails, you find another. I marveled at my aunt's brilliance.

After that summer, Sam would dismiss shell collecting as a tourist's game. But I would spend every vacation for years seeking coquinas on the ocean's edge, where waves wash away the sand, and little jewel-toned bivalves squirm to bury themselves again before another surge hits.

Empress
Mother

Unity

Let me fast forward to the summer of 1988, when Carleton College mailed me their annual *Zoo Book*, a black and white compendium of my incoming classmates' photos, along with hometowns and high schools.

In my photo, I wear no smile because the portrait artist—best in my hometown—wouldn't let me. It wasn't his style. His portraits were too expensive for retakes, and he was the expert. So I chose the iconic 1980s close-up. The young woman pictured is enigmatic—you could project almost anything onto her. She's a puppet and a muse.

My Korean-American roommate, Hanna, from suburban Chicago, must have taken one look at that photo and read me with precision, but I can't speak for her. Looking at her senior picture, I worried that I might not measure up to her expectations because I didn't know many Asians. So I faced my fear the only way I knew how.

I mailed Hanna a letter when I received our rooming assignment. In it, I appealed to my Swedish heritage and German expertise. I asked, "What languages do you speak?" I couldn't have named my query as white centering, but I was trying hard to get it right and did exactly the thing that I didn't want to do. My unintended message was, *Clearly you're Asian and I'm very white. I don't even know what I don't know. Please teach me.* It was very nearly an apology. I made it her job to educate me when she hadn't signed on for the role of Asian cultural educator.

For the record, Hanna had tested out of French, was as fluent in Korean as English, and quoted the Middle English of Chaucer (a poet I'd never heard of). I wanted not to be ignorant, to know as much as she did so that I could keep pace and connect. I kinda hoped she would be my first college friend. But there were so many basics to wade through. Our rooming situation brought me face-to-face with my discomfort over parts of my heritage that I'd always looked past.

I really did believe that I was raised to stand against racism. I learned about the Civil War and the Civil Rights movement in the second grade. When our teacher asked who won the Civil War, I'd raised my hand and announced, "We did." Since she looked puzzled, I added, "The North." We were Minnesotans, obviously, and Minnesota fought for the North. We were against ethnic bias. But my veteran ancestors fought for the South. I didn't know that at the time, or claim it when I did know.

Also in the second grade, Mom and I watched the miniseries *Roots*, in which Alex Haley traces his ancestry through generations of slavery to Africa. We understood clearly what we were seeing and rooted for the Black characters. Obviously.

I honestly believed that as a Minnesotan and a Christian, I was exempt from racial bias. If that were the case, then our common Protestant faith should have brought Hanna and me together. Consider this song from Sunday School at Grandma Doris's church:

> *Jesus loves the little children, all the children of the world. Red and Yellow, Black and White, they are precious in his sight . . .*

We white kids sang these words blithely each week, oblivious to the very white room. Jesus loved us all exactly the same. No further discussion required. Non-white kids were welcome to be one of us. When Hanna explained white centering, I started to see why that song was never my favorite. Minnesota Nice protocol frames things from white perspectives as if that were the proper perspective. We don't even know (or admit) that we're doing it, defining people of color as non-white, projecting our reality onto theirs. When called out, we can get defensive, proclaiming our good intentions rather than listen and learn.

I sincerely missed the days of banishment to my childhood room when I stepped out of line. Now my trespass *was* being in my room in the tiny vintage dorm. I wanted to love my roommate as myself. For a while we extended olive branches in each other's direction. When Hanna taught me how to make savory ramen noodles, boiled in my hotpot, served in Grandma Doris's hand-me-down pastel Tupperware bowls, I loved it. Hanna loved writing notes to her friends on my tablet of red paper hearts. But culture, it turned out, was more than just notecards and soup.

Such was the learning curve for a white woman, one generation out of poverty, one generation into women's lib, barely arrived at a whole new echelon of academic rigor. Hanna insisted that I enjoyed privilege as a white person nevertheless.

That fall, I received a series of postcards—cherry blossoms and pagodas—sent by two juniors studying off-campus in Japan. They'd seen my *Zoo Book* photo. Their notes said that I was extraordinarily pretty and instructed me on how to make the most of Carleton's party scene, as if they were looking out for my best interest. They laid it on thick. In conclusion, they wrote, they'd look for me at parties and check my progress when they returned. Such bullshit. Still that male gaze from Japan intrigued me.

Hanna remained unimpressed. "Amy." She stood beside my desk while I pondered the latest postcard. "When we're in the lounge watching TV, pay attention. People say hi to you before me. They notice you first. Because you're white and I'm Asian."

I was incredulous. "Really? That happens?"

She sighed. "Just watch."

It was a small dorm, with few first-year students on my floor of twenty-two people, but students from the whole dorm gathered regularly around the lounge TV, just outside our door. People occupied every seat for our afternoon *Jeopardy* rounds, notable among gameshows because you had to answer in the form of a question.

A stream of visitors flocked to the kegolator in the adjacent senior suite. (*What is a fridge with a tap on the front and a keg on the inside?*) Soon enough, someone passed by—for the life of me, I can't remember who. He said, "Hi Amy."

Maybe I said hi first. Probably I did. I made a point to notice my animated response, perched on the outer sofa, drawing attention. I looked over at Hanna, sitting still on a chair in the inner corner, body drawn into herself, waiting to be acknowledged. When at last it happened, she smiled, bemused.

Her theory may have been partially true, though upperclass women looked after us both. Some helped me to see my background more gently than she did. So much remained to be tested, so much unspoken. So much resentment seeped out sideways, head on, and every which way. I tired of Hanna taking my heart-shaped notes for her friends. She tired of spoon-feeding me. When I visited Germany the following summer, I bought Hanna her own set of the vibrant colored pens she liked to borrow. She in turn gave me a pair of the lacquered chopsticks her boyfriend had taught me to use.

We barely spoke again, even in the watercolor class that we shared senior year, spring term, where I was surrounded by friends. I knew that

I couldn't match their drawing skills, and Hanna was accomplished in that regard too. But I made awesome collages.

Hanna, if you're reading this, I want you to know that I heard you. While I've mourned that I didn't get what I wanted that first year, you taught me discernment. And for that I'm thankful.

You know what? I will always be white. I can't change what my upbringing was. That's what I have to work with, terms with which I must live. But thanks to that first year in college, with its ridiculously steep learning curve, I learned a ton, including how to entertain questions as much as right answers.

That was my set-up for the spring of 1992, when Rodney King, a Black man, was beaten on video by cops, and they were acquitted. The Los Angeles uprising began, and violence raged for a week. Sheltered by the cornfields of Minnesota, Carleton student activists made a list of demands, including that we'd all skip our classes and come to their Diversity Teach-In. I understood that this was a moment we couldn't ignore. I'd spent four years sorting through my ambient culture on so many levels. I knew that I hadn't arrived at any enlightened stance. It's just that . . . After four years of trying to integrate cultural lessons, I needed to breathe. I needed the respite of my art class, and no more words for awhile.

To get to class, I had to walk alongside the Bald Spot, a grassy field at the center of campus, where clusters of students attended the Teach-In. At the microphone stood a white classmate, whose words rang out through the speakers. "Look at those people walking past here, not stopping. Those people are racist." He lumped us all together, all of us random people on the sidewalk, as if he knew our motivations.

I knew him by name, *Zoo Book* photo, and a singular encounter.

The previous spring, I'd been randomly assigned to take a test with a small group that included him in a class lovingly known as Chemistry for Poets. He'd shown up late to the bench beside that same Bald Spot where the rest of us had painstakingly worked out several solutions to our test questions.

"Write my name on that, would ya?" he said and walked away, without contributing a single answer. God only knows why we added him.

When he labeled me racist on Teach-In Day, he couldn't have named me if he'd tried. I took a hard pass. Lectures from men like him wouldn't bring me closer to understanding the roots of racial division, nor bring about unity between disparate cultures.

I spent all that afternoon and several evenings afterward crouched on the art studio concrete, saturating giant sheets of paper with watercolor, cutting out shapes, piecing and gluing them into a fragmented yet unified whole. I had been given a paradigm; the paradigm needed to shift.

Paradigm Shift

"Remember how you were raised," Grandma Doris said in August 1992. It was the day I left Minnesota for graduate school, at the end of an otherwise unremarkable and therefore lovely phone conversation. She spoke as if she were the matriarch of a fine house. *Remember how you were raised,* indeed.

My paternal grandmother never ceased to confound me. My decision to study German Literature in St. Louis had nothing to do with her family ties to the city—previously unknown to me—and everything to do with a full scholarship and monthly stipend, along with the promise of study in Germany, all of which she approved.

I used the nine-hour drive to St. Louis to stew on Grandma's out-of-the-blue proclamation. Beyond Christian morality, I couldn't quite put my finger on why her comment bugged me so much, nor what she was getting at exactly. After four years at college, I found her admonition belated, outdated, insulting, and even hurtful.

I assumed that she meant I shouldn't engage in premarital sex, I should go to church, and I absolutely should marry a white Christian boy. I'd never forgotten the way I was raised, nor had I betrayed it, though I'd been very tempted. It was a constant ambient noise, which I'd steeped in for two decades by then. Remembering *how I was raised* and adjusting accordingly was the defining struggle in my young life, a struggle that was hardly limited to Grandma Doris, though she was a more vocal proponent.

Thanks to a quirky, outspoken family who espoused a wide range of competing and concurring agendas, I was a dutiful master of reading the room. As a consequence, her admonition made no logical sense to my way of thinking. I'd ordered my life to others' spoken and unspoken requirements for as long as I could recall.

German graduate school was my choice alone, ironic because not only was I not German—that I knew of—but the German language wasn't my first love. Even more ironically, given subsequent events, that first love was Spanish. Remember me reading on the sofa for Grandma at five and trying to do it in Spanish? My second language love was Swedish, chosen to make my family proud at a distance. German was my third choice, and technically speaking, German chose me.

Yet within two months, I decided to drop out of my PhD program, effective in May. I informed Grandma Doris of my new plans at Christmas, namely to move home and teach high school. I could get my license at the University of Minnesota. Officially, I'd take a personal leave rather than quit outright, out of prudence. I thought that I'd found agreement with Grandma, which wasn't required so much as shaping expectations.

Since she only spoke English—she thought everyone should—Grandma Doris didn't know what Germanic studies or language acquisition entailed. To gain the language prowess that made her so proud, I wrote copious notes during classes—the only way my hummingbird brain paid attention—and recopied them, streamlining down to the essentials, the way I witnessed her doing when I was a kid on the floor, playing with office supplies while she typed up meeting agendas and minutes. I never realized—I wish I could tell her now—that I was modeling my habits on hers. I'd learned that work ethic from her, equal to and alongside religion.

I could sit for hours, in quiet and loud places, meditating on the flashcards that I wrote in precise cursive. Kaleidoscope words became holy fragments, bits of the divine. Make no mistake, it's a practice and it's a prayer. Those were the learning habits that I wanted to teach in my future classroom.

Once I completed a stack, I narrated my life out loud in walking conversations with myself. This babbling part, which so defined me and drew unwanted attention to me as a child, I had reclaimed. I didn't privilege one kind of learning (drilling or babbling), I adored both.

What I didn't love, and what I soon realized a PhD required the most of, was the intensive reading and German textual analysis, which put me to sleep. Because like Grandma Doris, I could fall asleep at the drop of a hat.

But I did eventually find a church after a determined search—a high Episcopal congregation. The rituals soothed my soul and bypassed my brain, with all that kneeling and reverent bowing. And incense. And stained glass windows. And Anglican songs.

That spring, Grandma Doris and Hubert—whom I alone called "Grandpa Hubert"—drove to St. Louis one weekend on a genealogical tour; as she said in advance, their agenda was tight. On Saturday, she called from their hotel on arrival, already having made dinner plans with Hubert's granddaughter Cori and her boyfriend, both sophomores at Washington University. She invited me too. Once again I was present at a first family meeting with a potential future spouse, when what I really wanted was our grandparents to myself. So I invited them to Sunday worship. I fully expected Grandma to praise my good taste.

Instead she countered with the name of a small Baptist church. "My mother grew up there. I was hoping you'd join me." She offered to pick me up early; she had her heart set on attending the Southern Baptist service. I hadn't realized until that moment that Grandma had a genuine past in this city, not distant connections.

My grandparents had driven all that way, and I was seeking a suitable compromise. That's how I found myself in the backseat of Grandpa Hubert's sedan that Sunday afternoon, riding to a cemetery in a forlorn section of town. "This neighborhood used to be quite grand," Grandma said, wistfully. "My aunt and uncle lived in a great big house. We ate such fancy dinners around their table. Servants came when my aunt rang a bell." I tapped my fingertips together as she reached her conclusion: "It's so much fun to see how the other half lives."

I exhaled. "What other half, Grandma?" She didn't answer.

My step-grandpa entered at the towering black gates, and we wove our way around trees and stones until at last she told him to stop. She said that she'd discovered genealogical ties to a wealthy family of German descent who'd passed themselves off as Dutch during the World Wars. Meaning that maybe we actually were a little bit German, maybe even more than a little. These were those relatives' graves.

Tucked in among towering mausoleums and monuments, we gathered around relatively modest gravestones, given the surroundings. Grandma offered details about each distant relation. One flat headstone bore the name Winnie.

"Who's Winnie?" I asked. "Why doesn't she have a last name?"

"As I understand it," she said, "Winnie married a man against the family's wishes. She rather disappointed them." Grandma nodded in approval.

"That doesn't change the fact that she married him," I said. "She deserved her full name on the stone." Grandma didn't answer.

I was thinking of Vivian. Regardless of her marital status, she would

deserve a full name on her grave. I was thinking of an unmarried classmate who'd given birth to Baby Jesse. Several of us had awaited his
arrival that frosty night in January, then missed his sudden entrance
when we left for a bite at McDonald's. With the cord wrapped around
his neck five times, Baby Jesse's C-section was indeed a miracle birth.
Had the worst come to pass, Tricia would've deserved a full name.

And though I didn't want to admit it, I was thinking of me. Over the
years, Grandma had displayed snippets of ancient letters, scavenged
from various sources, as genealogical finds: private communications,
newspaper clippings, family Bibles. I imagined her snooping through
a printer-paper box of letters in my childhood bedroom, full of mis-
leading hints at romance.

Hidden among these was evidence of an intimate, honest romance
she might overlook because it lasted such a short time. But if she recognized it, she'd realize I did make concessions to how I was raised.
In college, I hid a long-distance relationship with a brilliant biracial
man. Tony had an Ivy League degree to his name and was working on
his PhD at Harvard. None of this had any bearing on me the summer
I met him—we were both studying German in Vermont—until suddenly we were falling in love, and I began looking for ways to make his
case to every single one of my elders. He'd visited me in Minnesota
that final winter at college, and then in a panic I'd broken it off. It was
too close to home. Grandma Doris wouldn't know that story though.

All the things that should've made her adore him would have been
nullified by his skin color. I worried how certain relatives might treat
biracial children, and frankly I didn't want to find out. So I didn't bring
Tony home.

We climbed back into the car and Grandpa Hubert turned the key,
wearing the same patient, pleasant expression. The canopy of leaves
obscured the sun as Grandma launched into a tender topic from dinner the night before.

"It's a real shame you want to quit graduate school," she said. "I mean, think of the honor you're losing for your family." I felt the blood rise to my face. Originally, she'd wanted me to go into the business world. Where exactly had she recently bragged about me? Certainly with her bridge-playing friends, but where else?

"It's not a lost honor, Grandma." I studied the salt-and-pepper back of her head. "It's a stipend and a scholarship. I've changed my mind. The PhD won't make me happy."

"A scholarship is an honor. Something to be proud of." She looked over her shoulder with an innocent expression. "Isn't it?" I glared at her, and she looked hurt. We rode on in silence, punctuated by Grandpa Hubert's small talk.

For heaven's sake, she'd dropped out of college to attend business school as her parents' precondition to marry the man of her choice. Clearly she'd published my academic credentials in some genealogical tome or such, but that was her problem, not mine. Certainly I would miss the scholarship and the stipend, which bought independence. That wasn't a strong enough reason to stay.

But arguing was pointless. No matter how either of us framed this discussion, the other would never agree. Nor would we think of disowning each other. Recognizing our impasse, I folded and unfolded my hands until Grandpa Hubert dropped me off curbside.

"Good seeing you, Amy," he said. And he really did see me.

Heirloom Frames

"You and I think alike," Hubert said to me often, in conspiratorial tones—on the phone, in person, saying hello, or saying goodbye. "I always tell Grandma: Amy knows what she's doing." He never offered context. I never asked.

Each time Hubert uttered his few cryptic words, I felt a preemptive sense of relief, absolved of presumed disloyalty to Grandma Doris. He saved me from defending myself and bridged the gap between Grandma and me.

We all knew that he doted on her—vacuumed and dusted, fussed that she needed to eat right, taught her how to play golf, folded her into his Lutheran church, accompanied her on genealogical tours, and treated her like a queen.

I hoped he was right about my instincts because the University of Minnesota education department had quickly rejected me. I'd feared they might, based on my over-the-phone German proficiency test and early decision to drop out of the Washington University PhD program.

Despite the countless drill sessions I'd led in college, the hours I'd tutored, and the weekly tests I'd proctored and graded, the U of M rejected me because I had no experience working with children in schools. This was a serious blow to my ego.

Back in Minnesota, my bedroom in my parent's house still waited to receive me, the same room where—faded photographic evidence showed—young Amy lined up her stuffed toys and dolls to teach them to read. My dollhouse still sat undisturbed on a pedestal there. Once again, my future was a blank slate.

I purposely didn't call Grandma Doris while I pondered my options. One afternoon, the phone rang and Grandpa Hubert's name flashed across the caller ID. After staring a moment, I picked up and regretted it immediately.

"My bridge group says you didn't get into the U of M because you're white," Grandma said by way of hello.

"Excuse me?" *Because I was white?* It was only a matter of time before this particular shoe dropped. There it had been right in front of me the whole time, but still it stunned me. That she declared the reason seemingly on my behalf made it so much worse. I snapped, "I never told you I didn't get in."

"You would've called if you had." Grandma sounded annoyed. "Honestly, I don't know why you're so proud."

I wasn't proud, I was protecting myself from her unwelcome opinions. And she was playing dirty. She didn't get to insert her friends into the audience of my life, let alone blame random people of color for my misfortunes. She was saving face after bragging too soon about my academic success.

"Look, Grandma," I pushed back. "This is why I don't tell you things. I love you, but no. My whiteness isn't the reason."

There I sat in my soon-to-be abandoned St. Louis apartment, bewildered. I slumped, head in hands, on my living room futon under a ceiling embellished with floral plaster designs. Across the room, a lineup of four Hummel figurines stared back from my tiny altar, housed in the built-in bookshelf. The room was practically an homage to her favored decor.

I sat in their deafening silence a long time. Beside the original Hummel girl claimed from Grandma, two new figurines watched over me: a girl with a straw basket in her hands, and a choir boy singing, sheet music outstretched. I'd received both as gifts from Eva. For all the narrow American stories I'd been fed and had grown up believing, Eva provided counterstories. She pointed to hidden—and painful—truths in my culture *and* hers. That's why I believed her.

A fourth Hummel sat knitting innocently, singing along with a bird at her knee. This Hummel was a vintage gift from my late step-great-grandma, Cora, who married into my family at eighty. Behind Cora's sweet Christian façade, she'd devoted herself to Holocaust denial. Magazine stashes in closets after she died had confirmed this.

After Grandma Doris called, I felt drained and defeated. I'd tried so hard to manage one elder's egregious blindspots, only to unearth another more subtle.

On my apartment wall, a framed crescent moon shone down. It was the image I'd pieced together from watercolor paper that final term at Carleton. Its inspiration came straight out of my childhood: Grandma's card-stock office papers, married with all the flashcards I'd made. Grandma used to sing us songs about the moon. She told us how *her* Grandma believed that the Man in the Moon was a woman instead. "Look. Do you see her soft wavy hairstyle?" Similarly, my artwork helped me reframe set beliefs.

My final months of college, I'd shaped leaves and five-pointed flowers into that crescent shape, capped at each end with lemony points of a moon. Evenings at the studio, I'd meticulously centered the pieces on a blank page, painting their backs with sticky glue, pressing them firmly into their places.

I'd spent countless hours down on the concrete studio floor, cutting, piecing, and pasting saturated violet and dark-turquoise squiggles, each tiny wave similar, each one unique, their angles, their sizes, their textures and whorls, each shape holding its own space, filling the white expanse. I cut and pasted until there was exactly enough room for all of them. I'd been thinking so hard about who I was according to everyone else. And I didn't need to.

In a momentary impulse, I'd cut out an emerald flicker, the color of a leaf, in the shape of a wave. The solitary fragment was all those things and none of them. That green ribbon was me: the synthesis of a great many things. I nestled the emerald flame into those flowing waters where the moon was reflected, or—if you see it that way—the sky. And I was enchanted. I didn't create this artwork for anyone but me.

During the solitary months of graduate school, I spent whole days in its shadow on my floral futon, strewn with jewel-toned remnants. There I shaped the wayward scraps into the semblance of wildflowers.

I was especially proud of one very delicate, thorny pink rose that became a gift for Grandma Doris. One day she would display it prominently in her home. Even when she had to downsize, she took it with her.

Simple Steps

To whom does a woman's ambition belong?

The same month my friend Tricia gave birth as a single mom, Zoë Baird was removed as nominee for Attorney General of the USA, not because of her qualifications, but due to childcare issues. She'd hired illegal nannies and owed back taxes. Soon thereafter, Kimba Wood—second in line—had her nomination withdrawn, thanks to less flagrant issues of the same nature. This shocked me because I always did want to be a mother, but I also wanted a fulfilling career, and I thought that I could do both. Vocation had brought freedom to my grandmother, my aunt, and my mom, so why not me?

Women could wield great power, I knew. When Grandma retired from City Hall after running elections all those years, they'd hired three women to replace her. But she wouldn't have hired a young woman like me, who might have babies and leave. She told me so herself. We'd discussed it. Heatedly.

I believed I could have both. And yet . . .

If established baby boomers like Zoë Baird and Kimba Wood turned to under-the-table measures to secure appropriate childcare, and the job went by default to Janet Reno, a childless single woman from the silent generation, what hope existed for Gen X wannabe mothers and scholars like me?

Of all the admirable women I'd been fortunate to have as professors, I couldn't think of any who were moms except one. I'd always wondered: *When did she sleep?*

My year in St. Louis put my ideas about motherhood to the test. Before college, I was vocally pro-life, focused on the cut-and-dried morality of reproduction until a sophomore woman on my freshman floor drilled me on arguments that I'd glibly dismissed throughout high school. Coming into the conversation, I was emphatic: "I would never get pregnant by accident."

She frowned. "What if you did get pregnant?"

"God forbid, if that happened," I sighed heavily. "My family would support me."

"What about women whose families can't support them?" She listed real-world scenarios that looked nothing like mine, women in tough-luck situations, poor women, women stretched thin.

"I can't speak for them," I had to concede; I felt like a jerk. "But I would never have an abortion."

"Right," said my neighbor, who was Jewish, not Christian. "Then don't YOU have an abortion. That's why it's not called pro-abortion."

"What?" This idea had never crossed my mind.

"Listen again," she said. "It's pro-choice."

That's how I reconciled myself with Roe v. Wade. By graduate school, I'd started to see that even pregnant women who chose to give birth out of wedlock benefited from the choice. But even then, I was more like Grandma Doris than I cared to admit.

Motherhood was hypothetical for me until I met Tricia. We'd agreed to rent a place in St. Louis when the German department flew us into town to woo us for their PhD program. Right before my parents and I drove down to St. Louis one weekend to find our apartment, she told me over the phone that she was pregnant. "So I can't live with you," she said. "I'm moving in with my boyfriend."

That's how I came to live in my own apartment for the first time.

I thought that would be the last I saw of Tricia, but she arrived in St. Louis the same day as me. My almost-roommate and friend granted me needed perspective on single motherhood, given my vows that I'd never put myself in that position. Tricia made it impossible for me to continue thinking in that vein. She was wicked smart, wicked kind, wicked funny, and we got along famously.

By the grace of God, Tricia let me be present for and with her in St. Louis, during that blessed stage of her life. By the time her son was born that winter, I could hardly wait to be—what would I be to him? Auntie Amy? Several weeks later, Baby Jesse's father drove away in the wee morning hours and was gone. Then I took on the role that defined my time in Missouri, as much nanny as student. I learned a lot about what I wanted in life by witnessing Tricia and her son.

Every time I watched Baby Jesse in the early days, he cried relentlessly and I didn't know how to soothe him. I feared that I would never be a good mom. "Please, Baby Jesse, tell Auntie Amy what it is that you want," I begged, offering him bottles in vain, rocking him, putting him back in his car seat, at a loss because babies don't talk. Tricia laughed at my stories, like the time someone looked at my license plate and asked, horrified, if I had driven all the way from Minnesota with the crying baby. Despite my initial cluelessness, I caught on. Baby Jesse came to trust me, and I came to trust myself. We sat on my living room futon, laughing, playing with toys. I took Baby Jesse on school errands and showed him off. He might as well have been Sweet Baby Jesus, for how his surprise birth transformed my life.

Here's how I started to frame the facts: Motherhood was exhausting. Motherhood was delightful. Motherhood would require me to keep my wits about me. As a mom, I'd need to leverage every advantage. In St. Louis I'd always be a transplant who struggled to navigate the landscape and culture, even before bringing kids into it.

There were lines in St. Louis I was told not to cross, places that white students said I should avoid for reasons of safety. For example, you don't cross Delmar Avenue. You don't go beyond the Arch. Those were the hard limits. More intricate lines were everywhere, across the surrounding suburbs. My friends and I unwittingly came up against them all the time. My Carleton friend spoke of staying silent when a barber railed against Jews. "He had a razor to my head," he said. "I felt sick." I would've too.

In University City, where streets were said to be tough, Baby Jesse's mom crossed those lines to get Women, Infant, and Children (WIC) support for cereal boxes, milk cartons, and bags of corn. Tricia and I had the same stipend, money that only stretched so far. She said that she was the only white lady in that waiting room. She got home fine. Meanwhile in my posh suburb where I thought I'd feel safest, Mom helped me to make the rent, cops were looking for something to do, and I was wary of parking tickets.

One day, a cop pulled me over for going five miles above the speed limit along a tree-lined boulevard. He took my Minnesota license and let me sit there a long time while his lights spun round and round. He let me off with a fatherly lecture, though he was barely older than me. Then he very slowly followed me all the way home. When I'd bought my pretty aqua-blue car for its distinctive color, emptying my bank account shortly before graduation, I never imagined wanting to hide. But now I waited inside the car, doors locked, parked outside my apartment where

I lived alone on a one-way street. My stomach hurt. It felt dangerous that he now knew where I lived. The pepper-spray keychain from my mom wouldn't work on a policeman, I realized. It wasn't so safe in the suburbs after all.

As a non-native, I had come to realize that I didn't want to make my home on the Mason-Dixon Line. Farther still was Germany, where I was slated to go for a year of study abroad. Yes, I had time, but I didn't want to miss motherhood or be a mom in a foreign place. What if I didn't want to marry a German and stay? The clock was already ticking, twenty-two to twenty-three. Where would it end? Twenty-eight, twenty-nine, thirty? (The horror! At this point, I can tell you: At thirty-three, I'd give birth to identical twins, and that would be plenty soon enough.)

My roots ran deep in Minnesota; I knew the lay of the land and could look out for myself there. With my horizons broadened, I wanted to teach German to bright, well-intentioned teens who could stand to question some things before they got to college. We'd dabble and babble and stumble into brilliant mistakes. In Minnesota, where I'd meet the Minnesota father of my future Minnesota kids.

That May, I had a scare that confirmed the depth of my motherly instincts. Tricia had buckled Baby Jesse's seat into my car in a service-station parking lot so that I could drive him to my apartment, while she tackled a few tasks ahead of a menacing storm. As I turned onto the main artery that led to my cross street, the heavens opened up with torrents of rain. I drove Baby Jesse the few miles home, secure in my back seat, through the pelting deluge. I couldn't see ten feet in front of my windshield. I couldn't see the periphery enough to pull over.

Instead I drove on, each green light coming mercifully into view, while I prayed to Real Jesus for safe passage, not worried about my pretty blue car, nor what would happen to me, nor a future back home that was far from decided, only knowing that I loved this precious child, whose mom entrusted him to me, and I had to deliver him safe and sound. When we pulled up to my sidewalk, I turned off the ignition and sobbed with gratitude for divine intervention.

Yes, I would face obstacles, but I would take the next steps in front of me, and I would arrive in due time. Baby Jesse and his mom were off to Germany the next year, where he would grow into a little boy. But as for me, I had unfinished business to tend to back home.

Student

Courage

Some say that you can never go home again, and that's probably true for some people. As for me, it seems a foregone conclusion that I had to go back, and I had to go back as a teacher. Long before high school graduation, people from my hometown had insisted I would become one. Random classmates in school and their mothers at church asked me about it.

"I'm never going to be a teacher," I said.

"Really? But your mom is a teacher."

People made assumptions about me as a highly visible teacher's kid, and I didn't like it. True, I could talk in front of a crowd and my voice traveled far. But school—the thing that put food on my family's table—was far from a comfortable place for me. Long before I was our projected valedictorian starting in the ninth grade, my classmates and their moms eyed my good grades with envy, while the moms took note that their kids weren't as unpopular as me, nor as gawky, nor as naïve. Each time I was selected for any opportunity, it caught the attention of mean girls and their lookie-loo moms. Anytime I didn't make the grade or the cut, it confirmed their bias: *Who did I think I was?* How do I know? Enough people made such comments to my face that I feared their sentiments were universal. Which begat more awkwardness on my part.

This is also why I worked so hard to redefine myself as a cheerleader. First I made it onto the wrestling squad as a sophomore through a special try-out to fill a vacant spot. For our junior year, my best friend, Terri, and I made the soccer and boys' basketball squads together. During soccer season, Eva came to live with my family for three months and attended my high school. Cheerleading didn't impress her. Eva took her own classes and joined her own sports. But she observed my life closely, rode everywhere in my car, and spoke the truth with me candidly, whether or not we agreed. In that sense, she became a true sister. Before we reunited at Eva's house on the edge of the Black Forest the following spring, I'd videotaped my early cheerleading try-out, traded addresses with friendly faces only, and prepared to leave my hometown behind until senior year.

While I was in West Germany, I received plenty of letters from various classmates, and not only the ones I expected. I heard both sides of fights between allies and adversaries alike, the inside scoop at last. I wrote back, sympathetic, with friendly reassurance, and discovered that in letters, I actually was quite socially adept. Also that I was hardly alone in my high school struggles—everyone was shitty to everyone. While I was gone, even my best friend replaced me. Then Mom wrote to me that Terri and I had been named to the football cheerleading squad.

Drama ensued. Some junior girls named to the squad with us planned to approach me when I got back, to convince me to trade places with their more popular friend, who'd made the soccer squad. Had I been home I would've headed them off, but Terri had already surrendered her spot. As her reward, the school named her soccer squad captain;

I could be her co-captain. All indications showed that mean-girl talk against me was rampant back home.

Huddled over a cup of peppermint tea in Eva's bedroom, I alternated between two painful refrains: *Why can't they leave me alone?* and *Why can't they accept me?* The desertion by my best friend, with whom I'd shared many adventures but who had resisted outings with Eva—and never sent any letters—was particularly painful.

Eva knew the truth. "You try so hard to please them." She sipped her tea. "You can't because they're competing with you. And Terri's not on your side either."

I took some deep breaths and paraphrased Eva's words. "They're never going to be on my side."

"No." She shook her head. "You know what else?" Eva smiled. "They can't stop you. Be yourself, no matter what they say." She was quoting her favorite Sting song. She would follow up with letters across the Atlantic once I got home. Having Eva on my side didn't make me less miserable, but it did mean that I wasn't alone in the world, even if it felt that way. Because when I returned home, all my natural allies had moved on—neither my older brother, nor my best friend, nor Eva were there to protect me as things grew progressively worse throughout the football cheer season.

At our final away game, I stood, shivering and isolated at the end of the formation, rubbing my mittens together to ward off the cold, when an angry male voice pierced the air.

"HALL-BERG!"

My last name sounded so ugly. It came from an anonymous spot in the stands. Startled, I scanned the crowd and saw only darkness. When I spun to my left, the other cheerleaders stood looking away, oblivious. The faceless voice lobbed my last name several more times. And I stood there, stunned into silence. He didn't even have the decency to use my first name.

That was the loneliest bus ride home ever. I cried afterward for hours to my mom. Nobody mentioned what had happened on Monday. I prayed that it was an isolated incident, that my harassers would tire of me and move on. Instead, they doubled down. The next game, the jeers came from brightly lit bleachers at home. "HALL-BERG!!!!"

This time, I stood caught in full spotlight, visibly startled, frozen, fighting back tears, while my last name kept coming. I knew damn well people had to have seen it, parents and teachers included.

As I walked through the cafeteria after the game, a sophomore grabbed my arm. "Amy!" When I turned to face her, I recognized her. "Amy," she said again. "I know who's calling your name." And then she told me exactly who said and did what, and just how long it had been going on. She named a boy that I had a crush on. Whose attention I'd sought.

"Are you sure?" I swallowed hard.

"Yes, it was definitely him." I was heartbroken to hear the truth, but I understood. He couldn't afford the reputation of liking me. The girl spilled all the details. The cheerleader I most suspected—but could never catch—started it every time, aided by her best friend, whom I also suspected. He yelled on their signal. All the cheerleaders knew. Had known all along, as they smiled their brightest cheerleader smiles.

Within a week, two squadmates voluntarily confessed what they'd done, or at least what they hadn't done to support me. They also corroborated my story, naming the ringleader, a pretty girl who'd regularly stood beside me on the track. I'd known she started cheers without telling me first. But I hadn't known that she'd often moved up behind me, waved her arms mockingly, and egged the crowd on all season long. I'd been bullied by mean girls before, but this was a whole new level of mean. To the people who spoke up because it wasn't right, please know that your courage meant the world to me. I haven't forgotten.

The athletic director gave me permission to skip the playoff that Saturday, so that I could visit Carleton College. She told the ringleader to apologize. As I heard it, a few cheerleaders showed up tipsy at the game, ready to confront me together. Not sure if it's true, but that's what people said. Soon after, the junior ringleader called me at home, as expected. "Where were you?" Her words dripped with righteous indignation. "We were going to apologize."

"I had permission not to go," I said.

"You shouldn't have told on me."

"I didn't. Someone else turned you in."

Silence, momentarily. "Well, you have to accept my apology or I can't be a cheerleader anymore."

And that was it for her. She didn't want to lose her privileges or spoil her senior year or, I now suspect, be publicly shamed. She wasn't sorry for how she hurt me, nor that I would never be a cheerleader again—something that I had formerly loved. In my mind, back then and still today, she should have been permanently banned from cheerleading, but I held a lower status in that hierarchy. She'd won. I was the one walking away. "Fine. I accept your apology."

Why did I surrender? I wanted to be done. I think she exhaled and may have thanked me, I don't recall. I weighed those scenes for years, wondering what I could have done differently. As difficult as that whole cheerleading episode was, it did help me to understand what it is to be an outsider, and what it feels like to hide in plain sight.

The resolution revealed my outsized status at our school. I went on to star in both plays—bookish, pretty girls like me had permission to do that. When I hosted cast parties in our basement, kids of all ages filled the room. Everyone was welcome, Mom provided abundant food spreads, and we all had a great time.

And I was valedictorian. I gave a well-received speech at the fifty-yard line. I couldn't stop smiling afterward. I'd craved that external validation, and I'd won the biggest prize. But if I weren't valedictorian, who would I have I been?

So I learned part of the lesson: how to build myself up. Except trauma from the end of high school lingered at college. Even away from my hometown, I was always looking out for the mean girls, vigilant against people who might not like me, blaming myself, and apologizing in advance. I never went off-campus, though I was accepted to study in London, because what if my fellow travelers there didn't like me? What if I returned to no friends on campus? I didn't take education classes, either. Teach high school? No way in hell.

It took me four years to reorient myself toward people who liked me, and whom I actually liked. At our college graduation I couldn't stop crying because I had a real group of friends.

Every so often, out of the blue, people have told me they're sorry they weren't nicer to me back in high school. I know what they're talking about, and if it wasn't the cheerleading thing, then it was something else that I really don't need to hear about. That isn't my business. It may still weigh on them to know that they watched me suffer. But they're forgiven. Rather than confess their past sins to me, I'd prefer that they step up elsewhere with compassion.

By the time I left St. Louis, where I'd made a whole family of friends in graduate school, I knew that I could be there for teens going through the difficult high school years. That's the only place I wanted to be. And that was why I wanted to be a teacher, underneath it all. I wanted to affirm those sensitive students who needed an ally cheering them on— not to rescue them, but to help them find their positions of strength.

As for me, the sources of my deepest wounding—my hometown and a suburban high school—were exactly the places I had to revisit. That I did return was an act of courage and faith.

Intersections

After I dropped out of graduate school with no discernible plans for the future, I took on a fundraising stint for our Lutheran parish. They had me photocopying form letters, slicing them in half with a paper cutter, and stuffing them into envelopes. Somehow I did this surprisingly poorly. Rather than talking to me about it, they quietly replaced me.

No matter. I had my heart set on being a German teacher, though my rejection by the U of M education program reinforced the need for a backup plan, and not the secretarial temp work I cobbled together. Now was the time to be practical in a different way: The Wall had fallen, and the question was being raised about what languages kids should be taught going forward. Was German relevant anymore in our American worldview? In fact, German was fast becoming a niche language. Whereas Spanish wasn't. And therefore in Spanish, there would be plentiful jobs.

So I retaught myself enough to start earning credits toward a piecemeal Spanish major in night courses across the Twin Cities, including

101

at the U of M. Meanwhile I got a provisional substitute license through my hometown school district, which allowed me to work as a building substitute in my old high school, teaching whatever classes they assigned, learning to hold my own.

After a few months of this holding pattern, I'd applied at a Catholic university in St. Paul—presumably to earn my license in both German and Spanish. I chose the University of St. Thomas as the most expedient of my remaining options, with certification I could complete in two years, plus a Spanish department. Which was important, since the commute from my parents' home south of the Minnesota River was a forty-five minute drive on a good day.

As long as we'd lived there, the closest bridge had snaked through the valley. During rush hour, it could take over an hour to cross, and that was before the rest of the route into the Twin Cities. Alternatively, there was a long highway drive to the north-and-south freeways. In years when the Minnesota River rose past its banks in the spring, passages would flood. We South Metro residents were then reduced to narrow freeways, gridlocked all day long in both directions. This wasn't happenstance but by design. The trip to St. Thomas therefore required big time investments as I navigated roadblocks. One of my courses—Diversity and Multicultural Education—soon helped me to realize that, as a white woman, I'd only had a very small taste of such things.

One day during class discussion, I was voicing my frustration with crowded bridges and rural projects that didn't get funded, when a white classmate jumped in. "Those roads destroy Black neighborhoods," he said. "Have you heard of Rondo in St. Paul? The I-94 freeway was built straight through the middle."

I stiffened, startled by his intrusion, and confused by his reference.

I'd never heard of Rondo before. It was in an entirely different part of the Twin Cities from my rural hometown. So first I had to reorient myself, both to the landscape and my moral compass. I-94 was an odd freeway, which I'd noted again that year when I started driving into the Cities. The road bridged the Mighty Mississippi, a cramped corridor between Minneapolis and St. Paul, with several left-hand exits and on-ramps.

"That's not what I'm talking about." My voice sounded edgy. I felt it catch. "I'm talking about a bridge across the Minnesota River. There aren't any neighborhoods there." I looked down at my hands, which I was wringing in my lap.

The conversation moved on, but visceral energy coursed in my veins. Not only had he missed the very real context of my rural, south-of-the-river community, but he'd twisted my words, sidelined my point to score his, and—as I heard it—implied I was racist. Given my college experience, I also felt shame that my ignorance was still showing. My face would have broadcast my heightened emotions.

Before she excused class that day, our Native American professor—a brilliant woman who didn't mince words—announced our term paper. If we wanted a B for our course grade, we had to write an essay centered on people of color, including primary sources. This, I could do. Then she added the non-negotiable requirement that terrified me.

"In order to earn an A, you'll have to interview two people of color." She looked around the visibly white room. "There's no other way to gain true perspective."

I glanced at my classmates, none of whom made eye-contact except Rondo guy. I looked away. If I'd learned nothing else, I knew it wasn't people of color's default job to help white people learn. I considered my options, which seemed non-existent. I wanted to earn that A to show respect to my professor, though.

She'd revealed ways she'd crossed boundaries and faced major discomfort, earning her PhD to teach mostly white students like us, so that we could be better teachers for students like her.

Ironically, I no longer saw grades as a measure of self-worth. College and graduate school had disabused me of that illusion. But as she so aptly pointed out, grades still unlocked opportunities or put them out of reach. Remember that German language niche? The grade point average on my transcript could make the difference between a rare German teaching position and subbing forever.

While the thought of interviews triggered discomfort, my heart said that not doing them would be a cop-out and a source of lasting regret.

I hesitantly raised my hand. "What if I don't know any people of color well enough to ask?" I heard my muted voice and gauged our professor's response.

She neither smiled nor frowned, but nodded, resolute. "Go to the Office of Student Diversity. They can connect you with undergraduate students."

I'd already chosen to earn that A. The only question was how. Ever the literature major, I went to the library and found a book by Alice Walker, *Living by the Word*. In her essay, "The Dummy in the Window," Walker relates how Joel Chandler Harris, a white author, created the character of Uncle Remus, fictitious Black plantation storyteller to reframe classic African folk tales, Br'er Rabbit and Br'er Fox. This then became the Disney film, *Song of the South*.

I knew "Zip-A-Dee-Doo-Dah," its theme song, by heart from a childhood record. I'd known there was some controversy about the film, something about Blackness, specifically about a tar baby story, but it had never clicked before. Reading Walker's essay, I understood why she and her family never told those stories again after they saw *Song of the South*. Their treasured tales had been stolen and passed off as trinkets.

By the next class session, I had a topic: "African-American Women Authors." More specifically, regarding stories about Black people, who had permission to use what kind of words? Zora Neale Hurston, I'd learned, was criticized during the Harlem Renaissance for using the same kind of Black language white authors fetishized, as in Mark Twain's *Huck Finn*.

I still hadn't figured the interviews out. I'd left answering machine messages with two Black students whose names I'd been given. Neither woman had called me back, which made sense. Driving into St. Paul, I prayed the whole way. Mercifully, the guy who spoke up about Rondo made a beeline for me when I entered the room. "Do you need help finding interview subjects?"

I sighed. "Yes, please." I told him my topic and asked if he knew any Black women who could talk about literature.

"I go to church with a lot of Black people." His brow furrowed. "I have two women in mind. Both teachers. I think they'd be willing to help."

That's how I wrote the paper that would linger with me throughout my life. I don't have permission to use the words of the Minneapolis women who spoke with me—both of whom are far more public figures than they were then. I'll tell you that both women were—in different ways—a generous blend of guarded, candid, and kind. I will always remember how, when I called one woman at the agreed-upon time, we were making introductions when she suddenly said she'd call me back.

When she returned my call, she apologized. "Police came to our door and I was afraid for my husband. He's supposed to be on his way home." He was fine, thankfully. With that shocking detail out of the way, I interviewed her.

Besides the fact that no one Black author speaks for all Black people, here's the conclusion I drew in my term paper:

"How can I as a white person ever hope to sum up the experiences of any African-Americans? The answer is, I can't ... This work has left me more convinced than ever that I can never truly understand what it is to be an African-American woman, but I can respectfully discuss what I have learned."

Moreover, the women I spoke with agreed that it was important for "non-African-Americans to include Black people in their writings, but at the same time, they need to respect the boundaries that they simply should not cross."

When I wrote "they," I meant white people like me.

And finally, white people don't get to write in Black English. Ever. That isn't ours. Nor are Black stories. But we should all—regardless of skin color—read more work by Black authors.

In other words, we all have to speak from our own perspectives, while acknowledging our limitations.

This got me thinking. The real arc of learning was not about grades. I could not in good faith write about anyone else from an outside perspective if I wasn't clear on my perspective, whatever that was. And that would set me on a wider path of translation—its power to transcend cultures, the limits of what we can translate, and the wisdom to know the difference.

Variations on a Theme

"Dime!" said the voice of Isabel in Seville, Spain, as she picked up. *Tell me.*

I was calling from Eva's apartment to discuss my arrival. My Spanish host mother's bluntness was so far removed from the German etiquette I anticipated with my prerehearsed Spanish that I sputtered, adding costly minutes to my international AT&T card.

Isabel then told me the exact amount I should pay my airport cabbie, and how many minutes the trip should take. I was grateful, thinking that at least I could come prepared. On arrival, the cabbie drove a block past her door, and I let him carry my suitcases back down the narrow cobblestone sidewalk.

I'd exchanged enough money for the required Spanish pesetas, which I handed over. The cabbie then walked back to the cab and pointed to the meter, dinging away. We hadn't agreed on the fare in advance, at the airport. It dawned on me that this was Isabel's point. I could feel the sweat dripping off me in the sweltering July heat.

Along the white stucco wall, the wooden fortress door opened. Isabel emerged in her housecoat, hair unruly. The two argued in the street until she thrust a handful of coins at him.

Once he drove off, I apologized, feeling panicked. "Lo siento."

Isabel waved her hand when I asked how much she'd given him, "No importa." She handed me a key and had me unlock the door. The air inside was significantly cooler. She made me unlock and relock the massive door, practicing several times from both sides. "If you don't have the key, no one will hear you," she said in very slow Spanish. "You'll need it when you go anywhere."

Ahead of us I saw a bright central open-air patio, but she and I grabbed my suitcases, and she started up the staircase immediately to our left. It was lined in vibrant mosaic tiles that I'd soon recognize as typical for Seville. She led me to the second floor, past a smoky dining room with an oversized wooden table. My room was down the hall, she said. "We'll always meet you here."

Starting the next day, I would attend intensive classes at a Spanish language school for foreign students, which I found and arranged through the St. Thomas Office of Off-Campus Studies. At twenty-four, I had three objectives for Spanish instruction:

1. Placement at a high enough level to earn credits toward my major.
2. Firsthand knowledge of Spanish culture.
3. Enough Spanish fluency to student teach it in tandem with German.

As for Spain, I chose it over Latin America because I knew Europe through Eva. Plus, it gave me an excuse to stop off in Germany on the way. Spain, I quickly discovered, was different from German life as curated by Eva.

In my room, Isabel opened the giant wardrobe and demonstrated the bathroom fixtures. She pointed to the chair, the bed, and the bedside table. "Es todo para ti." *All for me.* The rest of the massive house, I never saw, except for the open-air windows across from my own, all centered on the patio that nobody used.

After I unpacked, Isabel showed me the church plaza not far down the street, where there was a pay phone. Thus started my orientation to Spain.

Breakfast the next morning was a bread roll toasted over the gas stove flame, slathered with jam. Isabel brought it to the dining room where I ate alone, and she talked me through my route to school like a kid on the first day of Kindergarten.

It took time to settle into a more mature role. After a week of lunches together, the barrel-chested husband came down to serve me breakfast on Friday. "Buenos días," he said. *Good day.* Though I'd studied Spanish on and off for years, I realized that I had no words to say *good morning.*

In my broken Spanish, I asked, "Is there a special greeting for morning?"

He stared through thick glasses and spoke even louder. "Buenos. Días."

I felt a primal embarrassment rush through my body, which on the walk to school gave way to awareness around my language learning patterns. Early on, there was always great resistance. When things didn't go right, I felt exactly like a child in a foreboding house, afraid to touch anything. Anxiety arose when I couldn't express everything I wanted to say perfectly. I pushed forward, impatient and moody, as if that developmental stage somehow reflected poorly on me.

This ancient, flailing resistance, I now saw, was at cross-purposes with my goals, not just for Spain but as a future teacher, when I'd be the grown-up in the room. And so I put a name to it. Yes, I was like a child on sensory overload, which wasn't personal. Unlike with Eva,

Isabel and her husband weren't family. I paid for my private room with a bath and two meals a day.

Many more language students must have stayed in Isabel's household during more temperate seasons, as evidenced by a vacant room with several beds, directly across the patio from mine. Signs hinted that money was tight. Many mosaic tiles were cracked, and my bathroom sink wobbled on its pedestal. We were the family's bread and butter, and they were clearly used to our presence. I knew that their three grown children and daughter's husband were home when they shouted out open windows across the central patio, which in my family of origin would have meant fighting, and a reason for shame. To them it was efficient communication.

With the help of José, our language instructor, my classmates and I pieced together not only language fragments but Andalusian culture, and we started to understand Spain as a fragmented whole, far more diverse than we expected.

My classmates came from Atlanta and Alabama, Boston and California, Germany and Switzerland. We were women mostly, from twenty to forty years old, who spent our intensive mornings together at the school and met up around Seville for weekends and late afternoons. The Swiss woman and I had an extra daily lesson, so we stayed with José until one. By then, it was siesta time.

Walking home was surreal, like those paintings by Salvador Dalí where everything melted. The white-hot sun beat down on white stucco walls, metal rolling gates were rolled down, and meandering roads were deserted. I could have been abducted in broad daylight and nobody would have known, especially since the area was notorious for prostitution rings, the church in our adjacent plaza notwithstanding.

But I knew my way back, my key fit the lock, and the heavy door opened. Upstairs, I'd find the whole family gathered around the table for a delicious hot lunch. Good for digestion, they said. Fish. Paella.

Potatoes. Only their chunky gazpacho was cold. Isabel's meals sustained me the rest of the day.

"¿Vino?" they offered me after lunch. I refused, always dehydrated, religiously drinking my daily water jug purchased down on the corner to ward off headaches. They spent their afternoons at the table with friends, smoking and playing cards. I retreated to my room for a nap. When I awoke, I drilled my daily notes, and condensed them into a comprehensive record of key vocabulary and every grammar pattern I'd ever need to know. Those notes were also maps to adventure.

My classmates and I used the information to access ordinary places where almost nobody spoke English, despite the myth that all the world does. While the late-afternoon sun beat down, we met up to navigate meaning and shade. They pointed me to tourist attractions, fabulous music, and magical realism books. I relayed their medical needs to pharmacists. *En Español.*

Thus my compadres and I observed at close range how cultural lineage looked, translated in tangible markers across time. We saw how a mosque with a minaret could become a gothic cathedral when religious fortunes turned, and how the Catholic bell tower retained its Moorish flair.

Within walking distance from that cathedral, I lived in a fortress replete with contradictions. Its cracked mosaic walls repelled heat and crime, but when I kept sugary cereal in my armoire drawer, purchased at an air-conditioned department store, an army of ants marched in from the bathroom. Panicked, I smashed them. Then I had to hide the bodies and smuggled them out to the plaza. Open-air windows cooled me while I slept, but mosquitoes buzzed in my ears. One night, a mosquito bit my eye. By morning, the welt had swelled to gargantuan size. So Isabel told me the exact brand of insect repellent to request from the pharmacist.

All of these details fed the stories that we unpacked in class.

Eventually, Isabel told me that the house was ancient, in the family for generations, brilliantly built by Moors with natural cross-ventilation—those windows—that kept our rooms remarkably cool. Before the Spanish Inquisition, she told me, the Moors had come from Africa and built an advanced civilization across Spain with libraries, universities, and mosques. These buildings remained afterward.

José confirmed what she said and pointed out words where Arabic became Spanish. "Look for words with J or Z," he said. Foods like oranges—*naranjas*—and saffron—*azafrán*—had Arabic origins. "God willing" was *ojalá*.

Catholic markers were everywhere too. When we said *adiós* for goodbye, we were saying "to God." Even the unlikely nickname José never used—*Pepe*—had religious ties. As he explained, the initials PP—pronounced *pay-pay*—stood for *Padre Padrastro*, meaning Joseph, the stepdad of Jesus. God was Jesus's real dad, of course.

This kind of discovery thrilled me, and pointed me to markers closer to home. Wasn't *goodbye* short for "God be with you?" It was so obvious. Once you see such connections, you can't unsee them. It changes how you see everything.

One day, I walked past a tapas bar and overheard some guys sitting outside. "You figure she's German or Spanish?" I didn't hear the answer but laughed to myself, dressed in gauzy pants and a top, with Birkenstock sandals, flipping my fan open and closed, like a local. Biologically I was mostly Swedish.

They wouldn't have wondered if they'd heard me on *Onda Cero Radio*, interviewed with two classmates about learning Spanish in Spain. We almost didn't make it. After our taxi delivered us, we wandered the grounds of the 1992 Seville World Expo, a virtual ghost town in 1994. We were about to abandon the cause when the young producer came out and found us. She ushered us into the studio in the nick of time.

"Tell me the first Spanish you ever learned," said our host on the air.

My Southern best friend said, "Hola." The other American counted to ten.

With the obvious answers taken, an image popped up. There was a cartoon box on *Sesame Street* that opened and closed its lid. It said, "Abierto. Cerrado." *Open. Closed.* So I talked about that box, and how children's TV made me love Spanish. The host laughed and continued the interview, all in Spanish for a full hour.

Until that live broadcast, I hadn't thought of that box in years, only that I'd adored Spanish as a child. Now I could carry on conversations for an audience.

A door opened until the door closed. I was beginning to realize how this looked in my life, a labyrinthine progression. From English to Spanish, then bits of French, on to a first passion for Swedish, before high school German and Spanish. After I foreswore Spanish forever, I'd complemented my German major with significant Russian and French, and now I'd returned to Spanish once again.

What was it that drove me to learn all these languages, beyond the desire to teach them, which arrived so late that I never took an education class in college, when I had the chance? Doors closed. But the German major—*that* happened so easily. And college jobs—first as a German and Russian tutor, then as a German teaching assistant? Those landed in my lap. As with that radio show. Doors opened.

Not long afterward, José taught us the then-novel but now-ubiquitous game, *Two Truths and a Lie*, whereby you try to stump listeners about which is which. What surprised me was not that I could do it, but my instincts for blurring that line. One truth: I sang on a world-famous stage with a semi-professional choir. Another truth: Spanish was my first love. The lie: My parents had been through a tumultuous divorce. Tangentially true: Vivian got the divorce while we watched.

I found it fascinating when friends with whom I'd traveled from Portugal to Grenada guessed that singing on stage was my lie. And I started to see how many facets of truth I packed into my lie. We didn't know each other's backstories. This left more ways to reveal ourselves energetically. I started to see how we all had origin stories, writ large, beyond what we said with our words.

The details weren't as obvious, or relevant even. For example, Isabel told me she was born Venezuelan, which was why her accent was smoother than that of most Andalusians. My Spanish wasn't strong enough for me to notice. I did notice that she had a way of cutting to essentials to help an outsider like me see the much bigger picture.

Yes, I had much to learn, as Isabel's husband reminded me. But it felt amazing to make myself understood, with Spanish pieced together like mosaic tiles. Slowly a new understanding took hold, seeds that would grow for two decades. Language is never solely about performance. Language opens up doors.

And yes, language closes them. That cartoon box was a much larger—and more profound—metaphor than I knew what to do with at the time. But I'd grow to understand it. Within a year, my Spanish would be shelved, incomplete, waiting to be reopened again. When the time came, I'd reteach myself.

Curiously, Seville made me a better German teacher than I otherwise would have been. And it would, eventually, open doors to teaching Spanish.

My Spanish bears markers of that summer; specifically, that Andalusian accent won't ever leave me. But there are depths to the Spanish culture that I'll never plumb. Instead the journey pointed me in new directions back home.

Embrace the Detour

The day I flew home from Spain in 1994, I spent hours stranded in the Barcelona Airport, waiting for French air traffic controllers to break their strike so that I could fly back to Frankfurt, and from there, complete my round trip to Minneapolis-St. Paul. Unable to leave, I used my remaining Spanish coins to buy postcards of Antoní Gaudí's famed buildings around Barcelona, a fanciful hybrid of Gothic and Art Nouveau. Someday, I promised myself, I'd visit the actual city where they have their own vibrant culture and speak Catalan.

While Catalan is closer to French than Castilian Spanish—the Spanish exported around the world—they're all Romance languages thanks to Roman soldiers who occupied Europe and left a patchwork of Latin variants. On that day, French people couldn't communicate with each other, so I'd probably miss my German connection.

Because language is a living record of human history, how we use it evolves and devolves. You can try to moralize about it, but it's true, and you can't stop the process. The best you can do is to learn the baseline rules of a language at a given time and place, and apply them in real-life situations. From there, you adapt.

With no other way to kill time in the airport, I pulled out a slim yellow volume with deckle-edge pages: *Como agua para chocolate*, by Laura Esquivel, a Mexican author. My book reading session would span two airports and most of the way across the Atlantic. It helped that I'd seen the movie, *Like Water for Chocolate*, in a Minnesota theater with English subtitles.

The story takes place on a ranch along the Mexican-Texas border. Tita, the youngest of three sisters, is consigned by family tradition to serve her newly widowed mother from birth on—for as long as they both shall live. (And who says so? Her mother, the boss of the ranch.)

Tita grows up in the kitchen, where the cook nurtures and trains her. In time, the mother marries off her oldest daughter to Tita's love, Pedro, to punish Tita for daring to think she deserves happiness. To compound the pain, the mother orders Tita to prepare the entire banquet herself, including the wedding cake.

Thus Tita shows her feelings through cooking, the one language available to her. One of her tears falls into the batter. Everyone who eats the cake becomes suddenly, inconsolably heartbroken—and physically ill. The bride upholds the false agreement of her loveless marriage, knowing that she was the consolation prize and her sister the bait. This dynamic leaves her bitter and eats at her from the inside.

Their rebellious middle sister rejects the whole toxic mess and runs off with a notorious bandit. Yet Tita continues to serve not only her mother, but her oldest sister, the brother-in-law who still desires her, and the niece she's determined to save from a similar fate to her own.

Recipes infuse the book and illustrate Tita's path to beloved elder. I am not a Mexican woman, nor did my relatives ever expect me to cook, and yet in Esquivel's telling I caught glimpses of my family's saga and my place in it as a younger sister. I steeped in indignation at Tita's thwarted wisdom and felt the rapture of forbidden passion, all channeled into her cooking.

Language is something else for Tita because she absorbs her mother's poisonous words. They live on within her, unbidden as a betrayal that won't cease. Not only must she redefine and reclaim her power, but in so doing she blesses the whole lineage for future generations of women.

Thanks to my Barcelona stranding, I had time to devour the full book in Spanish. It was as if I'd spent those lost hours transported onto that Mexican family ranch. My mouth watered over the recipes, as if I were a guest at their feast. Stories of my family bubbled to the surface.

That's the power of one person's story. Here's one I remembered that day:

When I was four, Mom left me to stay with her oldest sister Betty, whose house backed up to a wooded pond. Everything about the place felt dark and dense. I recall wood panels, oriental rugs upstairs, taxidermied ducks, and an odor of oil paint. Upon my arrival, Betty dispatched me to the basement, where the darkness and odor were strongest, with her older son, Grandpa Oscar's apprentice.

Downstairs, my thirteen-year-old cousin drew animals in neon-pink marker on a sketchpad. "What's this?" he asked, voice lilting as he raised his pen from the page.

"It's a horse," I said.

"No!" He added forked antlers. "It's a deer. Now what's this?"

"It's a fish," I said. As I spoke, he drew a few more lines. A bird came into focus.

"No! It's a duck. How about this?"

I studied his goofy sneer, eyes shining behind an unruly cowlick. Clearly he was toying with me. My uncle and his sons liked to hunt, and I felt like the hunted.

I hesitated. "A sheep?"

"No! It's a goat." He drew horns.

I let out an exasperated wail. And I had powerful lungs. His game wasn't fair in any sense of the word. It was designed for me to fail every time, and we both knew it.

I ran upstairs to Betty, who scolded me for being a nuisance. When that didn't shut me up, Aunt Betty made me an offer. "If you stay very, very quiet, I'll buy you paper dolls. You can pick them out." She stared into my eyes. "But remember I'm a witch. I'll turn you into a frog anytime I choose."

Betty did indeed cast a spell with that story and silenced me through fear. I wanted her to stop talking to me. Which isn't, I think, what she wanted. She wanted to be a *grande dame* maybe. When my dollhouse appeared on my sixth birthday, Betty's beautiful artwork was ready to grace every surface. I couldn't let myself play with that dollhouse, though I kept it on a pedestal, neat as a pin.

Festive occasions reinforced my belief that I dare not speak up in her presence, lest I err, and far worse, draw her attention. She'd turn on me and make me the joke. It occurs to me that every tantrum I've ever thrown was a fear that my needs would be ignored and a cry to get those needs met. Every headache gave me permission to stop being good. But those were extreme measures, for last resort. Far better to find sanctioned space, apart from the fray, rather than give ammunition to Betty or her ilk.

Things that keep us safe when we're four or six or eight stay with us, long after they're helpful. Why did Betty feel the need to spar with a little girl?

Perhaps it's because she was once an only child, her mother's joy. Then at age six came Vivian. At eight, my mom. Two younger sisters, adorable and inseparable. Their mother was sick in bed for a long while, unable to stomach most foods. Their dad was an artist who worked constantly. It fell to Betty—only a child—to look after her sisters. It was clearly too much to expect.

When I came along, of course she didn't want to take care of me. She still complained bitterly that her piece of cake from my parents' wedding didn't have a rose on it. None of that was my fault, though. I just wish that she had taught me to paint.

Once you spot the parallel patterns in stories, you see them everywhere. When you get far enough away from home, home will find you. Those higher up in a hierarchy will say, *I navigated this system. Therefore so must you.* But a free spirit can't live that way. Detours are a way of making sure we see other options: the messages we otherwise wouldn't have gotten, the lessons we otherwise wouldn't have learned.

After I missed my flight out of Frankfurt, I refused to spend the night there. Mom and I had tickets to see Julio Iglesias in Minneapolis the next day, her sweet attempt to support my Spanish learning. I was determined to get there by the time curtains opened. So I talked my way onto the last flight across the Atlantic, toggling between three languages: Spanish, German, and English. In New York I discovered that my suitcases remained in Frankfurt. Since I had no baggage to claim, Mom picked me up at the curb the next afternoon, and we drove directly from MSP to the State Theater. We made it on time, but in the darkness, we realized that we didn't know any Julio Iglesias songs, and furthermore, if we had missed his tired, innuendo-laden, macho banter we'd have been fine. The concert was a mere footnote to the rest of my detour.

The detour was in fact the whole point. If not for that endless day, *Como agua para chocolate* would likely have remained a pristine foreign book on my shelf. Instead I fell in love with magical realism. There's something more going on in a detour than we're able to see. Call it the Divine. Call it the Universe. Call it Spirit. Call it whatever you like. The Universe conspired for me to read the book because I needed to read it at that moment in time, as a young single woman building her independent life.

Not only did it give me a new way of reframing family truth, but the book turned me onto an academic passion that remains to this day. No, not Spanish literature, but the fine art of translation. If this language, this flight, this idea won't work out, then what else is possible here?

Funny how I learned the skills of renegotiation thanks to people who acted as roadblocks—such as my aunt—and I learned to find work-arounds. Anything could be anything else. A fish could turn into a duck and a sheep could turn into a goat. A round-trip Minneapolis ticket could be a one-way ticket to New York, and connecting flights could be rearranged once you reached the other side of the ocean. One way or another, I'd find my way home.

I'll never reread *Like Water for Chocolate* in English. As good as the translation may be, it won't match the Spanish. Don't believe me? Watch the movie with English subtitles. Listen to the same movie, dubbed into English. Different choices will have been made. Something will be preserved, something lost, and something transformed.

For example, that word-for-word title translation, *Like Water for Chocolate*. What does that even mean? It's elusive in English. Translation is a series of imperfect choices. Will you preserve the form, keep the literal meaning, or bridge cultural contexts? You must prioritize. The same Rilke poem from two different translators, placed side by side, might be unrecognizable as sharing the same source.

I'll choose the English translation when I know that I'll miss too much context. My favorite childhood book was Astrid Lindgren's *Pippi Longstocking*, translated from Swedish, about a free-spirited child who has no grown-ups to boss her around.

Translation happens even within a common language. You'll never speak the same exact language as anyone else, nor tell the exact same story. Even if you're both speaking "English." Often the story you're telling isn't what you think it's about.

Sometimes, when you're forced to surrender your claims to the outcomes you wanted, the detour opens you up to what you really needed. I often think about how much I needed one day set aside to read *Como agua para chocolate* uninterrupted. That act of reading let me stare into a mirror and not look away. People have set expectations for me, sometimes for my benefit, other times not. Frequently their reasons had nothing to do with me personally, except that I happened to be there with my particular set of gifts that grew stronger as an outcome.

Sometimes I've changed the language and walked away.

Seeker

Acceptance

Starting the year I turned ten, I spent four summers in a row, two weeks at a time, Up North where Concordia College ran its language camps. I learned Swedish at *Sjölunden*, which means "Lake of the Woods." Our site was a rustic cross-country ski resort with handcrafted cabins and an expansive lodge, where we reenacted the heritage of my Swedish grandparents.

We greeted the sun in a circle to raise the Swedish flag with songs and gathered again before dinner for the Swedish national anthem. While the cloth descended, a sky-blue field with a yellow cross, we sang praises to our *old, free, quiet, mountainous, joyful* ancestral land. The words felt like church as we sang the Swedish: *I know that you are and remain what you were. Yes, I want to live and die in the North.* Then we filed inside to gather at long wooden tables and prayed our Swedish mealtime prayer: *In Jesus's name, to the table we go. God sanctify the food we have. Amen.*

If I wanted seconds, I only had to ask. "Kan jag få kyckling och små potatis?" Down came bowls of chicken and tiny potatoes. They trained us well in such things. During orientation, our leaders taught us how to say "ice cream"—*glass*, with heavy emphasis on intonation, to distinguish it from actual glass, which was *glas*. Strawberries were *jordgubbar*, which translated to "little old men of the earth."

There were also delightful pseudo-profane words: Leaders freely used the word *bra* as praise, the letter R heavily rolled, meaning "good," which made me laugh, as did *kött* for "meat," which sounded like *shit*. In my mildly scandalized mind, I harbored a playful suspicion that our counselors had made up a fictitious language to get children to say naughty words. That made their Swedish camp world more delicious.

Every day was a holiday in that world. For *Midsommar*, we folk-danced to fiddles beneath a Maypole, dined on *Smörgasbård*, and rocked out to ABBA—the only English lyrics allowed. That night, we put flowers under our pillows to invoke dreams of future love.

One surprising day, *Sankta Lucia* sang us awake wearing a crown of lit candles, bringing us cat-shaped saffron buns. That afternoon, Christmas songs played in the background while I wove paper hearts. What could be better than singing and dancing, the sagas, carving and painting and weaving, the lake and the woods, and especially ongoing praise for talking to hear myself talk?

Even on ordinary days, they regaled us with legends of fairies and trolls. I faithfully sent postcards to my elders in carefully scripted Swedish with promises of translations to come. My mom, brother, and grandparents wrote back in English. My Great-Grandpa Hallberg's widow, Cora, once wrote me in Swedish on a piece of pressed birchbark.

I was a good little camper, and counselors placed me in ever higher language-learning groups. I knew I was nowhere near the fluency of kids in the top group who'd lived in Sweden, and I might never catch up. I'd only ever be five-eighths Swedish, but in my family, I was the first Swedish speaker in two generations. Back home, I sang Swedish songs, one after another, words that nobody could touch.

Do you know that as you progress in a language, paradoxically, it often appears for a time as if you're getting worse? As your skillset widens, you know less proportionally. Your mind gets flooded like the overloaded computer it is. It's an ugly-duckling stage that you can't avoid, no matter how hard you try.

Disillusionment arrived for me the winter I turned thirteen, one Sunday at our Lutheran church. We were waiting to file out after the service when a family introduced their Swedish exchange student. Dad pointed to me.

"Amy speaks Swedish. Say something." He beamed.

We think that when we learn another language, it will be fun to use in real life, but in fact it's humiliating to be put on display for grown-ups you barely know, performing for an exchange student who's fluent in English. Suddenly I had no Swedish words. "No," I said.

Dad glowered. We shuffled straight out, my eyes fixed on the industrial carpet, all the way through the fellowship hall. I was about to demand an apology in the car, but he jumped in first.

"You made that Swedish girl feel bad, young lady," he said. "The poor girl is far from home. All she wanted was for you to speak Swedish." Since I refused to do that, he added, he refused to pay for Swedish camp ever again. That shut me up, but I was fuming.

I spent the afternoon venting, alone in my room. How dare he put me on display with no warning? But that's not all that the fight was about. They didn't teach Swedish at our local high school where I'd start school in the fall. Time was running short, and my family's investment wasn't panning out. I went one last time to Sjölunden after that. I wrote out the check to pay, and Mom signed it. We all hoped four summers would be enough to get me across the finish line. But the effort was doomed from the start. That's not how language fluency works.

The fourth and final summer, the staff put me in the top language group with the kids who'd lived in Sweden. When my report card came in the mail afterward, the Swedish guy who taught the lessons wrote that I didn't know enough words. I should apply myself more.

I felt as if I had failed, but that wasn't even remotely true. They'd put me in that top group for a challenge because Sjölunden had no other group that year for intermediate campers like me. And I eagerly participated. Fluency isn't a destination, or a single measurement that you've arrived at, but a progression.

German was the successor to Swedish, so similar that I had to make a point of forgetting Swedish to be successful at learning German. Except that German was really a broader education for me, thanks to Eva, my exchange sister. She was the one reason why I stuck with German long enough to get past that ugly-duckling stage. Later, I looked out for those in-between kiddos like me when I taught German.

There are plenty of benchmarks to measure success. Language is speaking and listening, reading and writing. Even in English, I communicate better in some ways than others. Eventually, the greater purpose for me to learn Swedish made sense. When Grandpa Oscar's health was declining, I was the one who knew his mother tongue. I'd prayed his childhood prayer at the camp.

Dad made amends for his Swedish trespass by welcoming Eva, and he even drove us to Disney World. I wonder if he knows how much I honed my language skills by standing up to him.

Here's something I didn't understand then: Those edgy places, beyond our comfort, are often where magic happens. That long-ago fourth summer, a fellow camper loaned me an authentic Swedish costume to perform under the Maypole at Midsommar, where we wove our steps with precision to a rollicking fiddle tune. We reprised our folk dance for the parents who drove up to get their kids, before I boarded the bus home for the last time. It was a beautiful send-off that prepared me to say goodbye to my first language passion. That in itself is a blessing.

Here's the thing I understand now, so many years later: All of my world language foundations were built on those Swedish camp summers. And my spiritual foundations too.

Sanctuary

I wasn't actually Lutheran all my life, only for a season. Grandma Doris wanted us all to attend her Congregational church, which we did for the first part of my life, even though we never lived in her town. This meant that I didn't go to school with the kids in Sunday school, and I didn't go to church with the kids at school until fairly late. Instead, I watched my local Catholic, Lutheran, and Methodist peers from the outside long before I worshiped with the Protestant kids. This shaped my sense of religion in significant ways.

I will say that Grandma's church was quite special, and I grew more invested in it when I was eight years old with the advent of a new building. One late-autumn day, Grandma Doris and all of her progeny walked several miles from the old building across town with our fellow modern-day pilgrims, carrying hymnals. At last we came to a bell tower on the edge of the wooded lot. Before us stood an enormous saltbox church, gray and white, with wings designed to look like a New England village. I've never seen the building's equal, before or since.

Entering through tempered-glass front doors, I adored the cozy window-lined lobby at first sight, perfectly matched to the outer façade, the ideal space to shake off the cold before you enter the crowning glory, the Meetinghouse.

White vaulted ceilings reigned over crimson pew cushions, white stucco walls, clear panes in windows, rich cherrywood trim. Shiny new Bibles populated the backs of the pews. No matter where you sat, you could look around the enormous hall and see people. You could also tuck yourself away, if you didn't want to be seen quite so much. When the sun streamed through the panel windows with too much intensity, there were shutters to shut. Everything was this balance of wide exposure and sheltered embrace.

What fascinated me most were the exposed organ pipes behind the choir loft, off to the right-hand side. The collection of giant and tiny copper tubes occupied a three-sided alcove that I liked to imagine as my someday dream house. This was the living embodiment of everything my dollhouse aspired to be.

During prayers, eyes closed and head bowed, I saw blueprints for my own future house in my mind's eye: stairs, bedrooms, a lofted hideaway modeled on the balcony, and a copy of the fireside room off the lobby. When I sat in the balcony, and the organ played its magnificent hymns, I was home. That graceful saltbox building gave me a sense of what it could mean to have a home church.

Sunday school was a different story. I barely knew the kids. We lived across the river, in a town they'd never heard of. Until I was ten, we made the trek every Sunday, whereas nobody back home had heard of Congregationalists. I couldn't explain, but I faithfully pointed out the building from the bus during field trips when we ventured north of the river.

Meanwhile back in my hometown, Christians with speedboats came to our neighborhood docks and ferried people, our family included, to island worship in summer. Some weeks the Methodists hosted. On the alternate weeks, the moderate Lutherans came. The Catholics and Baptists never attended. Seated on blankets in the grass, we sang hymns to guitar and recited messages from ditto-paper bulletins that rustled in the wind. I loved to pull up honeysuckle clover from the roots and nibble at the sweet tops. Island services didn't have communion or candles, but they served cookies and punch before we motored back home.

When I entered the fifth grade, Mom made a decision. From now on, we would attend church with local residents year-round. We spent one year as folksy Methodists. Then we joined the Lutherans for their structured liturgical style. That's how I came to the Lutherans at eleven, too old to absorb their worldview as a child, but young enough that they played an essential role in my faith formation.

If the Congregationalists had us memorize Bible verses by heart, the Lutherans unpacked the content for our minds. Sixth grade was the year that our local teachers' union, including Mom, went out on a bitter strike, so Lutheran Bible training was my sole education for three months. The teachers gave us actual homework.

Our focus was the lesser-read second half of the Old Testament, about Judges, Prophets, Kings, and the evolution of the Jewish nation. Every Wednesday and Sunday we took tests and learned additional names. In confirmation we studied Acts of the Apostles, the New Testament book where Saint Paul and the male Apostles interpreted *what Jesus meant* after Jesus was gone. From there we learned how Martin Luther reinterpreted *what St. Paul meant* and paved the way for a groundswell of Protestant churches.

If Lutherans provided me with theological grounding, then my agility at Christian code switching—matching phrases and tone to fit the context—developed as a consequence of all the varied churches I attended over the years.

When my friend Elizabeth married an actual German, the minister struggled to pronounce the bilingual vow he would prompt her groom, Martin, to say: "Ja, mit Gottes Hilfe."—*Yes, with the help of God.*

The minister kept pronouncing it wrong; Martin kept correcting him. This continued for a while. Finally, Elizabeth looked around. "Where's Amy? She can help."

I was seated in a pew of the stately Presbyterian sanctuary, doing whatever it is bridesmaids do while waiting for wedding rehearsals. For the two years we shared an apartment on Lincoln and Grand, I'd attended Elizabeth's childhood church on Summit Avenue in St. Paul, just down the block from the governor's mansion. I rushed up the side aisle to the altar. I absolutely could parse this phrase.

"Think of it like a goat with mittens on a hill," I said. "Ya. Mitt Goat-es Hill-fa."

Both men laughed and visibly relaxed. The minister spoke the words correctly. He never mispronounced them again, and that part of the ceremony went off without a hitch. Elizabeth says that the minister remembers me to this day.

I'm known for that kind of irreverent reverence. I am aware, though, that I have to tread lightly. If you peel back enough layers, you'll come up against fierce resistance. Often the deeper roots go undetected. This is the nature of en-cult-uration, the process by which a culture wraps us in its traditions, values, and practices. We're all subject to this.

For a while, I was a bridesmaid or wedding soloist—or both—plenty of times, often at Catholic weddings. Sometimes a bride alerted the priest not to serve me communion. Other times, I've participated when I was invited and done my best to blend in.

I'll never forget the wedding where I sang "Ave Maria," standing by the altar, all eyes on me, when the organist suddenly played a completely wrong progression of chords. I looked up toward the choir loft, where a circle of illuminated stained glass framed the organ. I knew the organist couldn't see me. My soprano voice hovered, lyrical, trained on the well-practiced melody while the notes clomped along, completely discordant. I stayed on the note, she caught up in a measure or three, and we carried on.

Afterward, on the steps of the church, family and guests—mostly Catholic—came to offer me praise. I'd learned to receive such comments with humility.

"Did you notice the part where I screwed up?" I asked the first lady who approached me, one of the bride's older sisters in a taffeta gown. I was laughing, but I genuinely wanted to confess the glaring error.

"Oh yes," she said. "You waved your hands and made a face. That was funny."

I was confused. I'd studiously kept my composure. I realized that what each successive person *had* noticed was how I—as the cantor—raised my arms in the wrong place to invite them to sing. It wasn't their turn to start yet. The priest kept chanting. I looked around, made a dramatic expression, and put my hands down. Everyone saw it. Almost nobody heard the out-of-tune "Ave Maria" measures. So I quit confessing that error.

The thing about a Congregational church, I now know, besides its New England origins, is that the members in each congregation decide what a church stands for, not a central organization. When they built the new church, congregants couldn't agree on how Puritan they would be. Specifically, would they hang a cross behind the pulpit? Or would that be too showy?

They compromised with a straight wooden cross that could be removed from the wall as easily as opening and closing the shutters. However, sun streamed in through the window panes and the surrounding cherrywood faded. Consequently the shape of the cross was burned onto the front wall. No matter what they did from then on, that cross would be there, in its presence or absence.

When I rejoined the Congregationalists as an adult, when I understood that I wasn't really Lutheran, or not entirely so, I would stare straight at that wall from my favored balcony spot. The building comforted me as much as it always had. The starter home that Dad helped me find in our hometown to my specifications would indeed echo its design: gray siding and white trim, windows divided into even panes, railings that evoked organ pipes, vaulted white ceiling.

I would always adore those features. But as for my grown-up theological bearings, I was like that wall: not exactly wearing the cross, but still fully bearing its mark, caught between religious traditions. Partially both and partially neither.

Discernment

The Thanksgiving when I was twenty-six, when I was considering the Congregational saltbox as my potential home church, I proposed to Grandma Doris that we attend a service together before our family gathering—just she and I.

We started out gleeful, on an elevated pew where we could both see and be seen. When we sang "America the Beautiful," I stood ever so slightly taller than Grandma in black flats, and I felt perfectly turned out as her modern and upstanding Christian granddaughter.

As the service ended, a friend of Grandma's greeted us across the stadium pews, rosy cheeked with perfectly coiffed white hair, her bright Sunday suit adorned with a glittery brooch. "Hi Doris!" She made her way over. "Is this your granddaughter?" Strong perfume wafted.

"This is my granddaughter Amy." Grandma's voice lilted. "She teaches German."

"You're so young and sweet." The friend grasped my right hand in

Seeker

both of hers. That perfume would linger on my clothing all day. "What a beautiful girl."

"Oh!" Grandma blustered. "You mustn't let her hear you say that."

"Why not?" The lady caressed my palm. "It's true. She's just lovely."

"Of course she is," Grandma conceded, then spoke in a forced stage whisper. "We don't want her to get a big head." It was like she was trying out lines from a play, awkward yet a noble attempt.

Grandma Doris was all about pageantry. She adored the Pilgrim cosplay—the family dressed in high-necked, black-buckled garb who greeted us at the entrance, and the teen boys drumming to usher us out. She found it cute that a Puritan man walked the aisles, poised to bump people with his stick if they nodded off during the extra-long sermon, prominently timed with an hourglass. The show was the whole thing. She didn't see her old church friends often. She was performing for a peer. What else was I expecting by going back to this church together, for which we both had deep nostalgia?

Unlike Grandma, I never anguished about being saved. Martin Luther proclaimed that *by grace alone*, I already was saved. I took him at his word. Maybe that was my problem because this church occupied a strange middle ground. They didn't exactly fit the Evangelical movement, but Grandma once described their approach as "Hate the sin, love the sinner." She wasn't wrong.

Nonetheless, that winter, I stood up front and proclaimed that I would covenant with God and with this congregation to walk with its members as God was pleased to reveal Himself to us. After that, I joined the choir. Because you need a place to belong and mark life's milestones.

If you were raised Christian, that's church. Where else will you turn for answers in case of birth, death, marriage, holidays, and large furniture purchases? I have to confess, when I put it like this, church sounds like a Magic 8 Ball.

For a brief while, things did align as if by magic. I bought that house in my hometown, but a new modern bridge had finally opened that year, and everything north of the river felt more within reach.

The following Thanksgiving, Grandpa Oscar was dying. He belonged to no church; Mom said he snored when he sat down inside one. But I'd never experienced God so closely as when I'd driven Grandpa on errands, seeing the world through his blind artist eyes in his last years. As I approached his death, sitting beside him after teaching all day, feeding him small phrases in Swedish, certain choir anthems felt blasphemous in my mouth. Their beautiful promises of salvation for true believers felt horrid. How dare Grandpa's worthiness for Heaven be up for debate. I started falling asleep, visibly elevated in the choir loft. I had to drop out, lest I be revealed as a hypocrite.

But I couldn't avoid conversation with well-intentioned Christians who said shitty things, things they meant to provide loving comfort, that sounded like, *Come, be more like me.* In my mourning, it took a hell of a lot of effort to make myself believe in enough of what they preached. I'd made significant inroads with the church Young Adults, particularly my *Koinonia* small group, which means "fellowship" in Greek. Indeed, I found myself torn between maintaining my social connections and parsing my too-progressive religious beliefs.

"Shouldn't we help other Christians—both the too lax and too rigid ones—to see their errors?" a woman asked our Koinonia group one Sunday. "Wouldn't that be the most loving thing to do?"

We sat circled in my living room; darkness peered through the transom. Since I'd been to many churches and never found this one's likeness, I was pretty certain that whatever conclusions we reached about God, they were not universal.

"No!" I said, too forcefully for our loving circle. "You respect their decision and leave them alone."

"But don't you think . . ." my sister-in-Christ continued, "that if a person is not a believer, we should try to convince them? They're living in sin. Yes, they have free will, but we're trying to save them."

"No." I said it emphatically. "You let people be who they are." Ironically, I'd spent hours cooking and cleaning before they arrived, trying to show off my worthiness. She backed off, but I'm sure she remained unconvinced. But then, I was trying to change her as well. This argument was a trap that you could never escape. Just like hell.

What would they have said had they known that I spent entire Saturdays upstairs in bed reading alternative spiritual texts? During regular phone calls, Vivian and I traded names of authors and titles the way that I imagined the early Christians recognized each other by drawing their Jesus fish. Except these books weren't biblical.

"Have you ever seen the *Course in Miracles*?" Vivian said. "It's a navy book. Looks like a hymnal, channeled by a woman in the seventies who wrote it all down."

"I've read books about the *Course in Miracles*," I said.

"Go to the primary source." My aunt's tempting voice drew me in. "There are daily lessons with one sentence each. The first one is, 'Nothing I see in this room means anything.' So you look around and say, *This table does not mean anything. This door does not mean anything.* Then lesson two is, 'I have given everything I see in this room all the meaning that it has for me.' And again you go around saying the phrase for the table, the door, etcetera." This idea—that nothing had any inherent meaning—kicked up all kinds of arguments in my brain. It felt sacrilegious. Vivian reassured me that I could stand to question my faith.

So I secretly bought a copy from the Borders bookstore new age section, and started writing cherry-picked lessons on slips of paper I kept in my pocket. *A Course in Miracles,* Lesson 29 said, "God is in everything I see." Lesson 127 said, "There is no love but God's."

One evening as the light grew dim on another Bible study, our host—the woman who wanted to save errant Christians—said, "I believe people are born gay." I almost laughed from relief. "But I believe they're possessed by demons," she added. She meant this unironically. We asked her to clarify. "Really?" someone asked.

"You can't mean that," I said.

"Yes," she answered. "I mean that literally."

Did she know who was sitting in her living room? An inadvertent ally to closeted gay teens. In the eighties, before the AIDS crisis, when self-advocacy became a matter of life and death, churches didn't say much about homosexual people. Thanks to taboos, these folks did their best to blend in and suffered in silence. Some Lutheran synods are quite homophobic. By the early nineties, the newly merged ELCA Lutherans openly welcomed gay and trans members.

Not to mention that I'd seen Carleton classmates come out as lesbian, gay, or bisexual. Brilliant, courageous, sensitive people. My host's ugly theology held real potential for evil—and justification for genuine damage inflicted on real people's lives.

At school, I was that teacher who stopped to call out random students whenever I heard them say, "That's so gay," same as I would any slur, except it was usually *that* slur. In the hallway or my classroom, I asked the teens with as much respect as I could muster, "Do you know anyone who's gay?" When they invariably answered no, I asked, "Are you sure?" Then I pointed out that they really had no way of knowing who was gay, or had gay family members or friends. I asked them to imagine how hard it must be to live with that secret and hear those hurtful words. The careless teens almost always backed down. For the most part, they didn't mean anything by it.

Truth be told, such damage cut deeper than words. I knew that from my cheerleader trauma. Unchecked, mean actions follow casual slurs, resulting in safety denied, talents hidden, and opportunities lost. LGBT students heard me. (Other, more nuanced letters came later.) Though

I identified as none of those letters, several students confided in me. They recognized me as a kindred spirit. That's not something I would have expected. Growing up in the eighties, I didn't know for certain that gay people existed around me. Now I did, so I did better.

Students waited after class to ask if they could come talk to me later, formal but vague, as if preparing me to receive their confession. My filters would lower, and I'd understand: This sensitive, beautiful soul wasn't straight. The teens who confided in me were some of the most thoughtful, self-aware people I knew. All they needed was a safe space to sort out their thoughts and just be.

Yet, I stayed on in the church Young Adults group. My show of devotion was so convincing—my Bombay chicken curry with chutney was a big hit at our potluck—that I was invited to join the Young Adults leadership team. I was a moth to their flame, eager to nurture connections.

A short-term Lutheran boyfriend forced me to take stock when I brought him to Palm Sunday to meet my Koinonia friends. They welcomed him warmly for coffee hour. He stood among us listening, wordless. By Easter, he and I had decided to celebrate separately, which for me meant dinner at Grandma Doris and Grandpa Hubert's condo after church. Then he got bored and called to ask if he could come over. Because I felt lonely, I agreed. When Grandma heard my Lutheran boy was coming over, she got this determined look in her eye and wiped the dish suds from her hands.

"Grandma! Please don't make a fuss," I said. "I'm pretty sure we're not going to last." Nevertheless, when he called up from the lobby, and I buzzed him in, Grandma slipped out the door and rushed down the hall. She wore a triumphant glow as she escorted him back. This was only the second guy I'd ever brought around, and Grandma was dying for a suitor, especially a handsome Lutheran boy.

After he met my relatives, proving he existed, he suggested a walk. Stepping into the fresh air, I asked, "What did Grandma say to you?"

He snickered. "She gave me a hug and said, 'Call me Grandma.'"

"Good God, how mortifying," I said.

"It was pretty embarrassing for you." Sun filtered through branches onto the sidewalk. The day was typical Minnesota Easter: pleasant, with a pronounced chill. After we walked many blocks out and returned, I went upstairs alone.

What made Grandma's trespass most painful was that I wanted the very thing she wanted for me, but she didn't listen when I said this wasn't it. Both of us wanted the white wedding with cascades of flowers. I never stopped wanting that love-and-life story. But I did expect my version of it to center on me, not on her.

Truthfully, both of us engaged in magical thinking, trying to force something that clearly doesn't want to happen, as if we could follow a formula and usher our will into being. I'm reminded of that classic game Grandma taught me, where you clasp your hands, fingers hidden inside: *Here is the church.*

You raise your two index fingers: *Here is the steeple.*

You flip your hands over to reveal interwoven, wiggling fingers. *Open the doors, and see all the people.* I was having a hard time accepting that those things weren't real.

Soon thereafter, my boyfriend invited me to meet him, impromptu, for an afternoon movie—with a hidden agenda. After the film ended, we lingered outside the Starbucks around the corner. "My meeting at church won't start for an hour," I hinted, hoping for a little more time. "For the Young Adults leadership team. It's my first time, so . . ."

"Look," he interrupted, "I know they're your friends, but I don't know why you worship with them. You don't believe the same things that they do. That's your grandma's church. It's not for you."

"I know." I looked wistfully at the empty tables through the window. We weren't going inside to share an intimate cup of coffee after all. We weren't in love anyway.

"I've been thinking," he said. "This isn't working for either of us."

God bless him, it was painful but true. After we parted—did we hug?—I took a circuitous route to church to waste time. As an ice-breaker, we shared our favorite Christian radio stations. I had none, intentionally.

My ex was right: This fellowship was too self-segregated, too proud to be *in* the world, but not *of* the world. To remain in their protective bubble would be my version of sacrilege.

What I understood, what I must always have known, was that I was like Grandma Doris, taking joy in ceremonial rites. But I was also like Grandpa Oscar and Aunt Vivian, who encountered the sacred world wherever they went, and immersed themselves in it. They required creative expression, unhampered by dogma. And so did I.

Was this saltbox church God's will for me?

Signs pointed to no.

Trust Yourself

That spring, an art teacher and the librarian were talking in the staff lunchroom about their church softball team when I placed my tray on the table. "Oh!" I pulled out a chair. "Where do you go to church?"

The librarian mentioned a vaguely familiar name.

"Is that in Minneapolis?" Something told me to listen up.

"Downtown Minneapolis," said the art teacher.

I knew the church they meant, one of those Progressive churches that my Koinonia group had specifically worried about. "That's too far." I sighed. "I need a new church. People at my current church say homophobic things."

The librarian flashed a wicked smile. After years of living in Minnesota, she still maintained her Alabama accent. "At our church," she said, her voice an upbeat lilt, "there are people who would argue that Jesus was gay."

This was the third time this downtown church had drawn my attention. When I was singing with the Minnesota Chorale, I'd gone there for a choir rehearsal of Carl Orff's *Carmina Burana*, which is by turns bawdy and regal. *O fortuna*, the opening song goes, *fickle fortune, the world keeps turning, and change arrives.* And the work twists and turns, between Latin and Middle High German, with picturesque imagery.

The downtown church organist was our conductor that concert, and he'd booked our rehearsal in the sanctuary, not far from Orchestra Hall. Given the secular content, it felt risqué, and refreshing, to sing the texts in a sacred setting.

The darkened sanctuary itself had surprised me as the lights came on because it felt so familiar with its dark wooden beams, red Pilgrim Hymnals in pew backs, and organ pipes right up front. This was the less pristine first cousin of my saltbox church, an inner-city oasis with parking lot guards, forty minutes from home in good traffic. But now I was willing to try it, knowing what really mattered: There is an order of service, a cadence that flows through religious observance. It doesn't require dogma, but rather discernment. Everything is intentional, and then the Spirit comes in.

With the invocation, we welcome God into our presence and make ourselves present to God. Lighted candles lead to processional hymns that give way to prayers. Songs give way to readings, announcements, call and response, and special music. Offerings. Sermons. Communion, which doesn't happen weekly in many Protestant churches, reminds us that we are many and we are one. The energy crescendoes. We receive the benediction, a blessing of good words. We carry love out into the world.

That was my dearest hope. I needed a place where I could mourn and celebrate in equal measure. Beyond that, I wanted tulips and lilies at Easter. The "Hallelujah" chorus. Christmas carols by candlelight. Daughters in pastel dresses on holidays.

I happened to visit on Children's Sunday; there were several choirs and bells on full display. Once the children had carried their hand-picked flowers up to the altar and done a liturgical dance in the aisles, the teenage confirmands took their turns in the pulpit. They were joining the church, unless they weren't, which they explained in faith statements printed in the bulletin.

The teens presented vastly different pictures of God. Some described standard theology. Some didn't believe in God. Certain beliefs were very esoteric or equally likely, quite academic—or both. They said things aloud that I'd tiptoed around. Adults listened as if that were normal. Biblical stained glass kept watch around us, and I admired their jewel tones. I could trust this congregation with my future kids.

On my way out of the labyrinthine building I noted the oversized embroidered scene of Pilgrims, prominently displayed on one wall. Ladies seated at opposite ends of a large dining table poured coffee from silver pots into porcelain cups. There were abstract oil paintings and a garden courtyard at the center of the building. The feeling was eclectic, historic, modern, multilayered, curated, cohesive. Decidedly Christian and probably haunted. On the outer lobby wall, a memorial stained glass tree in primary colors bid me farewell.

I felt certain that God had led me here. That I would marry and raise children in these hallowed halls. As for whether they'd bury me someday, that felt inconclusive. For the time being, I saw a wedding and baptisms. I hadn't met the groom yet, but I had a feeling that I soon would.

I arranged for Sunday mornings off at my summer bookstore job so that I wouldn't miss church. In subsequent weeks, I heard ministers, some openly gay, preach in prose and poetry. We sang traditional hymns and read Bible verses. The messages were eloquent, theologically sound, and firmly rooted in social justice. Yes, this was still a very white church, but they knew where their neighborhood was.

They'd already addressed my pronoun problem. We prayed to the Holy One, or Loving God, or our Mother-Father God, to whom we offered our thanks, and from whom we asked guidance. We didn't label

God as our Lord and King. My heart swelled to hear these inclusive, feminine words integrated with my faith tradition.

The downtown church and the saltbox church both initiate members using the Salem Covenant of 1629, an absolutely beautiful statement:

> *We covenant with you O God and one with another, and do*
> *bind ourselves in your presence to walk together in all your*
> *ways, according as you are pleased to reveal yourself to us in*
> *your blessed word of truth.*

It bears mention that by 1692, a mere inversion of two digits, the good people of Salem were trying outsiders and outspoken women as witches, based on hearsay. Mom always used to tell me that—given all the things I seemed to channel from another realm—if I had lived in Salem, I would have been burned as a witch. I only dispute one part of her assessment: Witches were burned in Europe. In the New World, colonists hanged them.

It was this sentiment, that you had to get the words right, that had haunted me until I found this place. By the time I left the saltbox church, I was parsing words, jumping in and out of the Apostles' Creed, the standard recitation of Christian beliefs.

Soon after I transferred my membership, the saltbox Congregational church that I'd left behind made a shocking ultimatum on my new congregation. If the downtown church wanted to remain affiliated with a Minnesota Congregational organization to which both belonged, then our downtown ministers would have to provide a statement of minimal required beliefs. Jesus as salvation from hell, I'd imagine. Probably a Virgin birth.

The saltbox church had no authority over our congregation. Still, when they wouldn't back down, our head minister withdrew us from the organization rather than debate. I found it shocking that my former church would deny me a Christian home and life-affirming that the downtown church insisted on giving me one. We talked in depth about our faith. They didn't make us pass litmus tests.

Within weeks, I met my future groom, Dave, when he started working at the bookstore. Once we had declared our affection, I discovered that I'd joined the only church he would ever have attended. During his teen years, his dad dropped him off at a local church and went home to write. I've heard him tell it many times, including when we met with the minister to plan our wedding. "I would go inside and wait for my dad to leave." His eyes lit up. "Then I walked to the comic book store until it was time for him to come get me." He laughed. Dave has the best laugh. Our minister laughed.

I love the story because it reminds me that if we'd met any sooner, Dave wouldn't have known what to do with my religion. Nor I with his rebellion. He chose to join this particular church, even though it required a major time commitment to get there.

Such is our family pattern. I make decisions that ground our traditions, but I always want to make sure that Dave is willing to follow my lead. And he lends me perspectives that I don't always see.

Not long after we started attending together, the picket line formed outside our building. Our church, with another downtown congregation, had purchased the empty nursing home across the street in order to convert it into supportive apartments for unsheltered people. Neighbors fought the project based on zoning. They rightly said that there was already a high density of support facilities. This would hurt property values, they claimed. True, they lived in this neighborhood, and we were a commuter church. But it wasn't that simple. People were already living there, in their streets.

Picketers greeted us every Sunday for months, careful to stay on the city sidewalk. They waved neon signs with clever, forgettable slogans. They made eye contact and smiled like good Christian greeters. They said good morning. We said good morning and kept walking. Once, we returned to find a flier under our windshield wipers, asking us to contribute toward legal fees to sue our church, to which we pledged financial support. Such tactics didn't sway us.

The church was within legal rights to renovate the building and rent to whomever they wanted. The city only required approval to provide supportive services for apartment residents, which would make them better neighbors. Purely related to property values, this was a sound investment.

Eventually, the downtown church won its case, and the picketers left. Our Minneapolis church had revealed exactly what I believed in. I knew that I was incredibly fortunate. I wanted to believe that people would look out for me and my loved ones if we required compassion. *Do unto others,* Jesus said, *as you would have them do unto you.*

Feed the hungry, house the homeless, love is love is love is love.

Dave believed the same things. Within a year we were engaged.

When Vivian came to town, I drove her to meet Dave for brunch at the restaurant where his family went instead of church. At my prompting, Dave told Vivian his comic book story. She laughed with abandon, and I was grateful for their connection. Vivian was at her most charming. She studied me afterward from the passenger seat.

"Your hair looks so pretty. You should always wear it that way." Vivian always said the same thing about my hair no matter the style, which delighted me.

"So you like Dave?" I said. "I knew you would."

"I do." She nodded. "And he's very handsome."

"Don't you think he'll make a good father?" I asked.

"Let me tell you something." She ran her fingers along the chain on her neck. "I like that Dave likes you for who you are."

"And you'll be such a wonderful great aunt." I was thinking about how often I'd ridden in cars that she drove. When I pulled into a turn lane, waiting for the light, she shifted her body toward me. "I don't want to live to be old," she said decisively. "I want to die when I'm young."

My shoulders tensed and I gripped the wheel. "What about your granddaughter?" As if I could bargain with fate. "You adore her."

"She's wonderful," said my aunt. "But I don't want to be one of those people who lives on and on. I've lived enough."

I want you to understand: My aunt hadn't given up on her life yet. She'd promised Dave and me over eggs that she would read Kahlil Gibran at our wedding. She was making her own plans, for herself and with her own kids—my cousins. It's more that she wanted to level with me, to prepare me for what was coming. She had that gift of premonitions. Later, after she went silent, she would send me a dream to show me how and when she would go. She must have known—based on decades of observation—that I was the kind of person who would skip ahead in a book to the end, read what was coming, then return to the page where I was, and follow the story development forward. It's why Vivian had insisted that I get the psychic reading. She knew that I needed forewarning to let go of my expectations.

You can't cherrypick predictions. You have to know what you know and take the shadows along with the happier parts.

I got the wedding album that I envisioned—actually two, one in color, one in black-and-white film—full of church vistas and loved ones. In that collection of photos I see effusive joy, hidden sorrows, contemplation, pure delight. And every other emotion.

I've never felt so happy as when I was married to Dave in that church. You'll see joy in both of our smiles. You see it in my parents' faces, and Grandma Doris's, and muted in Hubert's.

You see it in Vivian's face, but only from a distance. My aunt spoke so softly that we could barely make out the words. She is ethereal in my mind, dressed in gauzy white. There aren't any close ups. I've looked.

It's those images, plus the sounds and smells and sensations that stay with me from that church. Who could've predicted the volume of notes I would write in that sanctuary, phrases that I faithfully recorded when they moved through my mind, possibly whispered into my ear by resident spirits, mostly in the choir loft? They came to me when I knew what my aunt had meant about living too long. Those musings are here, in this book.

Sometimes, when I think about what Vivian gave me that I treasure the most, it was permission to acknowledge what's really present, without trying to smooth over shadows or push them away. To encounter challenging turns of fate and dwell with them. Not perfect, but real.

During our years in that sanctuary, I took solace on many Sundays: after 9-11, just before we all flew to Atlanta for Vivian's wedding; after an art teacher came to my classroom to tell me that Paul Wellstone, our Senator and a former professor from Carleton College, had died in a plane crash, eleven days before the election; after our Christmas Day miscarriage two months later; when Vivian died her slow, early death; when Grandma Doris went fast; when Hubert couldn't recall me.

In between sacred words, in the silence, I found moments of stillness in that place, if not the fabled peace that passes all understanding, then at least time to sit with the pain. There was nothing to do sometimes but let it be.

Puppet

Ease

My fourth-grade art teacher once demonstrated a special effect that forever changed my perspective. On sheets of white construction paper, she had us draw crayon jungle scenes. Once we finished, we painted over our drawings with watery blue ink that filled in white spaces, skimming vibrant flora and fauna to form a blue overlay that magically permeated all open spaces.

When my first monkey didn't turn out, I remade his head into a palm frond, a trick I'd learned from Grandpa Oscar's world of art: When you make mistakes, integrate them in another way. A yellow spotted giraffe rested her weary head on that sleight-of-hand broad leaf. That day, I learned that I could draw attractive—if imprecise—jungle animals. And I learned for the first time how filters worked.

My second attempt at a monkey shimmied up a coconut tree, looking more like a squirrel, tail cocked and no visible front hands. There was a baby elephant with black tusks and unfurled trunk, and a magenta toucan, wings tucked in, that hovered miraculously. If you looked carefully at the other palm tree, you'd see a snake, winding the length of the trunk, reenacting his temptation of Eve.

Nothing was in perspective, but nobody cared. My composition was beautiful, this company of wax animals held in the wash of indigo sky. What struck me were those watchful eyes. All of them were watching.

My teacher loved my drawing so much that she entered it in the 1980 Minneapolis Aquatennial Art Fair, a summer tradition in Minnesota. When they named me a finalist, Grandma Doris, Cora, Mom, and I carpooled into downtown Minneapolis. A fancy luncheon awaited us on the top floor of the IDS Tower, the tallest building in the skyline still to this day. Afterward, we descended to admire my prize-winning drawing at a makeshift gallery in a second-floor storefront.

It was matted on orange construction paper with a yellow-and-blue ribbon affixed to the top-right corner, above a handwritten placard with my name and hometown. My three elders posed there in turn beside me, beaming with pride. Then we wandered out to the balcony that overlooks the sunny Crystal Court atrium, and they asked a passerby to snap one last photo of us together.

"Let's call it *Four Generations of Hallberg Women*," one of the women in my family said. It could have been any of them. They all chimed in with their approval of this good idea. The reference was clearly a counterpart to *Four Generations of Hallberg Men*, a treasured family snapshot composed of their husbands and my older brother.

In the resulting images, I beam in a floral smocked hand-me-down dress from Vivian's daughter, my cousin Sam. Ironically, my artistic talents came from that other side of the family. It was undeniably a proud day in my young life, but I wondered what it meant to be a Hallberg woman.

At the back of my mind, certain details felt not quite right. Each of these women married into the family, Cora a mere five years before she became a Hallberg widow. Only I—a ten-year-old girl, not yet a woman—was an actual Hallberg, heir to that good Christian name, though I made no pretense of real affinity with those Hallberg men, other than by birth. Based on their own logic, these women weren't successive generations. I was their convergence.

Though I couldn't have put it into words back then, that's when I first had an inkling that we experience life on two levels. There was the catalyst: I copied a picture in response to an assignment because my teacher made me a template, and I liked creating. Then there was what happened afterward: storied display, with a layer of meaning, exhibit A for family worth. And that's performance art. Suddenly you're justifying your place in a family snapshot. Once that understanding's there, you can't strip back the overlay.

It would have felt so lovely if the moment had stood on its own. I want to rename the picture: *Women who loved me beyond measure.* That's the name it deserves. Instead there's a story implied that isn't necessarily true. Underneath that, what else is going on? And am I allowed to question it? Is that respectful to my elders, who love me so much?

Case in point: that "pure" Hallberg name derived from a bastardized change. Sheer happenstance. In the early 1900s, the wife of a fundamentalist Christian minister believed that our Swedish name—*Hellberg*—was evil and made it her mission to replace the offending syllable. Thus my pious Great-Grandpa Hallberg, an immigrant, became the first of four generations spared from eternal damnation in Minneapolis, Minnesota.

Hellberg wasn't original anyway. According to Cora, faithful gatekeeper of Great-Grandpa's history, that name was bestowed by the Swedish military when there were too many Olsons, Andersons, and such in their ranks. This was all accepted Nordic family lore.

Call me *Beloved Soundmountain*, the name I translated for myself from Latin and German derivations one day as a bored American teen studying in West Germany. Left alone, the ill-fated Hellberg would have made me *Brightmountain*. But Soundmountain suits me.

It's my identity, which I happily embraced as a young German teacher, Frau Hallberg. It delights me when language traditions bump up against each other, and I happily draw those distinctions. When I married Dave, I kept my beloved last name. Dave agreed, and Grandma Doris did not, for genealogical reasons. This is the crux of my eternal conflict with Grandma Doris. We saw the exact same evidence and came to different conclusions.

She was a genealogist who thought that *everybody should speak English in America*. And I was a person who spent most of my career fully aware of my language limitations in German *and* Spanish, even after years of dedicated study and practice.

Throughout our shared lifetime, our competing sympathies simmered and flared. I was her granddaughter, whom she loved dearly. Until I married Dave, Grandma Doris and Grandpa Hubert were my secondary emergency contacts, after my parents; I trusted them that completely. Grandma was the person I turned to again and again as a great source of comfort.

I was also an extension of her lineage. She was maddeningly unpredictable when sharing information about me with other people. For a long time I felt my only recourse was to pepper people outside my family sphere with personal anecdotes about her, as surely as she did the same about me.

Late in my high-risk pregnancy with my twin daughters in 2003, she emailed me a copy of a letter she'd sent to a distant relative she'd found on the Internet, in which she detailed all her descendants by name and date of birth, including information on my unborn twins. I called and yelled at her, transformed by impending motherhood into a furious banshee.

She begged me not to work myself up, knowing full well about my miscarriage, about which I'd sworn her to silence. These twins were her dearest wish for me, always. She also didn't want to surrender her claims to their records. She called her connections "Good People." I called them "Internet Strangers."

At a certain moment, she grew strangely quiet and cold.

"Fine," she said. "I will never again mention your children on the Internet. Or anywhere else. Now please calm down."

Victory! Or more realistically, détente.

I likewise guarded Mom's side of the family. When Grandma Doris asked about my dying aunt, I shielded Vivian's privacy with a fierce wall of silence.

And yet, through my daughters, some of the tensions between us released. Soon after I gave birth, Grandma and Hubert's turn came up at an assisted living complex a few miles north of the river from us, where senior members of their two churches often moved when their time came. This was as close to me as Grandma Doris would ever live, twenty minutes away. It was a beautiful facility, where the unit would be refurbished to her specifications before they moved in. So Grandma Doris got one last chance to select her decor.

Because we were parents with infant twins, a role that was exceedingly hard, the paring down and the move happened without Dave's or my help. We did swim with the girls one time in my grandparents' beloved condo pool that Easter—pictures show them floating in our arms, dressed in baby bikinis.

While they would never experience the big family dinners I remember around my grandparents' dining room table, my daughters got something far more special: personal attention. Grandma would make reservations. The girls and I would meet Dave at the apartment around dinner time. Hubert would grab his and Grandma's name tags from the table by the door, and we'd make our way to the dining hall.

"Are those your granddaughters?" every old lady asked Grandma.

She nodded knowingly. "Great-granddaughters." She announced their names with significant pride, then raised her hand to her mouth and whispered too loudly. "I can't tell them apart."

At Halloween, the residents delighted to see twin witch hats, tall as the girls themselves, bobbing along between tables and wait staff, making their way to the salad bar to snag chocolate pudding that would otherwise count as dessert. Grandma expected them to also order ice cream and a cookie.

Of course she insisted that we come back to the apartment afterward. As the girls grew, they performed private concerts on miniature violins, complete with handmade programs, each song written out and presented in the narrow living room in front of the floral sofa. I joined in for a few songs with my full-size violin, which I'd started to play purely for the fun of the lessons. Mostly we played fiddle and folk tunes, but there were also classical songs by European composers.

For the melodies he knew, Hubert grabbed his harmonica. Grandma Doris perched on the sofa, as if this gathering was all she had ever wanted in life.

In those moments of music-making, the idea of performance for the sake of appearance or identity melted away, into a shared experience of unconditional joy. Yes, there was a playlist. But there were no hidden agendas, no outsiders to impress.

When summer came around, Grandma packed picnic lunches and reserved the gazebo. We played mini golf. In a photo from that time, I see myself with her, leaning into her shoulder, shaded by a tree branch behind us, genuinely relaxed in the afternoon light of an ordinary day. I see a mom enjoying her twins through the eyes of her elderly grandma, who clearly loves all of us, equally, beyond measure.

It's everything I ever wanted from her.

Divine Timing

The winter I found out that Grandma Doris's cancer had returned, my designer friend, Christi, from choir—the same friend who turned me onto writing classes—gave me two pieces of quality upholstery fabric from her vast collection of samples. Pairing the two patterns together brought me back to my childhood. Eventually Mom sewed them into a banner, and Dad mounted a curtain rod on my writing studio wall to display it over my desk.

The resulting combination—white flowers embroidered onto a white background, and more white flowers on lilac—looked pretty but bland. For several months, its mediocrity disappointed me every time I sat down to write, given that it was exactly what I had requested. It hung there, dreary, all winter long.

That summer on a whim, I took the textile banner down and embellished it with metallic fabric paints in magenta, navy, and green, plus silver for outlines. This was a trick I learned from Vivian to spruce up furniture pieces, but the banner got ugly fast. That day, I was supposed to be packing for a student trip to Germany that I was leading, making sure that Dave and our daughters got packed, except that now I had this mess to fix. Time was running short.

Panicked, I threw the cloth into the bathtub and tried to wash the paint away. Failing that, I bundled my daughters, then age seven, into the car and drove across the river to a big-box craft store for a deeper shade of iridescent green. As we strode into the entrance, an elderly, wire-haired lady started to bellow.

The voice sounded inhuman. It took me a moment to register what she was saying: "Amy! A-my! Aaa-my!" I stopped in my tracks and turned to look. Slightly hunched in a jewel-toned plaid jacket, frail but fiercely determined, stood my grandmother glaring at me.

When the girls saw who it was, they ran to wrap their arms around her legs. "Grammy!"

She wobbled slightly, then steadied herself. "Be careful!" She was uncharacteristically brusque with them.

Grandma and her daughter, Sally, had stopped on their way home from her latest chemotherapy session. Our fortuitous encounter felt divinely arranged. We really needed to see Grandma before we left, and we needed forewarning about her condition.

We hadn't unpacked our suitcases from Germany in August when Mom called to tell me that Grandma's treatment was over. No more chemo, no more radiation. The largest tumor had grown from golfball to baseball size.

That day, the girls packed up their violins, and we stopped off to buy her lunch. Grandma sat in a white chair when we arrived, hair whiter than ever, face whiter too. She wore oxygen tubes in her nose, and an attendant was showing her how to remove and insert them.

"Amy!" Grandma said, delighted. "He's German!"

"Yeah." The man looked up. "I'm one of those Mexican Germans."

"A lot of Germans went to Mexico," I said.

I asked him to explain to me, one more time, what Grandma needed to do with the tubes and the tanks after we finished eating. The airflow nozzles had to point in the proper direction. That was the important part. Grandma needed to breathe.

What a beautiful day that was. She sent me home with an unopened package of festive floral dinner napkins. The leftover soup would rot in the fridge. Hubert's daughter-in-law said Grandma Doris was resting whenever I called to say . . . what, exactly? We left messages and never connected. Everything remained unsettled until the day I arrived after school at her deathbed.

I couldn't find a parking space. Exactly three spots remained in the front lot of the complex, reserved by signs as a reward for their most punctual employees. It was my second day of school, 2011, and I had choir practice, again. "What about relatives late for a deathbed?" I asked myself. My retort felt satisfying inside my car, where I didn't give a damn about being nice.

I looked again at the dashboard clock and started around the narrow private facility road. "Please let me do this right," I said under my breath.

Every time I'd been near Grandma Doris for the past week and a half, I felt the compulsion to weep, sometimes in front of her. Always in front of the blended entourage of relatives. Even when I managed to hold the tears at bay, a precarious wobble in my voice betrayed me. Grandma told me I mustn't cry. I told her I'd rather cry than stay away. "Only tears of happiness then," she'd said, resolute.

I pulled Mom's number up on my phone. *Breathe*, I thought.

"Mom," I said when she answered. "I have to drive around the complex. How's Grandma?"

"The minister's here. It's not good. Maybe today, maybe tomorrow."

I swallowed hard. "I'll be there soon."

"You should know something. Lucie told the minister she's worried about letting you sing."

"What?!" Lucie was Hubert's daughter-in-law.

"She said you can't control your emotions. She said you won't do a good job."

"Are you kidding me?" I practically shouted. "What did you say?"

"I told the minister you'd sung two songs at my father's funeral, and one verse was in Swedish. Dad said Doris asked for you to sing. He said you'd do fine."

"Dad or the minister?"

"Both. I brought you the music."

"OK." I sighed. "I'll be there soon."

I continued back past abandoned cement troughs, piles of pale beige dirt, and a vacant construction trailer until I got to the far end, where Grandma and Grandpa had their apartment. Orange traffic cones stood in a row across the paved road. I stopped, put the car into park, exhaled, and got out. I moved each cone to the side, got into the car and drove through, then got out again to put each cone back into place, and drove on.

Taken at face value, Grandma Doris chose a perfect funeral song, *Precious Lord*, a Black gospel. I recognized it, thanks to a choir project in my twenties that invited white singers into Black churches to educate us. It had been years, but those gospel songs stayed with me. At every rehearsal, my fellow guest singers and I made copious notes in our scores to approximate what probably came naturally to the Black singers for the hymns we thought we knew.

I suspected Grandma Doris had missed the song's wider significance, so neatly tucked into white Christianity that she wouldn't know. If only she had told me what the song meant for her. We should have talked about a lot of things, but it was too late to talk, although she was still alive, albeit not for much longer.

Two days prior, she'd summoned Mom and me to her apartment for a private audience. She slid five jeweler's boxes at me across the table, one after another, with sticky notes to go with each cryptic treasure, tiny annotations in my Aunt Sally's handwriting that I read aloud. Grandma Doris was so out of breath by then, and so weary, that she couldn't expound on the shorthand. Sally couldn't remember the details because she'd written the notes in case Grandma died during her hip replacement surgery the year before.

At last Grandma had raised her wrist and nodded at a floral watch I'd given her. "You'll get this soon."

I swallowed hard. "Not too soon."

She'd given me a sharp look. "I need to go now." Then we rolled her to the hospice wing upstairs.

Which brought me to this moment. I stepped into the mild, late-afternoon air and began to walk. Mom handed me the sheet music as I entered the building. "You'll have to sign in." Several people on the log-in had visited Grandma. I added my name and the time, and we followed the industrial floral carpeting down the corridor.

Dad met us coming the other way. He reached his arm around my shoulder in a hug. "You'll be great."

The minister emerged from a door down the hall, a familiar, charismatic man with jet-black Elvis hair. He shook my hand and smiled. "Good to see you." Warmth beamed from his face as we chatted about my brief stint in the choir, and I felt my shoulders relax. He said he'd see us soon and strode away.

My cousin walked by with my uncle, and both men patted my back. We continued.

Dad introduced me to an elderly couple outside a nearby room. They expressed surprise when they heard why I'd come. They said they were sorry. "Me too," I said.

Finally, I walked past that lounge, where four relatives sat in the exact same places from the last time I'd been here. Hubert was barely tracking anything these days. His daughter-in-law was with him. I didn't stop to talk. There were so many people present for something so private.

I entered the room next door that housed her nearly expired body. Grandma lay in the bed at the back, her mouth wide open, lips wilted against her gold-tipped ivory teeth. They'd finally moved the other old woman out of the front bed. For several days running, she had stared silently as we shuffled in and out to see Grandma. I wondered if I should offer an apology for our vigil or say hi. So I'd never said anything. How Minnesotan of me.

Aunt Sally reclined in an ancient family wheelchair with sea-green vinyl and heavy steel bars, broken leg propped up on a wicker basket from home. Mom moved to stand by my aunt, and I moved to Grandma's side. I held her hand, rubbed the mottled arm with tissue-paper skin, the watch I gave her still heavy on her wrist. I touched her forehead, ran my hand down her cheeks, told her in a pinched voice that *I love you. I'm proud of you. I know you're proud of me.*

I told her that she could go where she needed. That I'll always, always remember her. I leaned over to kiss her, stood up, backed away, but didn't leave. It wasn't enough.

Sally spoke up from the corner where she'd been watching silently until then. "Do you think you'll be alright to sing?" I opened my mouth to explain how I knew I'd be fine but stopped instead to look at the photocopied pages in my hands, which I'd read, silently, multiple times since arriving.

I glanced at the flimsy hospital wall, considered the relatives in the lounge, then looked back at my aunt. At last my eyes landed on Grandma Doris. I wanted her all to myself, the woman who'd chosen me to sing this song, the only person who mattered.

I opened my mouth, and out came my voice, clear and strong:

Precious Lord, take my hand, lead me on, let me stand.
I am tired, I am weak, I am worn.
Through the storm, through the night, lead me on to the light.
Take my hand, precious Lord. Lead me home.

And then I turned and walked out of the room, down the hall, and into the daylight. Grandma might go today or tomorrow. But I'd completed my vigil.

Margin Notes

Grandma may have found her way home, and we'd buried her properly as requested, but I was still tired, weak, and worn.

I never shared with Grandma how much my life was breaking down. I'm not sure I ever told her that I was now teaching Basic Spanish on top of a full German load. She would've offered her constant refrain that I worked too hard. By which she meant that I should spend more time with her. I didn't have the bandwidth to explain.

Before Dave and I married, we took a perfect premarriage test at our church. As in, we earned 100%.

"You aced it," the minister said at our appointment, as soon as we'd sat down in her office to review our results. "I've never had this happen, but I can't offer any advice. I've never met a couple more suited to each other." Mind you, this woman could wax poetic on social justice solutions for half an hour in the pulpit. "I honestly have no suggestions," she said, turning up her palms, smiling brightly.

I felt vindicated that it had taken me so long to find the right husband—a younger man, who cared as much about this test as I did. Plus, the uncanny reading from Vivian's psychic foretold his arrival. So this confirmed it. The problem with this approach to a test is that you don't often identify potential areas for growth, for when times are tough. And that would have been good to explore, especially since the psychic had foretold a heavy burden several years in.

In retrospect, our results were entirely predictable. As a student of human nature, I'd approached our romance like a case study. Working at the bookstore where we met, I'd curated a personal library from new age to novels to self-help to memoir and applied all that book learning—plus lessons from failed relationships—to our romance. I navigated the shit out of this thing and landed my man.

We planned our marriage carefully, methodically, the same way I did my career. When we met, I owned our first house, had tenure, was at the top of the pay scale for my years in the school district, and was on my way to seniority over nearly every world languages teacher, not just German, but Spanish. Which in theory ensured my job security until retirement in my sixties.

I'd taken the summer job seeking a compatible man. Even that part worked out: Dave's a language scholar who dropped out of a PhD program in order to teach high school Latin. Just as I did with German. He studied dead languages, I did the live ones. That was our running joke.

One particular bookstore coworker made an extended play for Dave. She'd ask to see my engagement ring and hold my hand staring intensely for a long moment, or ask offhandedly if we were still getting married. Once she reverently told me that Dave adored *A Prayer for Owen Meany*, by John Irving. He and I laughed about it, since I'd given him the book. She'd seen him reading my copy.

He joked about my "other boyfriends" too. He knew he benefited from my past mistakes and personal growth.

Shortly before our wedding, when we worried whether he'd find a job, I was driving home from an errand north of the river, and the sky turned green fast. I waited out the storm in the parking lot of the very high school where they were deciding whether to hire Dave or cancel their Latin program. Several light posts had tipped over and rolled menacingly around the car, but the rain subsided. I drove away unharmed.

I read it as a sign. Somehow we would weather even our scariest storms, and maybe that school would soon hire Dave, and they did, right after our honeymoon. Within a year, he added English literature to his credentials, at my suggestion. When you're hedging your bets against an uncertain future, anything can be a sign, and I read them all.

Our life was set up to be good. We wanted two kids. I had twins.

I was always a planner and always an overachiever. You have to remember, an honor student has achievement trained into her, even when she doesn't see the connection. Her rigor is, she believes, the very thing that makes her worthy—of love and belonging and security. She earns it by working hard. By the time we buried Grandma Doris, I was working incredibly hard.

I never wanted to be Saint Amy. I wanted deep fulfillment, balanced with a sustainable life. I prayed that it would happen someday.

Wednesday church choir rehearsals and Sunday services in Minneapolis offered me respite. On Sundays, Dave and the girls came with me. On Wednesdays, Dave drove our kids to his parents' house for dinner while he did schoolwork.

Not long after I'd found out Grandma Doris was dying, I'd met up with Dave on the way to church choir to run an errand; when I dropped him back at the Starbucks where he often graded, I saw that I had time to spare.

As he stepped out of my passenger door, I gathered up my courage and made an impromptu suggestion. "Can I join you for a while?"

"What?" he asked. Did he simply not hear me, or did he not want to? He sounded vaguely irritated, or disengaged at best.

"Nothing," I said to save face. "OK, goodbye." Did he see how I pretended not to have offered? I drove on to our Minneapolis church, the one where we had married, ashamed at what had become of us, feeling the vacuum of hard things unspoken, echoed by the frozen tundra.

After rehearsal, while I was walking into the darkened lot, I saw that he'd called. I watched my frosty breath materialize in the winter air and waited until I'd locked the car door before calling him back. He asked too eagerly when I'd get home.

He met me at the door, led me down the stairs to the basement, away from listening ears and looked me in the eyes. "A barista I talk to sometimes gave me her number." Apparently she was young and liked to ask about his Latin T-shirts and shared his musical tastes. That evening, she'd made a loop through the coffee shop and dropped her scrap on his table as she passed by.

"Let me see it," I said. He handed me the folded-up slip. There was her name. First name only. So shameless. So simple.

"What did you do?"

"As soon as she was out of sight, I snuck out the back."

"But you took the paper with you."

We stood there, leaning into and holding each other. Between us, we knew eight languages—six living, two dead—but we couldn't find the words to quell the chaos that was our collective life.

"What do I do?" He sounded small. "I'm supposed to be with you."

"She saw your ring." I gave him a meaningful look. "She knows what she's doing. Throw her number away."

And he did. But he did contemplate going back to explain. To her. I was a cornered beast, seething but keeping it under control. This woman was eying my man and our kids. And I'd made it easy, but I saw her for what she was: a dangerous threat.

He wasn't asking for reasons to leave me, he was looking for reasons to stay. I didn't know that for sure at the time.

Things were extra tense for a week. Our marriage was a cheerless, hollow shell, and there was no denying it now. I lived on the edge of tears, and he dissolved into distant silence, avoiding me while he showed open affection to our girls. Finally, we had it out over the phone after school, again before choir, at my insistence.

"You've frozen me out," I said.

"Things shouldn't be this hard," he said. "It's all so complicated."

"Another woman won't solve this." I paused. "You'll still have me and the girls to deal with. She'll just make everything worse."

Silence. "Then I should go back and make things right with her."

"You need to make things right with me." My tone was confrontational. Intense. "If you go, we'll never be rid of her. Do you want to be with *her* or with me?"

More silence. "I want to be with you."

"Then be with *me*."

He didn't go back to that Starbucks.

I promised to stop weighing him down with every bit of chronic school drama; I understood that I was my own worst enemy, stretched to my outer limits.

Our marriage survived.

Follow Your Feelings

When I became a mother of infant twins—already a seismic shift— other things started to change. Administrators who championed me had moved on. Men came into the district with their sights set on leaving their mark. They dropped in cute, casual jokes about adding Mandarin Chinese in conversations with me. They did not say, but frequently hinted, that German wasn't relevant anymore.

By the time my kiddos finished kindergarten, these new-to-me bosses had shut me out of backroom meetings, piled on too many mandates, and assured me when I tracked them down that they had the kids' best interests at heart.

At first, I conspired to make their plans work. Sure, I could teach four levels of German a day, two or three levels an hour, over forty kids some hours, running between multiple classrooms in the same period, all day long, two schools a day, every day. With a brand new overhauled curriculum and shorter classes than ever before. I wanted to be part of the solution.

Part of that solution meant giving a parent-teacher conference moments after I read the email from my cousin that confirmed Vivian's passing. It required me to miss Vivian's funeral because I was so far underwater at work that if I had actually flown there, I might never have come up for air. This is not hyperbole, but understatement.

The next year they assigned me five levels of German plus Spanish One for the first time ever. The September Grandma Doris died, I started my third year of this unsustainable progression. I had my school picture taken that morning. While I drove between schools, Mom verified by phone that she was gone. I left my sunglasses on, told students that my grandma had died, and taught for the rest of the day.

Truthfully, I couldn't manage, as evidenced by a fresh shock of white hair at my crown. Nobody could've managed the load they assigned me. But I had a home mortgage, young twins, and a teacher husband not so high up the pay scale. We needed my income. I couldn't imagine another career, although I had the luxury of savings from Grandma for emergencies only.

Save the principal, spend the interest, she always told me. The same value should have held true at work: guard my energy, guard my health, rather than run down my reserves.

I kept saying to anyone who would listen, "This isn't working."

Sometimes, when the going got really tough, at the height of my German and Spanish double-and-triple booking, I quoted Vivian's psychic to students. *I would do twelve things at once and have the energy of three. It would be very emotional due to the nature of the burden. But I could handle it, whatever it was. Be positive,* she'd said. My students knew I was a bit eccentric. We laughed. Gallows humor.

People around me—outside of education, and not the students who had to witness this mess—said, *They can't possibly expect you to follow this schedule.* Well-intentioned acquaintances shook their heads. *Seriously, teachers are saints. You aren't paid enough.* They would offer a brilliant suggestion: *You need to tell administrators you can't do this.*

I practically burst into tears but refrained. Administrators had knowingly done this to me. All evidence indicated that they wanted German gone. I could've helped them to add their Chinese and maintain our other language programs in more sustainable ways, but they tuned me out and called me biased toward German. I was the institutional memory that administrators chose to ignore.

Let's make it even clearer: I taught in German, which drained my brain exponentially more than teaching in English. Most of the men and women who left me no margins, and framed it as moral obligation, weren't fluent in any non-native languages. They called their uninformed plans "doing right by the kids."

What about *my kids*? The paperwork to support my career demanded endless hours outside of that ridiculous workday. That part never factored in. Then Grandma died, and another school year rushed on.

One Saturday afternoon, I dragged hoses across the lawn, past the perennial garden I'd planted by our front porch, straightening the hoses onto the driveway, to let the water run out so that winter ice wouldn't burst them.

"Girls?" I called out, my voice sharp. "Where are you?"

Mira, newly eight, popped her head around the corner. "Here I am."

I paused a moment to breathe in, breathe out. "Where's Olivia?"

"She's playing out back."

Another breath, in and out. "You were supposed to collect all the tools and organize toys in the garage." I sized up the front lawn, resting my hands on my hips. "I also need you to bag up the branches you cut and left in the garden."

"OK," she said too quickly. "Bye, Mom." She disappeared.

It was hopeless. We built our home on the edges of designated wetland where nature commanded our attention. The two times that day

I'd looked for our daughters, I'd found them hunched over frogs in the grass and chasing each other with butterfly nets. They were doing what children were meant to do: laugh and play.

I couldn't ask Dave to stay home and help. He was off at a new coffee shop correcting piles of essays. And he'd supported me during Grandma's rapid decline.

Standing in my weed-ridden garden I felt rage rise in my throat. "God help me." My tone was a blend of a plea and a demand. "Something has to give."

I entered the garage, where my gaze landed on the dollhouse.

My dollhouse.

When I was a kid, other girls who visited always wanted to play with it. I hadn't let them. I hadn't let me. I couldn't recall playing with that house, not even a single afternoon, only maintaining and straightening up all that furniture, an extra chore in addition to cleaning my room. One time I even tripped and fell into the corner and got a black eye.

Now as then, I'd done everything right. And yet my house and yard and marriage and motherhood and career and mourning all added up to an ungodly mess.

Mom had delivered that dollhouse unbidden when I bought my first house, furniture boxed up for my crawl space. I never asked for it, but still it followed me. When we moved into this bigger house, just shy of our daughters' third birthday, I'd set it up in the basement and let them have at it.

They'd enjoyed themselves, filling rooms with any toys they saw fit to include: ping-pong balls, random plastic animals, odd scraps of paper, pinecones, and seashells strewn about the floor with boxes of miniature food and tiny magazines.

It mocked me, that dollhouse. The problem wasn't my marriage to a good man, or my lack of time to be a good parent to really sweet kids. The problem was that beyond my broken career, I didn't have any real ways to play, nothing to bring me joy, few friends I could laugh or cry with.

Emotions kept piling up in me like so much dollhouse furniture with no outlet for release.

Recently, I'd hauled the empty dollhouse up from the basement and put it in the garage until I could decide what to do with it. The block that was the chimney still sat on a bookshelf downstairs.

All the furniture was gone, each chair and mirror thrown out as my daughters demolished pieces that fell apart easily, the glue brittle with years. They'd broken some of the window frames. I winced to see the girls' names scrawled across the front walls in crayon. Children's graffiti ran the length of the attic.

What a strange end for a dollhouse I'd dutifully protected for thirty-five years. My daughters destroyed it, lovingly, joyfully, in only five. And still I couldn't get rid of it. Even Goodwill refused to take it.

It was garbage. I carried it out, placed it on the driveway, and gave into the rage of the full-blown temper tantrum that my elders never would sanction, not in a million years. Because finally I could.

I began with the windows, snapping pieces of frame no thicker than toothpicks, and busted down that little fucking door from its hinges with a satisfying crack. Then I bent the front walls back so far that they popped off at the hinges. The attic too. I grabbed at the carpet and tore it away from the wood. The wallpaper as well. It tore away easily in spots but stayed firmly affixed in others. I stomped at the walls that divided the house into rooms. In short, I beat the ever-loving shit out of that dollhouse.

At last, hopped up on adrenaline, I stepped back to admire my handiwork: an empty shell that used to resemble a house. Now only the stubborn wallpaper scraps kept it from being anything more than two long rectangles bonded together.

After I threw the debris into the trash, I brought the shell into the garage and left it standing on one end beside the trashcans. I walked inside our real house and slammed the door.

I had never felt more alone.

Muse

Freedom

When I grappled with a cover story for why I was resigning, three and a half years after my permanent transfer to the Spanish department, I would recall how folks responded to the original news of that reassignment. As Frau Hallberg, I was known as a formidable, if emotionally weary, defender of the German program against all threats to diminish it.

But that struggle had taken its toll. That's why, when word got out that going forward I would teach only Spanish and leave the German department, well-meaning colleagues and parents of German students rallied with variations on a predictable theme: *But German's your first love—your heritage, your first language passion, and you should continue to teach it.*

And I'd correct them. Actually, Spanish was my first love, thanks to its prominence on *Sesame Street*. But really, my first language passion was Swedish. And I wasn't German, to speak of. (True, Grandma found German ties in St. Louis when I was in graduate school there, but I didn't give that much credence.)

"We're Swedish," I said. "I went to Swedish camp as a kid." It was a misdirect away from my qualifications and internal politics, and it worked.

"How many languages do you know?"

"Besides English? I've studied German, Spanish, French, Russian, and Swedish."

From there it was an easy dismount: *Say something in another language, whichever they asked about next, smile sweetly, shrug diminutively, move on.*

The truth was that I'd been trying for decades to become fluent in Spanish; something always steered me away. After the *Teach Yourself Spanish* vinyl record we borrowed from the library melted in the back seat of our station wagon, my first language instruction was Spanish summer school at six years old.

The teacher told me that my Spanish name was Anita because Amy starts with an A. I learned: "Hola. My name is Anita. What is your name?" We counted to ten and learned the Mexican Hat Dance. That wasn't what I signed up for. The scope was too small.

When I finally student taught Spanish at thirty-eight years old through the University of Minnesota, I could complete the required hours of high-school practice with a colleague across the hall between German classes, but I also had to practice teaching elementary students. This was a policy change in the state of Minnesota. When I earned my German license, I made sure that I could only teach seventh graders and older. Whatever it says on your license, administrators can assign you to teach it, and I don't have the temperament to teach younger kids. But rules are rules, and so to earn my Spanish license, student teach them I must.

El Lago del Bosque, the Spanish camp, said I could spend a couple of weeks working with a mentor there, but that would have taken me away from my own four-year-old kiddos. Thankfully, I got to student teach third grade at a Spanish immersion summer school in St. Paul.

This was neither summer school from the seventies, nor a spendy overnight camp. Kids who go to immersion school speak Spanish year-round. Some use Spanish at home. Either these kids needed to shore up their reading, writing, and math skills, or they attended summer school because their parents needed childcare. Or both. Every third grader spoke Spanish more fluently than I did.

So I leveled with the kids: I asked them to speak Spanish with me—not bypass my clunky Spanish with English. I needed their help to improve. In return, I could help them become stronger students. They had the fluency. I had the skillset. Mercifully, that convinced them. Elementary summer school Spanish exhausted me in unparalleled ways. But I learned a ton, including that Spanish does sound like dancing. That didn't mean that I knew all the steps, only that I could recognize them with great effort, and appreciate them.

That summer, when I wasn't teaching or taking classes, I crammed like nobody's business. The U of M required two standardized exams—one on language skills, one on Spanish-speaking cultures, including literature. Failure wasn't an option; the closest testing site was the University of South Dakota.

Thank heavens we could rely on my parents to watch our girls. Dave drove me past hours of corn fields while I flipped through flashcards. Once we arrived in the tiny town of Vermillion, South Dakota, we checked into our hotel and arranged our whole evening around my exam preparations. We scoped out the building on campus and ate at the Chinese restaurant on Main Street. After an early showing of *The Simpsons Movie* at the cinema to help us wind down, I tucked in early while Dave read his book in the lobby.

Around eleven, give or take, a muffled sound woke me up. Someone was talking on a cell phone just outside the door, and they weren't stopping. I stumbled out of bed and opened the door to find a tall blonde woman directly outside our room.

"Will you please talk somewhere else?" I said. "I'm taking a test tomorrow." She turned, and I recognized her as a fellow teacher from my school—not one I knew well. Startled, I called her by name. It was surreal.

She stared momentarily, waved me away, and moved down the hall. I went back to bed and eventually fell asleep, not yet placing this as a harbinger of people who would look past me in hallways, unsure of how to engage. Nor would I engage them.

The tests went well. I knew exactly which exam questions I'd missed, which I verified from my notes on the ride home. I prayed that I'd passed both tests, which I did with generous margins, and I prayed that I'd never need to teach Spanish. Within two years, though, I did.

As Profe Hallberg, I was known as a joke in the high school where I first taught Spanish One. With my many levels of German and daily travel between buildings, I didn't have the energy to get part-time Spanish right. A full-time position in the other high school was my semi-fresh start. I struggled to put a nice face on this.

Ah that brutal, nasty Minnesota Nice. What if I'd told the truth? That I worked my ass off and retaught myself Spanish three times? Also, I felt inauthentic because I wasn't Latina. Neither were most of my Spanish colleagues, but I digress.

We really should have talked about that, as well as the fact that I'd experienced loss after loss. How do you solve a problem like Frau Hallberg, once empowered, suddenly small? You make plans to contain her. You script her. She scripts herself. Things suppressed come out sideways. They have to.

She learns to be an incredible sleuth, which doubles as paranoia when every decision about her career is now made behind closed doors, doors she once freely walked through, and she reads the clues and trusts very few. Nobody tells her what they're doing.

Even my work role that felt most rewarding was hidden work, a volunteer as faculty advisor for the Gay-Straight Alliance, along with a fellow Spanish teacher. We held closed-door meetings where kids hung out, as kids do, safely out of view.

But I knew people were aware of us, and I worried about a time when that would become an issue. One could say that I was a volcano ready to blow.

Fortunately, I had a release valve. Soon after Grandma Doris died, the same day I became aware that my time teaching German was ending, I'd received notification of my writing apprenticeship in creative nonfiction with an award-winning author named Cheri Register, who serendipitously held a PhD in Swedish. Even as I handed off my German program, I'd begun sending Cheri chapters about that, meeting her for coffee to hone my perspectives, and arranging substitutes for afternoon classes so that I could attend twice-monthly Minneapolis workshops with writing peers. This required major investments of money and time.

To earn all that time off, I had to sub for other teachers during my prep time, write sub plans, and arrange for school pick-ups with Dave. I cared about quality Spanish instruction. But the sensation that I experienced when I drove down the freeway, away from school into the city, midday, felt way too delicious.

I'm sure that didn't go unnoticed.

When Hubert entered the hospice wing the following January, I almost didn't go to his bedside. I never mentioned his impending death to any Spanish teachers.

That Wednesday afternoon, I sat between my desk and the window sorting through as many papers as I could wrap my mind around, weighing how much still had to get done, and if I could get to Hubert before choir practice. In walked Jeff, my sweet custodian of the past few years, a big folksy guy with a salt-and-pepper beard. "Hi Amy!" His eyes sparkled. "How are you today?"

I sighed. "I'm not sure. My step-grandpa's gonna die." I felt my throat catch. "He doesn't recognize me anymore." The one time Dave and I dropped by the apartment after Grandma's death unannounced, Hubert was polite but also clearly terrified. So we stopped going. "I'm trying to decide if I should go say goodbye, or if I've already done that."

"I'm sorry." Jeff picked up the waste basket and carried it out to dump in his cart, then returned it to its place beside my desk. "Sounds like you might want to go. You could, you know. Maybe you should." It's all I really wanted, someone who cared, someone to convince me.

I always had the nicest custodians. On my way out, I saw his cart back by the locker bays, and I shouted to him: "Thanks for your encouragement. I'm going."

"You're welcome," he shouted back.

It was quite dark when I arrived at the facility. In the dimmed hallway outside Hubert's hospice room, I encountered Hubert's son and daughter-in-law, my dad, and my cousin Ellen. They'd all seen him. Such was my timing that just as I was the first person in Grandma's family to meet Hubert, I was also very likely the last person to speak to Hubert while he was still alive.

He lay alone in the room, and I regaled him with stories of our time together, especially this one:

"Remember the summer you taught me to golf? You drove me to a three-par course, bought a bucket of balls, and pointed me toward the driving range." In my mind, he stood watching, alert in his golf shirt and no-iron slacks. "You placed my hands on the club. When my shots went far, you said, 'Good job. Do it again.' When a ball landed badly, you teed up another. 'Try again,' you said. 'We have a whole bucket and nowhere to go.'

"You helped me to reposition my feet and line up the shot. No matter how impatient I got, you never lost patience. You insisted that I keep my eyes fixed on that tee while I swung, backward then forward, keeping time by saying my name, *Amy K. Hallberg.*"

I wanted him to remember who we were to each other, and perhaps he did.

Once I returned to the darkened hall, my relatives dispersed into the night and I went off to choir practice, as I seemed to be doing whenever a beloved elder died.

My parents planned to bring my girls to say goodbye the next morning, but then Hubert passed. I believe he left as I crossed the river on my way to work, when the sky was still a deep midnight blue, and the waning crescent moon shone bright.

His daughter-in-law, Lucy, called me with the news just as I reached my desk. Hubert was gone.

Lessons by Proxy

Hubert had an only child, a son, the one person with the right to call the shots. My parents told me he wanted a service in April, when the ground thawed. We'd reconvene then.

As for me, I wasn't satisfied with *Hubert's dead. See you in April.* I'd put mourning on hold for years—first Vivian, then Grandma Doris, and last my Frau Hallberg persona. The public-facing memorial service could wait, but I'd be damned if I waited for our family to get together.

The Jewish religion offers the practice of Shiva, a time of mourning where you do as little as possible except to mourn. Christianity soldiers on. Nevertheless, the death of someone close brings up all kinds of odd things that run deep in families, like stories that haven't been told. Who knows each mourner's pain points or even our own?

In Hubert, I had lost the first man who took me seriously. A man who said repeatedly, *Amy, you and I think alike.* In my family, people questioned my thinking and my emotions. But never Hubert. Over the years, I called on him countless times: in cases of emergency, when I needed rides to the airport, and for no reason at all. Hubert's son, a pragmatic doctor, lost his dad. We had different agendas.

"Here's the thing," I said when my step-uncle returned my call. "April's a long time away, and I'm going to need something sooner."

He repeated what he had in mind. He sounded weary.

"I need something now," I said. "Doesn't have to be much."

"OK, Amy." He sighed. "What would you like?"

"Could we meet just as a family? Reserve that room at the facility? We could say a prayer, read a Bible verse, tell a few stories, sing a hymn. Eat in the dining hall afterward. One last time." I laid it out like Grandma Doris would have expected, a proper service and a proper meal. She and I hadn't always found common ground, but I knew she'd agree.

So yes, I wanted a family gathering. I wanted to say all the things while we could, and not hold off before our family as we knew it inevitably went our separate ways.

And that's what we did. Hubert's youngest granddaughter, the only one born into our blended family, helped her dad put together programs. We prayed and read a verse. She read a short eulogy. He played piano. We sang. It was perfect.

When we told stories, here's what I said: "Grandma wanted me to call him Grandpa, but I didn't want to. Then after their wedding, Grandma found the money to fly us four grandkids to Hawai'i so that we could get to know Hubert. He made us wear heavy sunblock, so I stayed pasty white, except for a nasty burn on my stomach where I missed. They scheduled us the whole time on tours and luaus and scuba diving. We had breakfasts and lunches and dinners. And we got to know Hubert. After that trip, I asked him if I could call him Grandpa Hubert. He said he'd like that. And I did too."

It was a clean, well-lighted place with a door to the giant meeting hall where we'd held Grandma's funeral, and I felt my relatives listening, enrapt in what I was saying. We built on each other's memories as each person chimed in. But I didn't expect my cousin Ellen's response. We hadn't compared notes in years.

"I agree with what Amy said." She paused and looked up, teary eyed. "I was sixteen when we went to Hawai'i. I didn't think I needed a new grandpa. I definitely remember how he made us wear sunblock."

She said more, her own version of things, but I thought about that age gap. *Sixteen.* It was a detail I'd missed, a significant blind spot in my memories of us. The evening added up to countless ways Hubert had brought us together and was present for every one of us in our blended family, each as we needed.

After my step-uncle treated us to dinner in the private dining room, he thanked me profusely, and later Mom would call to chime in with the comments he made to her: "I didn't know how much I needed this evening. Amy knew."

But that evening, all evening long, I felt numb. As Dave drove us away in the darkness, I checked my phone and saw that my mentor, Cheri, had emailed to express grave concerns about my recent aimless writing. I fired back that I was quitting the apprenticeship. Mind you, I hadn't planned to quit the program. But out the words came, plain as day.

Shocked, Cheri suggested a come-to-Jesus talk at our usual coffee shop the following day, after our respective church services. We both arrived in our Sunday best. Normally we both wore jeans. Paradoxically, the usual formality between us was broken. I noticed how Cheri's salt-and-pepper hair and her proper manners resembled Grandma's.

"I challenge you because I hold high standards for all the writers I work with," Cheri said. "But I worry that you take critique far too personally. Everyone won't like your writing. I wonder if you can handle it." She wasn't wrong, I would hate it. But that wasn't quite it.

"I can handle suggestions." I looked down at my hands, intertwined. "But I need to ask follow-up questions." I swallowed hard.

"I know that everyone won't approve of me or my writing. But do you respect me?"

In retrospect, this was the question that I always wanted to ask Grandma Doris. So often, I'd felt under pressure to explain myself when we were at odds. Cheri asked me similar questions, and that was the likely cause of my outburst. And yes, for the record, Cheri genuinely liked and respected me. I needed to hear it. Then we were OK.

It started to dawn on me that while Cheri resembled Grandma—smart, reverent, independent, fiercely determined, took excellent notes—Cheri only cared that I knew what I meant to say with my stories, and that I wrote them well.

"Readers need to see your motivations." She took a sip of her coffee. "As the narrator voice, you have to show us that you're OK. Even if you the character aren't OK. Or readers won't feel safe. They'll worry."

I knew that Cheri worried most when I couldn't narrow the scope of my project. I had so much to say, and I wasn't prepared to kill any darlings. Only rearrange. "You can save some for another book," she frequently told me. I disagreed. I felt like I had to get this whole story told. I couldn't wait.

On one of my early drafts, Cheri had written, "Don't hedge." That's what she was telling me: Stop asking permission to say what I mean, including permission from her. Now I saw that she meant it more universally too. She was watching me watch her reactions to see if she approved.

See also: *fawning, a trauma response.* Cheri was merely the proxy though, eliciting tendencies that I had taken on very young. Bear in mind that creative nonfiction was foreign to me. But also, I grew up watching reactions, trying to get the words right for people who might have opinions. And in particular, my family. My whole, extended, eclectic family, into which I fit and I didn't. Yes, I tried to tell truth, *and* I sought approval from people with power over me.

It was a watershed conversation, perhaps the first time I realized why I was so much happier learning languages other than English, where I wasn't expected to formulate appropriate thoughts on demand. By comparison, in English I was trying so hard to anticipate expectations in order to protect myself.

After our emergency meeting, my writing started to land, and I made up my mind to take Cheri's one-day class on researching family stories. It was on a Saturday in April. Yes, the same Saturday that Hubert's son planned to hold a memorial service. Who knew when Cheri would teach that class again? My parents said to do what I had to; I was an adult.

My friend Katherine, also Cheri's apprentice, listened to my justification the following week at the Loft Literary Center in Minneapolis.

"We've had our service," I said, with certainty. "I'm done."

She nodded earnestly. "Sounds like you know what you want." Katherine was a children's neuropsychologist who was writing about ADHD, which I was starting to suspect that I had from reading her chapters. Her blond bob, her piercing blue eyes, her face shape, and even her manner of speech strongly evoked my aunt Vivian, so her approval felt official.

In February, my parents' generation cleared Grandma's and Hubert's belongings from the assisted living apartment.

Mom brought several items for me:

1. From the powder room, the framed rose collage I'd made in graduate school.
2. From a table in the entryway, a pewter candlestick of a wood nymph on a lily base, moth wings at her feet, and two flower stems that lifted up daffodils, wired by Grandma to light up opaque candle lightbulbs. We'd agreed that I would get this.

3. My long-missing VHS tape of *Amadeus*, which I'd recorded off of TV, painstakingly pausing at commercials, and since replaced with a DVD.
4. Two gilt-edge mirrors, one an octagon, one a rectangle.
5. A small cardboard box of colored paperclips. (OK, I claimed those for myself when Dave and I dropped by to move something heavy.)
6. Inside that box, a red heart sticker. (Clearly a message.)
7. A carved wooden chair with stained white brocade, to be redone. Dad gave me the phone number of Grandma's favorite upholsterer, who lived in our part of the metro, out in the country. He told me the yardage so that I could buy fabric.

I wanted my selection to be symbolic, something that Grandma Doris and I would agree on. I found the perfect material on the Internet, lavender crushed velvet roses on off-white. It was reminiscent of her mother's patchwork quilt that Ellen got from the back bedroom in Grandma's house. Once I knew what I wanted, it should have been easy, but the fabric was wholesale only, so I asked my designer friend, Christi, if she could get me the fabric.

When she couldn't access that supplier, I tracked down an Internet source, got swatches, and placed the order myself. That should have settled it, but the order kept getting lost, and payment stalled, despite email exchanges and phone calls over the course of two months.

During those two months I still refused to attend Hubert's funeral, citing the writing class I couldn't miss. Eventually, I had to concede that a class on how to research family stories—while skipping a prime opportunity for said research—sounded foolish. Still, I was taking a stand, and I suspected that Grandma was likely taking a stand from the other side of the veil, delaying my fabric's arrival.

There was precedent for this. She was always surreptitiously squirreling away mementoes. There was a time when Ellen and I taped a sign on the bedroom door that we shared. Eventually the sign disappeared. When Grandma sold the house, Ellen discovered our sign among a whole trove of paper scraps the boys had fished out of our waste paper basket, and stashed behind the television in Grandma's office in the room over the garage.

When we went to tell Grandma, she giggled. She'd suggested the hiding place. She thought that our brothers' behavior was cute.

Then Hubert's oldest granddaughter, Cori, became our step-cousin. With one more girl cousin to share duplicate presents at Christmas, everything shifted. We never became a natural trio, despite our grandparents' fondest wishes. I didn't start to get close to Cori until graduate school in St. Louis, where she was a sophomore while I attended. Grandma always wanted our whole family to be close, and she definitely would've expected me to show up at Hubert's funeral.

Would she delay my lavender velvet to get my attention? Absolutely. One Saturday morning I woke up with a new idea: I would talk with Grandma Doris, looking into her gilt-edged mirror.

"OK," I told the ghost of my dead grandmother. "I give up. If I go to Hubert's memorial service, can I please have my fabric?" I could sense her assent. Sure enough, the velvet appeared in short order, and the chair was ready on Easter Saturday, one week before we buried Hubert's ashes.

I was glad that I went to the memorial service, again at the assisted living meeting hall. When I told Ellen about the chair, she told me about a Scottish landscape that Hubert had painted and framed for her. She loved the painting, but not the frame. Recently, she'd chosen one that she preferred and had it reframed. Meanwhile, awkward photos from our childhood flashed across a giant screen at the front of the room, until the ceremony began.

Afterward, while my step-cousin Cori and I waited in line for the luncheon in the side room, I showed her a photo of my crushed-velvet chair and told her my saga. "So see?" I said. "I'm sentimental like Grandma. We both got what we wanted."

"You always were the most like her." Cori sounded as cheerful as always.

I shook my head. "I'm pretty sure Ellen was her favorite."

"I don't know about Grandma's favorite." She paused to give weight to the words. "I said the most like her. We all thought you were."

Before we left for the cemetery, Dad asked me the way to our family plot, and I told him the names to watch for on gravestones. I imagined Grandma nodding, satisfied. I was the one who knew where the bodies were buried.

And I was the one telling the family stories.

Shadow Work

That June, shortly after our phone rang, Mira, age nine, made an announcement. "Grandma Katy found kittens in her window well."

"I must have them," I said without thinking.

"What about Wolfgang?" Dave said. "It doesn't seem like a good idea."

My poodle, Wolfgang der Hund, had grown tired and gray. I didn't want to replace him when the time came, nor did I want an empty house. Meanwhile, Dave often spoke of his beloved childhood cat.

"What if we just go see them?" Olivia said, looking a bit like a kitten herself. Bringing Wolfgang to meet them was just a formality. We arrived at my parents' house bearing tiny baby bottles bought at a pet store on the way over.

Olivia held the fluffy black-and-tan girl, who hissed then settled on a serene meow that sounded like chimes. Mira cradled the boy, who was black with a white blaze down his forehead and little white paws. He watched her with his yellow-green eyes.

A funny thing happens when a beloved dies, especially if they'd become a shadow of the person they once were, especially if you were a relative who only ever saw them on special occasions. Stories from all of their ages flood back and run together. You see their presence where you never saw it before. That's why connections that might have seemed random are anything but. And so the story breaks open. Little by little and all at once. I associated cats with Vivian. Clearly, she sent the kittens.

I hadn't had a cat since I was nine, the year Vivian left for Florida. First our cat, Yankee, had died on the highway the same day they left. We replaced Yankee with a brother from the same breeders. We kept him as an indoor cat, but Dad grew allergic, so we had to give that cat away within months.

Why wouldn't Vivian bring us two kittens? That's exactly what she would do. The timing was flawless. Within days, my two cousins, Sam and Nick, would arrive with their kids and Nick's wife for Camp Hallberg, our annual reenactment of their summer visits.

A few days into Camp Hallberg, I talked my way into Nick's very full SUV rental to go find the house where they had lived as kids, somewhere in the community where I taught high school. In all my years working in the district, I'd never come upon the house, never had occasion to go there, and never tried to find it, but my first classroom looked out over the wetlands in its direction, and so it lingered in my mind like Narnia, that magical place that only exists if you find the right portal.

In the four years since Vivian's passing, I'd often thought about their house with museum gallery rooms all on one level, at the bottom of a treacherous hill that got muddy in rain and icy in snow. I recalled a shiny black corridor that ran the length of the house, and leafy green branches that peeked through skylights above a sunken bathtub of cobalt blue tiles. In my memories, Vivian entertained guests in candlelit elegance.

There was a dungeon too, a secret storage space beneath a trapdoor in the carpeted back hallway. "I'm going in," Vivian warned, "so stay back! If you fall in, you'll never come out again." Down the path through the woods was a lake. "Don't go in the lily pads," Vivian said. "People throw glass there."

Maybe it was the kittens or my dying curiosity to see if old memories served, but I felt called to see the old house. My cousins had some sketchy directions and a street name that had changed from when they lived there. There was road construction. Stoplights were out following storms that had swept across the Twin Cities the night before.

"I'll tell you what," I said in the backseat. "Shut off the GPS. I'll get you there."

Nick's wife drove, and together we figured out the path by intuition. Finally, she turned the SUV down a narrow crumbling road with a flight of trees above and a flight of trees below that skirted the lake. We looked up the hill.

"There it is!" we cried out in unison. The house was exactly as we remembered, but smaller. We talked over each other, narrating the journey of how we got there. But when we parked in their old driveway, I couldn't get out of the car. I was terrified someone would recognize me and rumors would start. About what, I couldn't say.

Even towering over everyone, with an impressive sunburst tattoo on his left shoulder, Nick still wore his impish childhood grin, and Sam was as fearless as ever, not fazed by ringing the doorbell. When nobody answered, Nick's wife and Sam's older daughter joined them to wander the yard and peek into windows. But I stayed with the younger two kids, where I ducked down in the backseat, riding out a panic attack.

"When will they be back?" Nick's son asked.

"I don't know." I rubbed my fidgety hands together and bounced my knees. "Have another cracker."

Sitting in that back seat, I realized I never really knew the aunt who lived there. We grew close when I was an adult. And I didn't want to enter that house, only orient myself to its location. Having seen it, I prayed for my cousins' return.

At last they emerged and climbed onto a giant boulder out front for pictures. Only once they slid into the car could I let myself breathe.

Driving away, they confirmed that the house looked much like they'd left it. They recounted details from their childhood that coincided exactly with my memories, and added several that I never knew.

"You found it, Amy," Nick's wife said. "How did you know?"

"I've taught in this school district for years."

From there I directed our tour with a running commentary past our maternal grandparents' former house, minus the picket fence. It was only slightly out of our way to the Minneapolis mausoleum, where I opted to wait outside. I sat on a ledge and looked across Lake Calhoun, which has since been renamed *Bde Maka Ska*, the original Dakota name. I thought about how my cousins were born here, but how only I identified as a Minnesotan and knew all these random tidbits, and how it all felt cohesive to me.

I thought about the day that Yankee died, and Vivian set out for Florida with her kids, and I lost the closest thing I had to a sister in Sam, but how instead I gained a penpal, and how that changed us. We faithfully wrote letters. I became a tourist in her life, and she was a tourist in mine.

In the seventh grade, I read every last Agatha Christie mystery in the junior high library paperback spinner displays because Sam read Agatha Christie.

You can learn a lot about narrative from Dame Agatha's plot twists. She points you in one direction; you're certain you know the score, before she points you in every other direction, until at last she reveals the culprit. You knew it! The obvious answer was there all along.

In high school, Sam pointed me toward John Cheever's short stories, about people who aren't as they seem. A writer can't find better training. You start to see all the roles that people can play.

This tour of significant places in their Minnesota life wasn't fiction. The contrast on our road trip was very, very real. My cousins had left our extended family behind—our emphatic, frustrating, eclectic family—that I grew up watching firsthand, where I played a central supporting role and was often my elders' confidante.

At the cemetery, I realized, possibly for the first time, that Sam must have missed our family. Our close-knit family. Unlike Sam, I never had to arrange my mother's living facilities and hospice care, far from any relatives to support us.

A year before her death, Vivian had visited me in a dream. I saw her spirit behind a window and opened it. She floated up over the pond by my house, into the inky sky, to a full moon ringed in frost. Her mother, father, and son escorted her into the light, and they all disappeared. They looked like four little pairs of white coquina shells. I woke up crying, unsure if she was alive.

Little Olivia, age five, stood outside our bedroom door, silent. Somehow I sensed her. "Olivia," I called into the darkness. "I had a dream about Vivian. Come cuddle." We nestled together, whispering under the sheets while Dave slept. Vivian had sent me forewarning. One year later I kept vigil, looking out the window over the pond at that exact moon. And I did see glimmers of angels.

The dream was as emblematic of her life as it was a foreshadowing of her death. Her children didn't get a metaphor. They got the real thing. And this cemetery visit was about their mourning. Their memories. Their mom. So when they visited Vivian's crypt, I stayed behind.

After their two families emerged from the building, I navigated us to the University of Minnesota for more sightseeing. On the freeway back home, Sam called me the family storyteller. I've always been one, but my cousin wasn't here to see that talent develop.

When Sam comes around I am thirteen again. She is forever one grade—and yet light years—ahead of me. And I am forever the age when I read Agatha Christie's books, idolizing my cousin in absentia.

Another story took shape that day, of what I was missing and why I cowered in the backseat: I'd built longitudinal relationships, not only with my family, but with students when I taught German. Teaching scripted Spanish didn't let me do that because I was only one among many teachers whose job it was to plant seeds that other teachers would harvest. I trained students. They moved on, just as my cousins moved on. I stayed behind.

But like Vivian, I too had a plan to reinvent myself. I was preparing to become a peer coach who mentored fellow teachers to develop their teaching skills, a special assignment for which I dreamed of applying when the position opened back up in two years.

Meanwhile, I'd found my place in my cousins' adventure. When we got back, my brother had taught my twins how to waterski. Mom had made two pans of Grandma Lillie's Swedish meatballs. We sat around the dining room table and devoured them all. Vivian would have found the scene delightful and poignant.

Dig Deeper

I often think about those coquina clams I adore. When they die, they leave these tiny seashells for us to enjoy. We use them in decorations and marvel over their natural beauty. But while the shells contain their breathing bodies, bobbing up and down in the sand, they're simply living their lives.

That's the way I felt in my final years of teaching. For a long time, I'd focused on my legacy, and what I wanted students to remember about me. By the end, I was looking for a place in education where I could survive.

I had spent two years building up stellar credentials, mentoring peers all over my building to show that I could. Among the peer coach candidates, I was seen as a frontrunner. Despite steep competition, I made the first cut of twelve candidates. Going into the interviews, rumor had it that I was the person to beat. There were six openings. I only needed one, and they'd train me. My time teaching Spanish, wandering the proverbial desert, would end.

One colleague already in a peer-coach position was a wild card, someone who still had another year to go, with whom I found it hard to work, and who undermined me. I'd vowed never to work with that person again. But peer coaching was my alternative to a Spanish position, so I couldn't wait any longer.

On my interview day, a secretary gave me the page of questions to look over before my turn. Somehow I couldn't wrap my mind around them. At the conference room table, a wound opened up on the back of my hand and started to bleed on the paper, like some strange stigmata. Picture the mortified faces while I uttered garbled reasons why I was a good enough Spanish teacher, hand bleeding. I barely mentioned my qualifications to coach.

By the time I received the bad news the next afternoon, my wound had healed so completely that I had to search my skin for a scratch. Among the people at school, only I wasn't stunned at the outcome.

In his rejection email, the supervisor offered to meet and debrief. Over the weekend, I prepared the strong statement of purpose that I should've given in the interview. That's what I led with when we sat down in my classroom to face each other in student desks.

"This isn't a second chance." He looked me dead in the eye. "I want to make that perfectly clear. Everyone in the room agreed: You made them highly uncomfortable. You're not in the running as an alternative should another position open up."

"Oh." I sank down into myself. Everything was as bad as I thought. But I'd been playing a long game for years, so I would continue. "Please tell me what I did wrong so that I can improve."

As a consolation prize, he offered me a spot at coach training that fall, so that I better understood what coaching entailed. I could reapply the next year.

"You won't find a better peer coach," I said, rallying my cheerleader side.

That night, I developed laryngitis like never before and never since. My body gave me no choice but to stay home all week. By chance, that week was the Tapping World Summit on the Internet, where EFT talks were available for free for twenty-four hours each, to release trauma stored in the body.

All day and all night, I wavered between sleep and tapping exercises, tapping about myself, tapping about my career, tapping about being scripted with Powerpoint packets in Spanish, and tapping on how stuck I felt.

But I made sure my sub plans were stellar so that I fulfilled my contractual obligations. People are willing to help you uphold the illusion. For example, regarding the teaching profession with its too-long hours, chronic overwork and underpay, mandated testing, and assigned tasks with no correlation to learning? They'll say it's a shame that you have to live that way. They'll say that you aren't paid enough. For this required sacrifice we call teachers *saints*.

Here's an open secret I couldn't ignore: Grading rewards a very narrow subset of skills. And the measure of skills is perfection. This diminishes everyone's gifts. It's the law of averages. If you're lucky—and work hard enough—maybe you can excel beyond others and work your way up the hierarchy. It's a losing proposition, with haves and have nots built into the system. Nobody wins though. My Spanish classroom observations consistently earned top ratings from my peer coach and administrators. Before that, I had perfected my one-woman German improvisational show.

So the interview panel was the worst possible measure of what I could've done as a peer coach. Once I was hired into the district, I'd never interviewed for any position I held. Still, I learned more from that cascading failure than you can imagine.

My experience paralleled what we say to students: Yes, grading is academic. This system isn't set up to measure your growth. But keep going in the same prescribed way. Don't mess up or take risks; you'll tank your grade point average. If you don't get fifty percent, you'll get zero.

All week I wrestled with old demons until I reached a decision. I'd listened to district officials talk about grading reform for several years. Some pockets of teachers were piloting new systems for grading, but the language department wasn't among them. Since my reputation was shot anyway, I was going off-roading.

I would pilot what our letterhead touted as "Exceptional Personalized, Standards-Based Learning." Essentially, if your grades improve over time, we don't factor in previous failures. Every student doesn't have to achieve at the same pace to show growth. The teacher provides clear, flexible standards to measure learning. However—and this is key—students don't have to perfect every advanced skill to excel. And isn't that true of all of life? Enough advanced skills will suffice.

My struggles only showed how resilient I was. I don't have to be the best interviewer to be a strong coach. And that failure notwithstanding, I'm good at helping people to figure out what they want to say, and what that looks like, given their language skills. That's what I wanted my grades to reflect.

Many parents disliked the new practices. They liked being able to calculate grades by the first few weeks of a term. They liked predictability. To them, my experiment was highly chaotic and unpredictable. I innovated as needed. But I could stand by the final outcomes like never before. Every student had multiple opportunities to pass with no less than a C. Because if you truly passed the class, why shouldn't you earn a decent grade? If you're a strong student who takes enough risks, then you absolutely will hit your limits and fail at some advanced skills. But that's why you deserve the A. And you deserve rest in between. Nobody should work all the time.

Not only that, but I built in extra time for students who needed help, and those who finished their required standards got to do passion projects during class. We held a Spanish fair in the hall that drew connections to Spanish-speaking places. I had piloted the whole grading system that the administrators were talking about and taken them up on trainings. I hoped people were watching.

At the end of the year, an official district policy came out of committee exactly as I'd worked out in my Spanish classroom, down to the smallest detail. Never in my career had I felt so confident that my final grades represented actual student achievement and real fluency. Never had I felt so successful. Now other teachers would have to abandon their broken grading systems. Or that's what I hoped.

That June, Mom's and Vivian's families convened for a week on her Florida Island, where I was happy for one shining moment in time. Dave, the girls, and I found ourselves the perfect pairs of flip-flops. Dave, who likes to stay out of the sun, spent his days reading in an air-conditioned coffee shop that served maple bacon donuts. The girls roamed free in tropical nature with their generation of cousins.

I moved between island spaces, sometimes with family members, sometimes alone, treasuring thoughts of Vivian, fellow tourists over the years, and myself on former visits.

A framed portrait taken on the beach, a gift from my cousin Nick, shows my family of four walking hand-in-hand in an impossibly blue paradise. Dave and Olivia look straight ahead. Mira watches the seashells. I march forward, eyes closed, at the edge of the surf in a private reverie, on a beach known for riptides. I have no clue what's coming.

Vivian couldn't have known when she packed up and left Minnesota, how fully she would recreate that world on her Florida island. Everyone was changed on both sides of my family when Vivian broke out of her perfect mold and went off-roading.

She saved her money, bought the Post Office, and turned it into a deli. Then she bought the dress shop next door, the oldest house on the island. She built a whole shopping center around them, where she recreated the white picket fences that Grandpa built, except these fences were walkways, and instead of an arbor gate, there was a gazebo that overlooked a pond with a fountain. Vivian's jewelry boxes were delicate silver cardboard like Grandpa Oscar's glitter, and her paper bags were floral prints like Grandma Lilly's garden.

Vivian started over with next to nothing and reshaped our horizons. Would I have known how to break down my career and repurpose the good parts if I hadn't seen Vivian do it? She taught me how to read the landscape, look for shiny objects, and amplify them. At our island reunion, I took copious notes on the kaleidoscope fractals, and spoke very little about teaching Spanish.

One morning, Dave went out predawn to watch the sun rise over the Gulf of Mexico. The next day, Mira and I got up early. We three walked down the path I'd traveled since childhood, over a footbridge that spanned grassy dunes. We saw the darkened figure of my mother sitting on her walking cane that doubled as a foldout chair, set against a vibrant sky the color of plum jam.

On the third day, my brother stood by our mom.

"Ben thought he'd join me," she said sweetly.

"Mom threatened my life." Ben arched his eyebrow the way both of them do. "She said, 'Get up if you want to see sunrise.'"

Dave, Mira, and I ambled down the beach. Shells crunched under our feet. Coral sparks crowned the city. We squinted and shaded our eyes with our hands.

On the way back, I asked Mira if she'd seen the coquina colonies at the edge of the shore, entire extended families where the surf washed away their cover, and the rainbow bivalve mollusks wriggled back into the silt.

"I know. I've seen them."

We'd just gotten back to Mom and Ben.

"Why do they do that?" I asked Ben. "The coquinas."

"They're filter feeders," he said. "So it looks like they're struggling, but actually, that's how they get nourishment."

It was the perfect metaphor to carry back into my teaching world. For all the struggles I'd weathered over the recent years, I was the strongest I'd ever been as a teacher, thanks to my lack of apparent success. Let me restate that: I succeeded beyond my wildest dreams, and I'm proud of what I accomplished.

But I think about those beds upon beds of tiny coquinas, each living their tiny circle of life. And afterward their beauty—all they leave behind—stays on as tiny altars, wherever they land. We study them and worship them.

Here's something I was starting to realize: education, religion, and ancestor study are all ways of preparing to live fuller lives. I had spent too much time educating and too little time living.

Fool

Love

Back in my Minnesota garage at the end of that summer, Dad and I took some measurements. We went to get a couple of two-by-fours and big hooks to fashion simple racks. We planned to hang up garden tools I'd gotten from grandparents, now piled in the corner: shovels, rakes, hoes, and brooms.

He drilled holes, sank anchors in the drywall, and made sure the boards were level. When I stepped back to admire his handiwork, I tripped over the shell of my dollhouse, still upended beside our recycling and trash.

"Dad," I said.

"Yeah?"

"Will you help me to take the rest of this apart?"

He gave me a meaningful look before he smiled. "Sure." With three taps of a hammer, the pieces fell free. I stood the panels upright in the empty garbage bin and noted the irritating twinge in my arm that would soon morph into a full-fledged frozen right shoulder.

Then I bent down and picked up one tiny wooden drawer with a gold-toned handle the shape of an infinity symbol, a stowaway artifact that made it through my destruction. I'm not sure where it came from. I pondered the drawer in my palm and brought it upstairs to my bookshelf. It felt as if we'd released something more, as if I'd stood at a precipice and set something in motion.

The day that I returned to work in August for our back-to-school workshop, I found out that a group of parents had hosted the superintendent for an informational meeting in one of their homes, and instead of listening, shouted him down. Administrators got spooked and unilaterally walked back their expansion of every new thing I had piloted for them at the high school level.

Those of us who voluntarily forged the path could continue doing what we'd started. Those who'd stayed behind would continue with practices that I no longer believed in. And I had to partner with fellow Spanish teachers again. I knew that I'd run out of options.

In desperation, I turned to our newly elected union president, whom I'd known for two decades. We met for coffee, and he suggested a retreat, which doubled as professional development, based on the work of Parker Palmer. *Courage and Compassion for Teachers*, it was called; I could use a hefty portion of both.

If nothing else, this retreat would give me some respite away from teaching. So one brisk Friday in October 2015, rather than going to school, I drove thirty minutes in the opposite direction to a Lutheran retreat center located at the end of a dusty road in the woods. The air was chilly in the lodge when I checked in before anyone else had arrived, and I brought my overnight bag to a small private room that contained a bed, a table for writing, and a sizable metal cross on the red brick wall.

In the room where we gathered, there was wood in the fireplace, morning light streamed in through the full wall of windows, and our host, a friendly retiree with a long career as an educational mentor, pointed us toward a circle of chairs, each with a folder of papers.

When all of us were seated with our random steaming mugs in hand, our host rang a bell. "There's something wonderful about moving slowly," he said. "We're going to read poetry and see what speaks to us." We read deliberately, line by line, in turn. Once we finished reading, we voiced our favorite phrases into the circle, whatever words or images registered most strongly. Nobody responded with conversation but simply let the various words echo out. We spoke so slowly that the better part of an hour passed. Out on the meadow, birdsong punctuated our silences.

Next we went around the circle, to introduce ourselves and say why we were there. I had so many fragments of reasons, all sad and scary. My knees bounced as I clasped my hands together and awaited my turn. What could I tell them? So much, and nothing I wanted to say.

During the nascent school year, it had slowly registered that there wouldn't be a second chance at a coaching position for me, not in that school district, not even after the training they offered me as a consolation prize. Even though I'd created an entire shadow position as the equivalent of a peer coach, checking in with staff members throughout the building, pointing out ways that I saw them succeed, making my daily rounds to balance the "real" position I dreaded.

There was also this: Multiple participants at the retreat came from my district, teachers whose names I knew, even if we'd never met. Some actually were peer coaches. They likely knew all the key players—possibly well.

Perhaps I could talk about the dad who emailed me all in caps that WE ALL TALK ABOUT YOU. There was the fact that my colleagues refused to let me teach Spanish Three, even though teaching the upper levels was exactly how I got so good at German. They *Minnesota Niced* me.

I was trapped at Spanish class basecamp, seemingly forever, while everyone else progressed. And my book about Germany—my escape plan—was a mess. So did I really want to talk about that? None of these stories that I might tell them were pretty. They were petty and victimy and small.

But if I hadn't told the tales, I might well have burst. When my turn came, everything spilled out in a pinched voice, along with fat tears. My glorious past as Frau Hallberg, my thwarted present as Profe Hallberg. A funny thing happened next. Our facilitator had specifically told us not to comfort each other or interject. Silence echoed out, but everyone sat at attention, and I felt heard.

My confession about teaching—that I felt the solitary sting of unbelonging—became the truest thing I could admit. When that lonely veil dropped, then a still, persistent voice hummed with deep knowing within me. I was not—had never been—alone.

A woman across the circle likewise volunteered her painful story. She made eye contact with me when she cried, nodding at me with appreciation. At the first break, she and I crossed the circle and laughed as we hugged.

I'll let the secrets of that weekend remain in the circle, but I will tell you something magical that took place. A lovely teacher who worked with special-needs students listened to more of my saga in a break-out session.

"Can I offer an observation?" She waited patiently. I nodded. "You're writing that book from your head. What if you told it from your heart?"

I didn't exactly know what that could mean, but it felt very true.

We had a long break after that session, and I went out to wander the woods. The trees reminded me of a walk I had taken in Germany, all pine cones and hills, rushing water and fallen trees by the path, and I realized how much the Minnesota landscape resembled Germany.

As I wandered, I let myself meditate on a painful question. Why had I struggled so hard to master Spanish, despite a lifetime of admiration and trying? The doors slammed shut so often it would have been comical, if it weren't so traumatic. Opportunities were everywhere. By contrast, why was German, universally known as a hard language, and a genuine niche, so accessible in my life? I already knew.

In German, I had mentors who invested in me. First Eva, who was my earliest life coach, before any of us knew what a life coach was. Then German professors. Then the assistant principal who hired me—herself a language teacher—and other school leaders who cared about my success. I became known as the German expert and learned what it was to succeed in that way.

With Spanish, I forged my own path. Administrators treated me and other teachers as placeholders that they could move around at will. Since I was never considered a Spanish expert, I had nothing to lose and could take bigger risks. So I went on adventures. With Spanish, I followed a path of growth through failure, trials, and detours into uncharted territory.

I took advantage of huge opportunities that fell into my lap. I never would've tried the amazing things I've done without that supposed Spanish failure. I learned how to teach myself Spanish so that I truly understood how languages work. I learned how to break open and reenvision educational systems. I learned to navigate technologies that never existed until long after I graduated from college. Suddenly, knowing all that, I had an additional knowing: Teaching Spanish had served its purpose. And now it was over.

On Monday, when I got back to school, a longtime colleague sent me an urgent message. We needed to talk. Parents had been complaining about me to her. Some of them were coming to confront me at Tuesday's parent-teacher conferences. Her forewarning saved me.

Let me tell you how I ended my career.

Life Review

When I look back on the miracles of my life, by far the biggest is that people have always looked out for me. It took Eva to help me see it, but ever since she came to be my exchange sister, I've known that I'm not on my own. There are people who help me bridge gaps.

Eva provided German context to my American life, and this informed my teaching. As teens, we watched President Reagan's "Mr. Gorbachev, Tear Down This Wall" speech live on West German television in her living room, weeks after I visited both sides of the Berlin Wall with American teens who mostly drank lots of beer.

Eva and I both thought Reagan was pandering, though I was his fan at the time. Without thinking about the timing, I gave a high school graduation speech nearly a year to the day from Reagan's speech, insisting that the walls must go—in Berlin and metaphorically, the walls we build in our own lives, holding ourselves back because we fear strident responses from others. East Berlin in 1987 stands out as one of my most colorless days ever. How did people live with government doctrine that scripted their lives and wouldn't permit them to make their own meaning? But there's always that tension in the human condition.

Sometimes if we feel safe enough, we find our meaning and our medium to access creative flow. German was that vehicle for me because Eva helped me to make the connections until I could on my own. The graduation speech came to and through me. I didn't overthink its message, but simply found powerful parallels from my experience and captured them so that listeners could make their own meaning. It's exactly what I'd done in my best moments of teaching German. I couldn't unsee the contrast with Spanish.

The conference debacle mostly died down, thanks to allies who looked out for me and smoothed things over behind the scenes. Mercifully, I could avoid another night of conferences, when my choir appeared onstage with a traveling show at the world-renowned Guthrie Theatre. Frozen shoulder notwithstanding, I threw myself into full-body improv. That I could do. But parent-teacher conferences terrified me.

As if on cue, Eva had started to send daily WhatsApp missives from Hamburg. They arrived as I drove up to the school, as if she sensed that I needed hand-holding to coax me out of my parked car and into the building. She texted a stream of pictures and stories.

She'd been sending me headlines for decades, and I'd been writing my book about our friendship for five years. When I asked about names to hide her identity, she wrote back: "My name is Eva. Any questions?"

Recently she'd registered shock at the rising xenophobic star of the GOP presidential primaries, who promised to build a wall on the Mexican border.

His reality series framed him as a serious business man, but I still remembered his bankruptcies, plural. No way could this joker win, I assured her. We'd learned our lessons from Germans.

Another time, she sent photos of a giant Hamburg tent city for Syrian refugees, to shelter them over the winter. Angela Merkel had welcomed them.

One day it was a voice memo: "I know you're a good teacher." Eva's familiar voice sounded guarded. "But do you remember when you told me you were going to teach high school? I told you then that I didn't understand why. I hope this doesn't hurt your feelings, but I think there are other things you can do." Her faith in something more lifted me enough to get through the day. Eva always could read me.

I'd begun scaling back on committees after my peer coach asked why I was scheduled within an inch of my life. The previous spring, I'd handed over my volunteer position as faculty advisor for the Gay-Straight Alliance. I'd considered that ally role the highest, if most subversive, expression of my Christian faith, such as it was, because I knew what it was to be othered. For that very reason, I understood that the role drew animosity toward me. Still, in this age of marriage equality, another colleague wanted to march with LGBTQ+ kids in homecoming parades, and I was happy to let her. I only needed to hang on long enough to plan my escape route in June.

And then one morning, a miracle happened. I arrived at my parking spot to find Eva's question: "Dear Amy! Do you happen to be in MN Nov 6–7?"

My heart leapt. Though our friendship spanned thirty years, Eva hadn't returned to Minnesota since 1989. I texted back on the spot.

"Definitely. Will you?"

Now—when I needed her most—she wanted to schedule a layover in Minneapolis, on her way to join her husband at a medical convention in San Francisco. Twenty-four hours with Eva in person would do me serious good.

I had schedule conflicts all over the place, but that weekend was surprisingly open. The weekend of Eva's visit, I prepared for Monday in advance to eliminate homework. Soon after the bell rang at 3:15, I pulled out of the parking lot. By 3:45, Eva was seated in my passenger seat as I drove away from the airport.

"Wow," she said. "This really does look like the Black Forest. I'd forgotten."

"Doesn't it?" I beamed. We had our own shared vocabulary and knowledge curated over the years. Her hair was short and wavy, not in a ponytail, but here was the same German exchange sister I'd met for the first time at the airport at sixteen, with her same pensive expressions. I was driving us back to my hometown, on the freeway bridge across the Minnesota River. First on the agenda, meet up with Dave and the girls at home. Second, go to Minneapolis. Third, spend the morning exploring my hometown, eat lunch, and go back to the airport again.

"So tell me." Eva cut to the chase. "How is your book coming?"

I glanced sideways. "It's a challenge to capture myself as a teen."

"Mmm-hmmm. Why do you think?"

"High school." I scrunched up my face. "What on earth was wrong with me?"

"Oh. Well you were a teenager." She smiled, and I could see her formulating. "And you were a teacher's kid. And your mother was not an easy teacher. So kids took that out on you. And you were really smart and cared a lot about doing well in school. So kids didn't like that either." I nodded. As a teen, I'd prayed that she wouldn't notice my lack of connections, but she did notice, and we talked about it. What a relief. "And of course your brother was a genius. He made it hard for you, I think."

I shrugged. "That's true too."

"But you were so proud of being a cheerleader."

I laughed. "Yeah, that was a mistake."

"I always wondered: Why is she trying so hard to be a cheerleader?" Eva shook her head. "It wasn't who you were."

It was classic Eva. If only my Spanish colleagues could be so insightful and open. Recently, I'd started telling the cheerleader story again. It had worked with LGBTQ+ students to gain their trust. Now it reflected my growing anxiety.

Still, for twenty-four hours here was Eva, who understood my motivations, sometimes much better than me. For those short hours, it felt so incredibly easy to be me again, joyful even. There's no greater gift I could think of. Not even German chocolate and a heart-shaped key ring that said *Viel Glück*, or "Good luck." That phrase has a double meaning in German. It also means "Be happy."

Driving home a few hard workdays later, I called Mom. "I need to quit. Now."

"Why don't you?" she said, to my utter surprise. "Quit after this term. Sort things out later."

"Really?" I felt like crying. "I can do that?"

"Amy," she said, "I've been praying. This is the answer to my prayer."

She didn't mention my children. Or that when she looked at me these days, Mom thought of Vivian constantly.

By that Friday, terrorists had attacked Paris. Nothing in life was certain, certainly not my union-protected job that was killing me, where I would never feel like I was good enough.

Dave met my announcement with acquiescent silence. I'm sure it terrified him. Fortunately, Mom talked me through it. She never let me rethink my resignation. "Your life is too important," she said. "And you've worked incredibly hard."

When I stopped teaching German, a young trans father and former student had reminded me on Facebook that we started in the school district on the same day. He was the first person to teach me where the pink triangle symbol came from. He was also the first to teach me how he found safe spaces, which meant that he skipped lunch and went to the library instead.

Back then, he hadn't transitioned, and our conversations were coded. As a man, his soul was at peace. Since his time, so many LGBTQ+ students had come knocking at my door so that they could unburden themselves of their hidden truths. I knew—because I had witnessed it—how healing that was.

Now I was the one seeking safe spaces and closing doors so that I could talk.

Liminal Grace

"I'm quitting. In January."

I looked across the desk at the peer coach who had helped me to believe in myself. She blinked a few times. "Wow. You're serious." She inhaled deeply. "If you're happy, I'm happy for you."

"I'm sorting out the details, but yeah, I'm going."

It was the first of many quiet conversations. None of my coworkers ever asked why. They only called me courageous. And I started telling them the exact reasons why I loved them.

I began speaking out in coded language to students. "You know, I won't always be here," I said. "You need to know how to use these resources yourself." By then the Spanish department was already sitting in on interviews for my replacement, alongside the formerly distant, possibly disdainful principal who eagerly welcomed my resignation and promised to make it easy to leave.

Sometimes I asked my students to envision their future.

"Can you picture your future self in a Spanish-speaking country? You're there, and you're grateful to this present you for learning Spanish today." All around us were maps and flags and grammar charts on the walls, which I'd adapted from my colleagues' work. They would remain on the wall for my successor. "Where is that country? The future me is standing at the top of Machu Picchu. And the Galapagos. I want to see blue-footed boobies with their blue eyes. Have you seen those birds? Their beaks are blue too."

Most laughed it off. They seemed to notice that I was having fun at long last. In the evenings, I walked right past cheerleaders practicing in the hall, and I didn't hide the small batches of belongings I cared to take home.

"¡Hola Profe!" they called out in chorus.

¡Hola Amigas!" The cheerleaders were some of my favorites. I noticed how many I had now that my outlook had changed.

As long as I didn't let myself rethink my decision, everything felt magical. The second I doubted the logic of leaving because things were running so smoothly, instantly my online grade book would crash or a class would revolt. My body was also making it clear that I couldn't stay on forever. My right shoulder clamped down, and I'd gotten a cortisone shot when my left hip went out.

But I could say and do absolutely anything, as long as I kept my agreement with the Universe that I was leaving. For example, nothing happened when I called bullies out on their rude behavior patterns, except that we found common ground. It was as if I had a window of grace to notice every beautiful thing one last time and to offer my traveling benedictions. None of it was a lie. I just didn't say that this was goodbye.

One student wasn't buying it. I'm certain that he saw right through me. He was a six-foot Somali student with an unruly Afro who walked into my room sometime after the start of the semester and announced that he'd joined my class. He asked complicated linguistic and cultural questions that delighted and challenged me. He didn't enjoy flattery, for reasons he only hinted at. He was one of my absolute favorites.

"Profe? You speak about Spanish-speaking cultures as if there were just one." He tipped his head. "But isn't that oversimplifying to group all the people together?"

He had a point, and I said so. I never hid my lack of real-life experience with any of those cultures outside of America, beyond my sampling of Southern Spain and two day trips across the Mexican border as a kid. I relied on local Latinos to fill in gaps, though I did harbor visions of myself in the places that I'd mentioned, along with Oaxaca, Barcelona, Costa Rica, and places I hadn't thought to think about yet.

"What did you major in, Profe?" he asked one day from his desk, a few feet from my own, where I sat entering grades at my computer. He was supposed to be practicing irregular present tense, but this felt more important.

I got up and walked over. "German literature."

He nodded. "Have you been to Germany?"

"I made my way home from the Berlin Wall twice."

He leaned forward, eager. "Did you get a piece of it?"

"No, I mean the real thing before it fell." I'd recently written this story, so it was fresh. "I got left behind by my tour bus when I was off buying souvenirs on the western side. And I spent a day behind it on the Soviet side. My friend was detained by their border guards."

I watched his eyes widen, genuinely impressed.

I thought about the Black Lives Matter protesters I encountered in the streets of Chicago when I was there to study translation in 2014. "I can't breathe," BLM chanted. "I can't breathe," echoing the dying words of Eric Garner, choked to death for suspicion of selling loose cigarettes. And who could ignore the attention-seeking man who'd become the Republican nominee for President of the United States, actively campaigning on the promise of a travel ban on Muslims? As Eva predicted, he had gained ground by overstating his qualifications, getting his foot in the door at the hands of a vocal minority, and consolidating his power.

The media claimed to be shocked, but we'd watched this wave rise for years. And after all, that's the historical pattern: Authoritarians give plenty of forewarning before they do exactly what they've always promised. I got very quiet. I thought about the German resistance and my hero, Sophie Scholl, who smuggled literature to counteract official doctrine. Did you know that the German resistance were writers? *The German resistance were writers.* They were storytellers. They knew they weren't alone. And like them, I was the unlikeliest rebel, until I wasn't.

"Have you ever heard of the White Rose?" I asked my student. He shook his head, blinking. "OK. You're going to want to read that. Some Rilke too. You'll like it."

I started to explain about Sophie Scholl, not much older than he was when her faith called her to action alongside her brother, as members of the White Rose, who used revered texts, even the Bible, to get through to the German people.

His face clouded over, and he cut in. "I just don't get it." He hesitated a moment before he asked his question. "How can Christians say the hateful things they do?"

"That's not my version of Christianity." It was a knee-jerk response. I stopped. That wasn't what he was asking. I had to do better. "Listen." I said, quiet, intent. "Your voice is important. Don't forget it."

Then he asked the question that proved he was onto my plans. "What do you think of public education?"

"Ask me when I'm no longer a teacher."

That Thanksgiving when my brother was in town, I had a major panic attack in the gift shop of the American Swedish Institute. My family of origin was Christmas shopping, and here I was, about to lose my source of income. Wandering among candles and linens, toys and treats in sleek Nordic designs, I tried to fix my attention on something—anything—to distract me. I had to get out.

I rushed to the door, into the frigid night, shaking uncontrollably in the parking lot. Mom unlocked the car and I crawled into the backseat, sobbing. My parents and brother let me cry. When I needed to vomit, they passed me a green plastic shopping bag as we raced down the freeway, and they delivered me home.

I didn't actually say that I was leaving until winter break. By that time, the whole staff knew. I'd started telling them that I was leaving to finish my book, so that's what I told kids and wrote in the few direct emails I sent to parents with whom I was in contact, before the blanket email went out from the principal.

Some parents let me know that they'd miss me. Some students made a point of saying goodbye. Some surely were happy to see me go. Some people said to my face what we all knew: Someone as dedicated as Amy Hallberg doesn't leave education, her security, her connections, and her entire social network, unless things get very, very bad.

Everyone should have known that I was the canary in the coal mine.

Read the Signs

The morning after I'd made my decision to quit, a colleague stopped by to say hi. He was a kind man who'd come out of retirement after holding high-power positions to teach history. Everyone liked him.

"Amy," he said. "I haven't seen you for a while."

"Your timing is perfect. I have a secret." I motioned him into my empty classroom and closed the door. "I'm quitting and starting over."

His eyes grew wide. I could see the gears turning in his head, grasping at words. "I have a career coach for you," he finally managed.

With that, he set off to get the business card. One look at the website told me that this coach placed very important people in very important positions, whereas my career consisted of twenty and a half years in a classroom. We weren't a fit. But once I knew that career coaches existed, I easily found the right one for me.

The day after I gave the principal two months' notice, I drove straight from school to my new coach's office, where I sank, exhausted and relieved, into the waiting room sofa. That day during my last hour, students had finally enacted the nightmare that all teachers dread. Class devolves into chaos while you're still talking. You try to yell over their voices and nobody hears you. Everyone talks amongst themselves and they call across the room. You stand and watch, helpless. Time slows to a standstill.

"Are you Amy?" The coach had entered the waiting room. She stood beside me, exactly as pictured on the Internet, a free-spirited woman with vibrant strawberry-blond curls. I gathered my heavy school bag and oversized purse, avoiding my frozen right shoulder, slinging both over my non-frozen left one as I rose up. She waited for me to regain my composure, then reached for my right hand. "I love your necklace."

My left hand involuntarily traveled up to confirm its shape: a beaded silver square pendant. My fingers tested the rhinestones. Oval aquamarine, round ruby red and carnelian orange, and a small turquoise dot.

I looked up to meet her eyes. "I bought this at a ski resort because it reminded me of my Aunt Vivian. She sold necklaces like this." I paused, weighed the story in my mind, and stepped into the hallway beside her, not wanting to overshare, afraid that I already had.

"Really?" She smiled and tipped her head. "Where was her shop?"

"Florida." I ventured the name of Vivian's island.

She raised her eyebrows. "I went there this month."

Words began spilling out of my mouth.

"My aunt used to live in the town where I teach. I think about her all the time. When she was forty, she moved to Florida with her kids and started over from scratch." I glanced at the career coach beside me, and saw that she was tracking my story. "Vivian built a whole shopping center."

I described its location and its walkways like white picket fences, like my grandparents' house, mere miles from this oddly shaped office building that I'd driven past a thousand times before but had never noticed.

She reached a door and stopped walking. I realized that I was still holding the pendant. I dropped my hand by my side. "Vivian died the same year that the district opened the high school I'm leaving."

The coach studied me a moment, smiling oddly. "I want to show you something." She slipped her key into the lock. "I visited that shopping center."

The door swung open to reveal her sanctuary space—clean white walls, window onto trees, exactly as pictured on her website. Except, in the corner, a mobile hung from the ceiling. Threaded with beads and crystals, it cast rainbow glints, even in the gloaming light. A rush of energy ran down my spine. She pointed. "I bought that suncatcher at a store there."

I knew the one. "That particular store started out as Vivian's children's shop. She had a rocking horse out front and another inside, big enough for grown-ups to ride."

"Isn't that wild?" My coach met my eyes and nodded. "Now. Would you like a cup of tea?" She talked me through varieties and how to run the machine, then gestured to the sofa. "Please make yourself comfortable." Thus Vivian made it known that this woman would look out for me.

Before I left her office that day, we had acknowledged what nobody else seemed to want to admit: that I had lost so much at work, and I had been mourning for years while also trying to fix things; that she understood the shame I felt; that I was much more than the one broken thing that (I thought) everyone saw; that I deeply loved this school system that was also steadily killing me; that it was, unquestionably, time for me to walk a new path.

Education had broken my heart. I tried to be my best self every day, yet it seemed that every foolish mistake lived on in perpetuity.

It's worth asking the question: What's your payoff for staying on in a hard situation? After I quit teaching, I wouldn't miss spending my days at school and my evenings correcting papers. I wouldn't even miss teaching teens with whom I could relate. I had my own twins verging on teens, and if I could have avoided their schools and their teachers forever, I would have done that.

No, I would feel heartbroken about what I'd lost, which was my extended social network, my professional purpose, my identity as a teacher, and all that entailed.

In the best of times, I loved that my gifts felt meaningful; that I could capture the attention in a room when I had something worth saying; that I could mingle among curated groups of students to hone their communication skills, collectively and individually; that I could witness their struggles and delight in their self-worth; that I could tell them flat out that I loved them; that some loved me.

My new coach watched me cry without flinching. When I was ready, we started a plan. First: We'd find a way for me to walk out of that high school in under two months with dignity and grace.

Second: I'd take notes on jobs I saw people doing. And I wouldn't limit myself to titles or particular fields. "Think of them more as archetypes," she said. For any jobs that caught my attention: What about them called to me? What didn't? "The answers are all around you," she promised. "What lights you up?"

Third: I'd grant myself the sanctuary I desired for the time being. For good measure, I went home and signed myself up for life coach training with an author I admired. Might as well learn a new trade while I healed, always the honor student, now without feeling the honor.

I always suspected that Vivian was the one tripping me up from the other side, whenever I was tempted to stay a bit longer, say until the end of the school year. She would've had no problem crashing my computer or inciting brief student revolts if she felt justified. At the same time, I trusted her instincts. Vivian never let a woman walk out of her dress shop with anything that didn't suit her. Smiling sweetly, voice dripping with honey, she redirected the customer to a fabulous new ensemble. The woman would end up buying a necklace and earrings as well.

I had a strong sense of Vivian on the other side, steering me into the paths of people who had the wherewithal to help me grow. I also remembered when my aunt lived in our basement, seemingly stalled out permanently. That was my energy during that season of change. That's why I needed the career coach—to help me escape without further wounds. The woman that Vivian led me to did that in spades.

What I really wanted after that was to be a real writer. Specifically, I wanted to be an author who earned a living from my writing.

My longtime book writing partner, Katherine, wasn't the least surprised when I quit because she'd been reading my stories of teaching. She declared that from now on, she would take Fridays off from client work so that we could meet up at Open Book, home of the Loft Literary Center in Minneapolis, and we would parallel write our books together.

Not only that, but I kept running into a former colleague, Roseanne, who lived near my in-laws' house. She was a trusted acquaintance who'd walked me through some thorny dynamics before she left her English position to be a mom. Every time I saw Roseanne, she'd taken several more steps as an emerging author. By the time I resigned, she'd published two young-adult books and was the marketing director at her woman-owned indie publishing house, Wise Ink.

Naturally, I gave her a call.

Over coffee, Roseanne said to finish my book draft and send the manuscript when I was done. Later, she would confide that friends often asked her to look at their books, and she dreaded those conversations when the books weren't quite ready. But I didn't know that. In January 2016, I only knew that I'd found my publishing path, even as I was moving into seclusion, wrapping up my work as best I could.

Fool

On my final day of teaching, three skater boys stayed after the bell to demonstrate concepts that they'd been trying to conquer all term. I'd earned their trust when I name-dropped my cousin Nick, an artist who's a big deal in the video game world, and they knew who he was.

"You know what?" I looked up at the boys. They stood in a semicircle around my desk while I finalized their grades on my computer. "You get this. It's solid. So I'm not averaging in your lowest grades. I can't defend that kind of grading anymore. This is B- work. That's what you've earned."

"Can I have a hug, Profe?" one asked, a scruffy blond boy.

So I hugged him. "I'm proud of you."

The other two looked sheepish.

"Do you want hugs too?"

"Yeah."

I hugged them too.

There was a party after school at a bar called Heartbreakers, which the librarian organized. Our longtime professional development coordinator brought chocolate sheet cake. People I'd known from my twenty and a half years in that district came to celebrate me. There were presents and flowers and cards. I felt beloved as I savored the bittersweetness of brief connection on my way out the door. The party continued, but I had another engagement and needed to leave.

After I said my goodbyes, I bundled up and took a few steps, then turned around at the threshold to scan the full room. With that, I exited Heartbreakers for the last time.

Witness

10.1 WITNESS

Patience

You would think I would have felt nothing but relief after quitting—but that's not how it works when your animal body has puffed itself up to look strong for too long.

Even before I resigned, when I'd entered the places where I felt safe— the choir loft, for example—I'd been breaking down. One Sunday, I had suffered a gushing nosebleed. Another week, my hip went out. Dave and Christi even had to carry me out after the service, and Dave drove me to urgent care. And all along, my right shoulder was hopelessly frozen. When you're finally feeling safe is when you fall apart.

As ever, I turned to my church. In the choir loft on Sundays, I staved off sleep by writing book fragments on Grandpa Oscar's old invoices, tucked into my black folder with the choir music. I'd rescued the box of pages from his garage when Betty told us to take what we wanted.

I'd learned a name for the meditation on words that took place for me during church services: *Lectio Divina*, Latin for "Divine Reading." Words call forth images, which evoke messages that yield to mystery.

I loved that mysterious realm, even as it terrified me. *Tell me how this ends*, I often wanted to scream at the Divine. But I had to live into it first.

I was at once confused, curious, invigorated, and deeply, deeply tired on a soul level. That's what those earliest days were like after I quit, and what life felt like to me for a very long time. I feared that I might mourn forever. I might have, too, but Christi and our friend, Julie, a gifted social worker, insisted we go on a road trip.

As it happened, there was an upcoming life coach retreat in Pismo Beach, California, and I wasn't sure I could afford the travel costs on my own, but it was entirely affordable with two friends to share the expenses. Christi had lived in Central California during her twenties, where she started her design career. She'd worked in beautiful homes throughout the region and knew the hideaway places that locals on a budget would visit. In no time at all, she'd booked our itinerary. We'd fly into SFO together and drive down the California coast.

At our first hotel in Carmel, German-themed for me, we opened the door to see a salmon-pink velvet chair in the shape of an S with two parallel seats, bathed in window light. "Oh!" said Christi, delighted. "It's a *tête-a-tête*."

As the name suggested, two people could sit head-to-head and heart-to-heart, intimately close, while looking in opposite directions. A shiver of recognition ran through me. It symbolized Grandma Doris, and our loving, fierce tussles over a shared legacy.

It was as if my dollhouse pieces—now released from containment—were all over the place, writ large, all intermingled. And all these bits and pieces of real-life dollhouse were here to help me, I knew.

One morning in our breakfast café, the song overhead was the one I sang as Vivian died. *I'll be seeing you*, the song goes, and I did—in winks from Grandma and Vivian: in our German hotel, boutique windows, sea, sky, forest, and tiny delights throughout the trip. What else could I do but take copious notes and ramble on obsessively about family stories, while my friends reminisced about loved ones of their own?

As we wove our way down the coast, we drove the oceanfront road to Big Sur, where we took shelter in our cottage under majestic trees that evoked fairy tales; then we went off in search of a happy hour at a place called *Nepenthe*, which means "a way of forgetting sorrows and pain." I remember it fondly, how we sat—perched atop tremendous bluffs—drinking ginger beer and sharing a cheese platter on a patio over vast sunlit waters—cerulean, cobalt, azure, periwinkle, turquoise. It felt so expansive and so joyful that I couldn't believe this was me.

That same day, we drove down a narrow, forested road to park in a shaded clearing. The sandy path opened out beneath twin cypress tree fronds. There we found a different kind of beach than the seashell-laden Florida ones. Our guide book said that the sand was purple, but I couldn't see it.

The sun's low rays flooded through the keyhole of a giant rock mass, a portal at its base in the shape of Minnesota, which you could see if you tried. That's where the mourning caught me so hard that I had to surrender.

The wind and surf washed over us. Their sound echoed off of the rocks so loudly that we couldn't hear each other speak. We wrapped ourselves in our jackets and sat while energy swirled. And I felt everything. Thoughts arose in my head—crashing, piling up, in painful aftershocks, mourning even this fleeting moment that would never come to pass again in exactly this way. My friends had set aside everything to be with me before they returned to their everyday lives and their well-established careers.

In that California grotto I found the physical space to grieve. I keenly felt the overwhelming sensation of shame, the grief over what never was and never would be, the fear of no forgiveness, and the overwhelm of infinite possibilities, knowing that we don't always get to decide.

My friends provided what I needed before my soon-to-be initiation into the life-coaching world. I needed that space away from my husband, who still wrote me love letters despite everything, and our teenage daughters, who desperately needed their mom to be OK. How did my friends know what I needed?

Maybe because Christi and Julie have weathered personal loss. They knew that sometimes you have to sit with your sorrows, and gentle company helps, even when you feel the least worthy. That evening—as I cried eating soup on our return from the beach, miserable about my misery in such a beautiful place—Julie said something incredibly helpful: "We can't walk somebody else's road to Damascus." Yet these lovely women walked beside me.

So here we were, briefly suspended in this magical, in-between place. My two friends drove me to Pismo Beach and delivered me to my life coach practice partner, Saadiah. While I took my first baby steps into that esoteric realm of love and light, my companions visited the opulent Hearst Castle and other notable places without me.

During breakfast on our last day, Dave texted a view of our back yard dusted with March snow. Since our family was going skiing in Montana the next week over spring break—a gift from his father—I didn't feel too sorry for him.

"Must suck to be in California," he quipped.

I shot back the view from the cliffs of Nepenthe. "It really does." I laughed. His emoji laughed. My friends laughed.

When Julie and Christi returned from shopping and lunch, ready to take the fast road back up north, they'd assembled us each charm necklaces on bullet chains. Inside the box they brought me were two die-cut bronze circular charms. One was tiny, stamped with a capital letter A.

The second, larger circle with typewriter letters said Brave. I would need that reminder. Sometimes I would even believe it.

Even those heavy moments would find me where I needed to be. They would require great courage. And I'd have plenty of time. I have been blessed in unusual ways. When Olivia broke her arm in Montana, not only did we still have Dave's health insurance, but I got to stay home with Olivia until the wounds healed into interesting scars. While I felt deeply unsettled, I got to be there. And I never had to phone in sub plans.

Indeed, my creative practice felt divinely inspired, and it spilled over into every other part of my life. An old now-married boyfriend recruited me to plan our twenty-fifth college reunion because I was available, and suddenly I was co-leading the events planning team. Plus, I had life coach training calls. And regular trips to Minneapolis for choir and writing and violin lessons. With all the creativity and volunteering and motherhood on my plate, I wondered how I'd ever found time to teach.

Though powerful waves crashed over me in the aftermath of my self-exile, moments when I could barely breathe through the panic, I've known another truth on the other side of those emotions. I'm guided by the Divine. I have nothing to fear.

I have air to breathe, water to drink, food to eat. There's a secure roof over my head, thanks in part to Grandma, in part to Dave, and in part to the fruits of my own labor. Inside my sturdy chest cavern, my brave broken heart continues to beat.

When I was young, penpals used to send me letters, full of pure love on a page—things that felt too tender to say out loud in each other's presence. After I quit teaching, people said such things directly, intentionally, to my face. I experienced moments of bliss when people saw me clearly. Not everyone, obviously. But enough.

Though I left many, many people behind, not a week passed before a friend—long-lost or current—reached out to offer me coffee or lunch. The fact that they knew my foibles helped me more than I ever expected. They sat across tables from me and listened. They offered small details to verify what I had been through, and as I required it, disillusioned me of hard beliefs.

Slow down, little camper, they all said, each in their own way.
You've done well. Rest now.
Let me tell you who I see.
Pure love. And.
Listen, be-loved.
You're a born teacher.
You'll always be a teacher.
(Yes, even if you don't believe it.)
You've shone brightly. You'll shine again.
You'll teach in the world soon enough.
For now, take comfort.
Let yourself be.

Living Museum

I fondly remember a conservative student early in my teaching career. "You're such a nice person, Frau," she once told me. "I can't believe you're a Democrat." Her eyes sparkled.

"You are too, Hildegard," I lovingly said. "I can't believe you're a Republican." (That's not her real name, obviously.)

Minnesota isn't red or blue. It's purple. Besides, when I was her age, I'd been extremely pro-life, and most of my extended family had been Republicans. It was a huge relief that I didn't have to navigate politics with students during the 2016 election cycle. No matter the outcome, I wouldn't have to teach the next day.

Eva had this brilliant idea that we should meet in Washington, DC for Election Day. In normal times, I would have jumped at the chance. Our long and storied friendship drew heavily on shared historical and cultural reference points. Besides, Dave didn't even want to watch the election returns.

My manuscript was with the editor, and I was wrapping up basic life coach training. Nothing was keeping me home except apprehension over the outcome. Did I mention that I have a history of experiencing pivotal American moments in a German context? The year I took my first group of students over to Germany, I heard Michael Jackson's funeral on German radio. Moreover, Al Franken won his months-long contested election for Minnesota's Senate seat the day we landed.

Then there was the summer I visited Eva in her apartment on my way to Spain. Navigating a non-native language and culture can be incredibly draining. How else to explain my mid-afternoon fixation on episodes of *A Different World*, the iconic sitcom set at a fictitious Historically Black College? Thanks to Eva's American cable channel, I could track Whitley and Dwayne as he interrupted her wedding to somebody else, and they married each other.

Rather than visit with Eva's apartment mate when he arrived home, I scooted up to the living room screen. Eva didn't say much about all the TV, but from her silence I sensed that she was annoyed. That's how I realized the depths of my introversion. I can only be social for so long, and then I require story time—especially in language that I can absorb.

That's also how I came to catch *The Today Show* when O. J. Simpson made history with the slow-motion white Bronco chase after his ex-wife Nicole and her friend Ron were found murdered in LA. Watching it happen in real time, I tried to explain to Eva and her friend who OJ was. I'd grown up watching this All-American football superstar famously running through airports on car rental ads.

"He's on television," I told them in German. "And in movies." They nodded, but their blank faces showed that they weren't tracking. Above all else, being in Germany let me watch my homeland from the outside. I was watching, watching, watching. Observing the cultures, comparing the two.

As we moved through 2016, I dreaded another one of those historical moments. So I leveled with Eva. Washington, DC, a city I know decently well, was the very last place I wanted to be on Election Day. As in my younger days, I had money fears and anxiety about my future.

"I'll take care of everything," Eva wrote back. "All you have to do is get there."

And after all, when your dear German friend insists on flying across the Atlantic for the sole purpose of spending a historic week with you—you go. I even reached out to my long-lost ex-boyfriend Tony, who works in DC. He invited us to watch the returns with him and his wife.

Election Day was sunny but cold. Eva and I walked and talked about many things. "I remember something you once said," I told her somewhere between the Martin Luther King, Jr. and FDR memorials. "You said that I knew a lot about your history. You did too. Perhaps I should learn more about my own."

"Did I say that?" She turned and smiled. "I don't remember that."

"I wrote it down," I said. "It made an impact." We meandered through FDR's four monument rooms, one for each presidential term. This monument was new to me, and my favorite by far. I smiled at Eva. "It's good that we're here."

Sunset was at hand. It was already dark when Tony picked us up on the Mall on his way home from the office. I could hardly believe this full-circle, perfectly fated evening that brought these two pivotal, dear friends of mine together. The house was welcoming, the food festive, and the talk convivial. And yet.

Eva and I sat mostly alone in their basement home theater while Tony, his wife, and their friends moved between the kitchen and us. Each time they came down, things looked worse than before. We tried to spin it, to hold on to hope.

"Tony," I said, too early that night, "Please take us back to the Airbnb."

On the drive to Georgetown, he let out a frustrated howl. There was nothing to do but hug him goodbye, unlock the door, and go to bed. As I lay in the darkness, I prayed for *deus ex machina*. I longed for God's hand to reach down from the heavens, scoop up my piti-ful nation, and set us on higher ground before morning. That prayer went unanswered.

Eva happened to be friends with the head of the German press corps. So the next morning, we walked from our Airbnb to his hotel. It was the most bizarre moment of my life when I sat in that lobby bar and watched Hillary concede the race on the corner TV. Tears streamed down my face. Eva stood beside me in silence.

Afterward, we went upstairs to the hospitality suite, where the press corps was broadcasting my American shame for all Germans to see. The German that we spoke in the makeshift newsroom made more sense to me than any English I heard or read that day. How exactly did "we" (it wasn't me!) elect a misogynistic, xenophobic man with an unapologetic record of hate and failures? For one, he promised to over-turn Roe v. Wade. And I'd underestimated the sheer vitriol directed at Hillary.

Eva kept me walking that day. We went to see the Constitution, the Declaration of Independence, and the Star-Spangled Banner. When I saw them as a kid, once on our way home from Florida, and twice on high school trips, those patriotic artifacts were vibrant. Now they looked washed out, barely legible under dim lights in dark rooms, and so very small.

My heart hurt and my head felt hollow, yet DC with Eva was the perfect itinerary. We spoke in German and English, whatever served best. As I walked through DC, surrounded by monuments to the fore-fathers, I absolutely feared evil. Yet my German sister walked beside me on that punishingly cold day.

It was so very frigid. She gave me her extra jacket, since mine was too thin. I don't know why I'd packed that jacket. I'd also brought inap-propriate shoes. Why did I do that? And why the hell did I buy that hot-pink Hillary mug?

We didn't go to the Holocaust Museum. We both knew German history too well. Instead we reserved tickets for the National Museum of African-American History and Culture.

That next morning while we waited for our entrance time at the museum, Eva and I were walking down the street, sipping hot lattes—Eva's treat—when men in black with serious weapons started screaming, "Get on the curb! Stay on the curb!"

Eva approached the closer man and asked why. She's German, remember?

"Normal part of the job," he stammered.

We crossed the street as directed and looked up to see the White House, where America's first African-American president resided behind black iron gates. It looked unbelievably small, diminished.

We heard the sirens. We'd passed the procession earlier and forgotten about it. The gates opened up to receive an enormous black SUV that looked like a hearse. Here was the victor, being delivered to Obama's doorstep for their first meeting ever, in the White House built by slaves. Eva and I both loved our first Black president, whereas his successor was singularly unsuited for office. Oh, to be a fly on that wall.

It was entirely reasonable, based on this man's words alone, to think that his actions would harm my daughters and future generations. My feet might hurt due to my bad shoe choice, my shoulder might be frozen, but I was nearly past the age of needing reproductive rights. What of the millions of young American women who weren't?

When I came to DC at seventeen—between Eva's time in Minnesota and mine in Germany—the Close Up program took us behind the scenes to see how government works. Two boys in our group led us in an abortion debate. My best friend and I, both heavily pro-life, tag-teamed our opponents. Whatever arguments they raised about family members who'd actually had to make that horrible choice, or people out of luck for any reason, we twisted their words with sanctimonious pride. I literally felt smug at that time, felt it in my face, like a kind of angry, self-righteous pressure. We were pleased with ourselves and thought we were doing God's work. Later at college, people would challenge my thinking, and semantics games wouldn't do then.

In time, I would come to understand how Roe v. Wade was of benefit to me, too. I had a high-risk pregnancy directly after a Christmas Day miscarriage, and I needed access to all the information to make the best decisions for my health. I was angry for a long time even after I got pregnant a second time because God isn't pro-life, in the sense that every fetus must live. My fetus had died.

People have opinions: Will you now adopt? Fertility treatment? I didn't want them to fix my body's failure to produce children or manage my feelings or say the helpful things that they needed to think. I wanted them to show compassion, and to let my loss be about me. Not their projections onto a wanted child that wasn't here. When does a pregnant woman stop being a person and become a mere vessel? So we don't talk about our pregnancy losses. But we still have them.

Dave was my full partner, but he deferred to my body, as he well should. Take away our bodily autonomy, and you've taken away a woman's freedom. He also grieved, in his own way. It turns my stomach to think of anyone facing police inquiry as the follow-up to a miscarriage. Without Roe v. Wade that would happen.

The day after Christmas, the white-haired Ob/Gyn on duty at my clinic was cold, stiff, and condescending. He said nothing could be done. When I checked in with my new female doctor a month later (because damned if I'd ever let that man treat my uterus again) she asked me how I was doing emotionally. She listened. Only then did she check me out; she said that I could try again after one period.

The day after that appointment, I took a positive pregnancy test.

In other words, my twin pregnancy dated to my Christmas miscarriage, and because a twin pregnancy is high risk to both mothers and kids, it was essential to know all the risks to assure proper care for my babies and me.

Mercifully, I had female doctors who trusted me with information and laid out all of my options, the same as any decent cancer or bone doctor would. Pregnancy was hard on my small frame. I couldn't breathe deeply. I barely walked without passing out. Thank God for access to reliable healthcare, whatever kind I needed, whenever I chose. None of this pain was some random churchgoer's business, not even a little.

I wasn't ready to talk abortion the day I stood across from the White House, watching the preamble to our transfer of power. I feared not for myself, but for many others already singled out. That terror felt real. I'm a German major, so I know the playbook.

This was a man driven by demons, and the demons were ours. However, my German heroes taught me: It's not enough to be against something. You have to know what you stand for. I asked God to make me an instrument for those who would soon have no voice.

Then we saw the African-American Museum.

There are volumes of books on that subject, written by people who know a lot more than I do. If you haven't seen that museum, go see it. If you're white like me, go humbly, ready to feel, and ready to learn.

That was the day I learned the name Emmett Till. Mamie Till's baby, killed for being a fourteen-year-old boy from Chicago who was visiting relatives and didn't know how to be Black in the South. Maimed beyond recognition because a white woman cried white woman's tears. Emmett Till's mother made an unthinkable choice: She let her once beautiful, now unrecognizable Black boy be photographed in his open casket, to be published in *Jet Magazine*. I read the story and saw the photos.

How had I never known that name? But then again, I never knew about the annihilated Black Wall Street—destroyed by a white mob in 1921—until the school district sent me to Tulsa for training in 2010. And I'd never heard about Juneteenth until it showed up on my iPhone calendar.

I entered the inner sanctum to see the original coffin, now empty, which felt like the funeral procession it was. Then I returned to the outer room and looked at the photos a while longer, to look at Emmett Till's original face. Two dark-skinned women stood on either side of me. "How have I never known the name Emmett Till?" I asked, confessing my sin, profoundly ashamed, knowing full well it was too much to ask. "I should have known his name."

"Mm-hmm," said the woman on my left.

"Now you know," said the woman on my right.

It was their benediction. Go forth and sin no more. Eva and I walked at our own pace that day, but it meant everything that she was there. As we moved to the upper floors the mood shifted. There was a celebration of Black contributions to American culture. This was something else I didn't know nearly enough about. I resolved to learn more.

The rest of that week is a blur. Eva took me to a basketball game and a movie, though. I needed that escape too. I could escape because I was a white woman. Part of me understood that because my life had been upended in January of that very year, I had the privilege of being in the Capitol, watching history unfold, learning to understand. The world would move on, quicker than ever, whereas I had nothing but too much time and the prerequisite knowledge for what was to come— what was already arising.

Which brings me to something I know for sure. German authors and artists had three choices during the Third Reich: They could sell their souls and join the Nazi cause, half-or-wholeheartedly. They could escape—leave the country and live to tell stories another day—or if it was too late, commit suicide. That happened too. Or creative people could stay to bear witness so that someday they could tell the tale. Inner emigration, they call it.

When the time came to speak up, I'd have my stories ready.

Lacuna

Here's the simplest definition of story. You set out at point A, expecting to land at point B. But you don't. And you won't. True, you may end up at that destination, but it won't be the way you envisioned. Or you'll end up at point C, a place that you never expected. Or you end up back at point A, and everything will have changed. Maybe you'll accomplish all three.

Despite what you want, your story isn't about what you think it's about. It's often the thing you're avoiding. The story is in the *lacuna*— the gap in the story. The thing you don't want to admit to yourself, that part that goes untold. Looking back, you'll see it was there all along.

When I was in the eleventh grade, visiting teaching artists from a non-profit organization came to our English classes to work with students on creative writing. Due to schedule constraints, they only showed up in my hour once, so we merely dipped our toes in. The writers said we could submit a story for their contest anyway if we liked. Our school's winner would be published in their anthology.

I went home and typed up a recent vivid dream, proofread it carefully for grammar errors, and handed it in the next day. The English teachers chose my story as one of three finalists, which my teacher read in class. The other two stories were polished, yet the organization chose mine.

"The Dream" was so strange that when the COMPAS Organization published their book, *Three Magics*, they placed it first in the final section, entitled, "Completely Out of Hand: The Bizarre and Inexplicable." Three decades later, I would realize in retrospect that my published dream was a forecast.

In this story, an angry man rushes into the wood-paneled room where I sit reading alone. He hits me, but the blows hurt his hand, and he winces. I'm startled but feel no physical pain. Furious, he drags me by the hair into a hallway where candles flicker, and still he hurts only himself. I have a sense that he has the power to close every door to me or hurl me like a ragdoll over the railing. At last, unable to break me, he becomes an ugly clown, laughing until he breaks down and cries. None of this is my fault. I know this for certain.

One snowy Saturday in December of my senior year, I gave my first public reading with the other young winners. Grandma Doris and Grandpa Hubert met my parents and me at the Landmark Center in Downtown St. Paul, a historical building with marble balconies that could've been the site of my dream. I felt smart and respected. Being a writer of fiction, I decided, was heaven.

On the way to the elevators afterward, a dignified woman flagged me down. "That was a powerful story." She watched my response closely, as if she needed confirmation, something that felt familiar from ladies at church.

"Thank you," I said, elated.

She leaned in, determined to latch onto the moment. "I'm so sorry that happened to you."

"What?" I blinked several times. "But that didn't happen to me. It was a dream."

"I thought it was real." She looked embarrassed and scurried away. But "The Dream" was its actual title!

Walking into the snowy, white afternoon, Mom confirmed that I read with dramatic flair. But that wasn't me acting. Energetically, I told my truth: I'd known the wrath of random sad clowns.

That day I learned that not only could I write, but I could speak with conviction. My published story sparked visions of being an author that never materialized. I hoped to major in English and become an author, but all I wanted to write about was Germany and family stories, not fiction. My essays about English literature turned out to be simplistic. Instead, I majored in German and made that my life.

Writing a book was only a dream, after all. I accepted that I'd never be an author. It was bizarre to look back at that thought once I was doing the hard work of writing my book. This time I was not giving up. My writing peers and friends in life coach training took me seriously. They said to keep going. And that kept me going.

It's important to note that subconscious resistance still tripped me up in maddening ways. For example, I failed the ethics portion of life coach certification. Mind you, the examiner assigned to me was also the lawyer-turned-master coach who wrote that section of the manual and taught ethics classes. Given that detail, my behavior made no sense. I'm an excellent test taker, and this was an open-book test, but I hadn't bothered to double check her resources. Uncharacteristic. I failed so badly—while acing the rest—that she insisted I go back and listen to every class recording and reread all ethics readings before she'd think of certifying me.

It probably didn't help that I fell asleep in her ethics classes, which I shouldn't have told her. I'm not sure it's sleep, exactly, but a response I've always had to experiences that I feel too intensely. My conscious self checks out. Seriously, when I go to superhero movies with my family, I sleep through initial battle scenes and wake up the moment they start the group huddle. That's self-protection, not sleep. But I always follow up online with synopses to get clear on the story. I assure you, I did all the readings.

The whole thing baffled all the people who'd happily let me practice on them. They trusted me with deeply personal stories, but here I was, officially an unethical person. I unpacked it on the phone with Saadiah, with whom I'd spent countless hours practicing. "Of course, it's ridiculous," she said. "You've spoken with plenty of people who told you as much."

We sorted out my technical problem. On the coaching forms that I'd submitted as evidence of my prowess, I'd written the names of coaching subjects beside their personal details. The examiner pointed to this as a huge breach of ethics for a life coach. I would be in business for myself, and I needed to guard client data. Whereas in education, when sensitive situations arose, it was my responsibility to inform all relevant stakeholders on a need-to-know basis. Which often involved forms. There was a space up top for a name, and I filled it in by dutiful force of habit.

"So the policies that I followed for teaching don't apply here," I said with a sigh.

Saadiah's voice was measured. "Right. What's relevant in one situation is not relevant elsewhere."

"And as a teacher it was my duty to make sure kids learned the curriculum, whether they wanted to or not. I was committed to certain outcomes. In coaching, that isn't my business. My OK-ness with how a client lives their life isn't the point."

"Yes, exactly."

I love hearing such things confirmed in Saadiah's Australian accent, weathered by her time in Germany, New York City, Seattle, Wyoming, and all corners of the world. When I met Saadiah, she was dogsled-ding, before she moved on to sailing. She translated my favorite Rilke poem to English for the fun of it. Now she was pursuing the study of Kazakh—the language—and riding horses in Outer Mongolia.

She was also a strategic consultant with a law degree and an MBA. Of course Saadiah would understand that the question of ethics was highly contextual. Intellectually, problem solved and lesson learned. We both knew I could now pass the test and get certified fast.

And yet, this quibble ran deeper. I couldn't let go of this particu-larly painful thought: *People have called me unethical.* That's where her Shamanic studies came in.

Saadiah teased out the sticking point, which went back to prever-bal Amy as she learned to speak. It ran through my religious training and forty-one years in schools, exacerbated by my recent exile from teaching: I managed people's opinions of me, especially those who disapproved, as if that were mine to decide.

As we played with variations on the thought, the stranglehold loos-ened. I felt my mind relax.

"So really, you are an ethical person; you need to know that for your-self," Saadiah said. "I think that's your answer. How does that feel?"

"I'm a bit lightheaded. But that makes sense. Some people will always question my ethics, and I can't win them over. I have to be the one who knows that I'm ethical."

"Yes."

"Because I am."

"Because you are." Saadiah laughed. "You're too ethical sometimes."

Just then a text came in from a former colleague. She wrote that the principal had been arrested; she asked me to call her.

Instead I texted. "What did he do?" I couldn't imagine.

"Child porn."

I texted back. "Call you in five."

It was as if I had received this shocking information at the moment when I was ready to know how close I'd come to evil. I'd considered him untrustworthy, juvenile, and eventually downright nefarious. Still, I never would've guessed that he was a sexual predator. The charges were already all over the news.

"Wow. The timing on that," I told Saadiah.

"Yeah. Wow is right."

I don't want to say a lot about him; this isn't his story. I do want to point out that his behavior was only a part of me leaving teaching. It's a red herring. I chose to leave a bad situation, although this man definitely helped to derail my career, empowered by many others. This bears mentioning: I predicted when I left that he wouldn't outlast me by long. Support staff all over the building had let me know how he undermined them as well.

He showed up at my final teaching observation with a big smile, wearing a suit. He never wore suits. In our post-observation meeting he pointed out several things I'd done well, but he was clearly toying with me. He'd been too attentive.

"I'll be honest," I said. "I'm surprised you admire anything about me."

"Here's the thing." His expression grew mean. "Kids don't like you. And the things you say!" He launched into a litany of things I'd said, out of context, editorializing without citing his sources.

At last I interrupted and showed my hand, sooner than I expected. "I'm going to stop you right there. I have an appointment with a career coach tomorrow. I'm leaving."

His face lit up, and the smile returned. He outlined steps for me to leave at the end of the term, and he promised to keep it confidential until I was ready, before he sent the blanket email announcing my exit to all stakeholders. Meaning: *everyone.* "I have to do that," he told me. "You understand." He promised to make it all easy. He'd hire a candidate quickly, and he'd make sure I kept my teaching license, even though I was breaking my contract. He was nothing if not a politician. My written reviews were solid, remember. Because I'd navigated backchannels in that system long enough, I had the ear of insiders I did trust, who supported me. From that day forward, I made sure he knew it. And he watched me closely.

In his sorry-not-sorry editorial in the local paper, my former boss blames everyone and everything but himself, including problematic teachers—like me, I presume. But I experienced misfortune too while I worked in his school, including family death and overwork like he describes, and I never did what he did, or anything remotely like it.

Name It

When Eva and I were in the DC airport waiting for our flights home, she gave me an assignment. There was a Martin Luther exhibition of artifacts on loan from the Luther House in Wittenberg, which was closed in preparation for the five-hundredth anniversary of his earth-shaking 95 Theses.

"It's in Minneapolis. You have to go."

"Oh yeah. Minneapolis Institute of Art. I've been there plenty of times."

Mia is a museum that I visited with Grandma Doris and Cora when I was little. I've brought my kids to play in the labyrinth out back. But my mind was worn out from the election, so I didn't grasp exactly what this exhibit was that Eva was talking about. Fortunately, she's persistent. "No, Amy, this exhibit is very special. You should go." Priceless relics from the Reformation were sent to Minnesota—due to our many Lutherans—and nowhere else in America.

Here's one reason for my resistance: Late in life, Martin Luther committed his greatest sin in a book he authored, *The Jews and their Lies*.

In it, he proposed that we should kill off all Jewish people. I first read about it in a novel called *German for Travelers* by Minnesota author, Norah Labiner. Look it up. You'll see that it's true. And the Luther House confesses it freely.

On January 6, 2017, shortly before the exhibit closed, I finally got there. The timing must've been preordained, as it often is with me, because when I walked into the lobby, Martin Luther's portrait stared at me from a giant reproduction. It could have been my former principal's mug shot.

I shivered. There certainly was something here for me. I wondered at that face, superimposed on each portrait, on each guidepost sign throughout the museum, all the way up to the special exhibit gallery at the far end of the second floor. Over the entrance was a vibrant celestial archway, dominated by an impressive, white-bearded Lord Father God in the Sky. *MARTIN LUTHER: Art and the Reformation,* bold letters proclaimed.

In a room up front was a prominent ceiling-to-floor family tree assembled from individual pages. Albrecht Dürer, master woodcutter, had carved the blocks for the Habsburg emperor so that his people could print stacks of posters. They sent them throughout the realm to be plastered onto building façades. Subjects in the streets could then admire the emperor's noble lineage. Dürer's elegant woodcut prints were delightfully observant. Only thing is, the family tree was a lie. It name-dropped people that made the emperor look good, but they weren't related at all.

As I read this detail on the placard, I got goosebumps. The artifact perfectly summed up my growing societal qualms. In an increasingly fun-house world where everything is connected, and nothing is as it seems, I was looking for places where I still belonged. The worlds of education, church, and politics weren't what I once thought they were, and I wasn't so sure about the life coach world either. At the

Luther exhibit I was looking for meaning, just as I was everywhere else. Albrecht Dürer's block prints would stay on my mind, I should note, not the nameless emperor who wanted to be remembered forever, nor the other Habsburgs, nor even really Martin Luther. I longed to emulate Albrecht Dürer, *the creative*. But detached from the dogma.

Five hundred years after the genesis of the Reformation, I needed new language for the Divine. *A mighty fortress is our God*, Luther wrote as he took on the Holy Roman Emperor. The God I sought in January 2017 was a welcoming door. That's where I was placing my faith, in those opening doors, even as I was eying the exit at our Minneapolis church.

The closest thing I'd had to a meaningful religious experience since resigning my job was a pilgrimage the previous summer to see an Indian Holy Woman at an ashram outside of Chicago, as guests of family on Dave's side.

When Amma, whose name means "mother," hugged me—that's what she does, and I've never before or since experienced such an enveloping hug—she called me *my daughter*, and later *my darling*. Amma says, *Love is my religion*. And I felt loved. But I'm not Indian by any stretch of the imagination, and Sankrit isn't my holy language. I tried to feel it, but I didn't. I'm too firmly rooted in Protestant Christian tradition. Olivia had come along for the ride. At thirteen, she had a passion for the paninis. We split several before I drove us back home. I'd wanted Amma to miraculously unfreeze my shoulder. But that's not what she did.

She sent me a cracker crumb by way of her attendant while I waited in line for that second hug. "Amma sent this for you," the attendant said to three of us in chairs at the base of the stage where Amma sat embracing people, gathering them against her white sari.

"What is it?" I asked in hushed tones.

"It's a *prasad*. A gift. She wants you three to split it." The other recipients were two women who had said nothing as we moved forward in two parallel rows of chairs set up for procession; I could sense that they didn't want me processing with them.

When we'd reached those three front chairs, one asked, "Could we sit together? We're friends." That's when Amma sent down that tiny prasad; I read this gesture as an act of healing communion, not physical, but at a soul level. What if miracles happen when we let go of our attachment to outcome?

What if I could start my own sanctuary—not a church—where writers could say what they believe, or don't, or are sorting? It's not a religion, and there aren't set beliefs, but there's a culture of coming together. It's bearing witness, which you undertake as a storyteller living into your story. I wasn't there yet, but maybe, I thought.

Given my recent history, I was terrified of blind spots. I confess that I felt trapped in perpetual sin by what I had done, and by what I had left undone. Namely, I hadn't yet landed a paid occupation. But it was a good pilgrimage. I bought a teal Om T-shirt that says Inquire Within. Olivia still talks about the paninis. Perhaps the greatest gift of that weekend was that I accepted the invitation, accepted the hugs, accepted the tiny prasad.

Do we ever get past the belief that we must have something meaningful to show for ourselves? I wonder how often the need for significance is the source of our downfalls. Is that why we play small and diminish our God-given gifts? Why we deny larger truths?

I remember once, after I sang at a wedding, how the groom's elderly grandpa spoke German with me at the reception. His parents had immigrated from Austria when he was little, and I naïvely thought that meant he knew Nazis were bad. He asked if I knew what the German people did wrong in World War Two.

"What?" I leaned in politely.

"They didn't follow their leader." He used the word *Führer*.

I understood exactly what he was saying; so did he, cloaked in the shelter of German, but mercifully nobody else did. Since this was his grandson's wedding, I excused myself from the conversation without debate.

Two weeks after my museum visit, Trump predicted American carnage in his inaugural speech, lending credence to the German stories I foresaw him enacting. One thing connects to another, all the way down.

What if Christians didn't believe—passionately—in God's chosen people? Much bloodshed and heartache would've been spared throughout our history. What if the Empress Maria Theresa hadn't sent her sheltered, German-speaking daughter off to marry a French king? Then she wouldn't have been there to suggest that they eat cake. What if Archduke Franz Ferdinand hadn't been assassinated, after generations of inbred Habsburg empire building, and thus sparked a traumatizing World War?

What if Woodrow Wilson, an avowed white supremacist, hadn't premiered *Birth of a Nation* as the first movie shown in the White House, a blockbuster production that revived a nearly dead Ku Klux Klan across the United States? What if there hadn't been a raging pandemic during his presidency? What if he hadn't caught the flu in Versailles and hidden his illness? What if the Versailles Treaty hadn't damned the nascent Weimar Republic, the most progressive government in the world to that point, bar none?

What if Wilson hadn't, in his enfeebled state, allowed the French to punish their German neighbors—and only the Germans—so harshly for a war that was complicated and provoked living conditions so bad for everyday Germans that they would enable a lowly soldier, failed artist, and known xenophobe to become their leader? What if Luther hadn't planted his seeds for the German Final Solution?

This was so much bigger than me. That winter, as it happened, an invitation to master coach training fell into my lap, along with a well-timed tax return that paid for it due to my lack of employment. My book was with the editor, well on its way. So I saw this training as the perfect opportunity to build my business. Despite the signs of rising trouble in the US, at least I had that.

Soon after training began, and I'd introduced myself as a soon-to-be author, I had a call scheduled with the editor, who was ready to tell me what I should revise. EVERYTHING, it turns out. I had interwoven twin books, one on my family tree, one about Germany. The book she found intriguing was the German-themed one. Either way, I had to unravel and sort out chapters, from the beginning.

A title came quickly to me. *German Awakening: Tales from an American Life.* With this revelation, my neat agenda for master coach training had fallen apart, and I had not one book, but two to write. As I'd invested so much time and energy in being an author *and* a life coach, I felt that I couldn't quit either.

As I curated my stories—which ones for this book, and which for that—revision meant getting clear on what I didn't want so that I could turn toward what I wanted instead. But it wasn't that simple.

The day I sent my daughters to Eva in Hamburg without me for the first time, American Nazis wielding tiki torches in Charlottesville marched all over airport TV screens like some brownshirt rally. "Jews will not replace us," they shouted. The President of the USA proclaimed them "very fine people" in looping sound bites.

The young girl in me found this terrifying. The former German teacher knew that I was here to bear witness and probably still had wisdom to offer. But the freshly minted life coach in me struggled with mindset work (*questioning my thoughts to dissolve old beliefs*). Painful stories were holding me back, I'd learned in master coach training. As I understood it, I had entered a world of love and light, set on vanquishing shadows by not giving attention to them. Except I thought I was a writer, and shadows in stories were the bread and the butter of my trade. I couldn't reconcile those viewpoints.

I didn't dare to bring up Nazis with my master coach training peers. They had been at this longer than me. Nobody mentioned the Nazis in Charlottesville, and I didn't either.

I would've given anything to step away from this book, but it was the one thing that I knew was mine. If not, why did these opportunities keep falling into my lap that made it hard to let go of my stories? So I kept going. Still, all my façades were fragmented irreparably.

The problem with dissolving beliefs is that we tend to replace them with something else we can believe in. Often we hold these new values with the same intensity as before. As for me, I'd burned through so many beliefs, so quickly, in so many intersecting realms—academic, religious, linguistic, love-and-light, political, literary—that I'd exhausted my sacred ground.

It all came down to a single question. What did I want? I wanted there to not be Nazis in Charlottesville. I wanted American Christians not to perpetuate white male supremacy. I wanted a president who wasn't a boldfaced charlatan, and I wanted my fellow Americans not to play disingenuous semantics games. I wanted to know what was true in this world.

I desperately wanted, more than anything, not to be writing a book about Germany when the fun-house mirrors revealed why we were so obsessed with those stories of state-sponsored horror. Those stories were also about our own American homegrown original sins.

I wanted my daughters to arrive safely in Germany and to have a wonderful time in Eva's care. Luckily, at the exact moment their plane landed at Schiphol Airport in Amsterdam, hours past midnight, our cat Serena jumped up onto a chair in our bedroom corner and awoke me by ringing some wind chimes. I do believe she sensed their arrival. Eva sent a photo of our daughters the next day, delighted, eating German ice cream. In the absence of anything better to do, I told Dave that I wanted a Dairy Queen Blizzard. That evening, we drove down to the shop, where we sat outside eating our melting ice cream quietly on a bench in the humid darkness.

I wanted vanilla ice cream. I would never voluntarily choose rocky road.

Advocate

Memory

Como Park is known to Minnesotans for its giant zoo. We went there with Vivian when I was a kid. There are amusement park rides, golf, frisbee golf, and picnic grounds. Then there's the Conservatory, a giant greenhouse where my college watercolor professor once drove a vanload of us to sketch flowers. Outside the ground was still thawing, but inside the historic glass walls, tropical plant species thrived. I remember our professor looking for a parking spot and reminding us to keep track of where we left the van. Every memory I have of Como Park from childhood on includes parking.

In August 2018, I had boundless energy by day, and people were eager to talk. *German Awakening* had shaped up fast once I wrapped my mind around it, and my editor had signed off on publication. With my book in production, I could start to focus on my work as a mentor to writers. By sundown, my energy drained away.

The life coach in me understood that emptying out was necessary to be refilled. And refilling was necessary to be emptied again. A natural ebb and flow, under normal circumstances. But since I was reinventing myself beyond the bounds of institutions, I had even fewer reserves to rely on. Knowing this, I limited evening engagements to special occasions, such as my friend's choir performance.

Kiki and I knew each other through Reunion planning; we'd bonded over shared connections and literary references, becoming fast friends. So I definitely wanted to go. But the morning of Kiki's concert, I'd picked up another Carleton friend at the airport for an extended brunch before I drove him to Northfield. By early evening, when I arrived in St. Paul, torpor had set in.

I parked my Forester in one of the smaller lots along the winding road, within sight of the Conservatory. My mind flashed on long-ago gold-and-white koi fish bobbing at the edges of their shallow containment, smacking their lips in the air.

I willed myself to catch a second wind. This was a singalong concert, and I wanted to feel joyous and carefree. Grabbing my phone, I locked my car doors and tucked my keys into my pocket. Then I set out in the direction the signs indicated, crossing vast swaths of lawn until the Pavilion came into view, an open structure with minimal shelter against the elements, nestled on the lake's edge.

I'd met my friend Elizabeth near there once, pushing strollers on a walk when our daughters were just babies. It was yesterday and forever ago. Kiki's pre-teen daughter sold me a ticket, and I greeted Kiki, who was setting up near the stage. She pointed me toward wrought iron and wooden benches, arranged into rows.

Night fell and stage lights went up. At least the songs were familiar, harmonious, good, and if I couldn't sing the lyrics without reading from my phone, they still resonated in my bones. Abba's "Dancing Queen" and Prince's "Raspberry Beret" were staples from our Gen X youth.

I sang tentatively in the breezy lakeside shelter. Kiki glowed, ebullient on stage, singing solos, blending with her ensemble. She looked my direction and smiled. I imagine I looked fine, but I wasn't.

The lyrics were everything I had forgotten. "Dancing Queen" was Midsommar dances at Swedish camp during my early teens. It evoked parties from my early twenties with Elizabeth in our apartment on Lincoln and Grand; it signaled the home in my early thirties where my tiny twins danced to it, suspended in Johnny Jump-Ups. "Raspberry Beret" had confounded me from the beginning, but Prince was Minnesotan and he was ours and now he was gone. The reminiscence was its own kind of circular despair. It was almost betrayal that the words brought no comfort.

My mind drifted to the Conservatory. I was what became of koi fish who escaped their makeshift pond into air they couldn't actually breathe. What was a raspberry beret to me or a seventeen-year-old dancing queen? Maybe once I wore berets. I was definitely seventeen once, dancing in Germany, but nevermore. It didn't matter that the songs were joyful. That was the exact problem. The doors had sprung open, I had walked on, beyond institutions, sovereign. And now what? Disconnection.

On and on my mind spun out stories. It was an ancient wound. Every time this particular despair came over me, it dragged me under as if it were the first and eternal time, and not a pattern. Afterward, I thanked Kiki, told her the music was amazing—which was true—and walked briskly into the inky night.

Back at the parking lot, my car wasn't there. It took a moment to grasp what had happened. Nobody had stolen my car. I had simply taken the wrong path into the darkness, and this was not my parking lot. I thought about calling someone and saw a notice on my phone that showed my parked car's location, a quarter mile away. Who knew it could do that? I was already so tired and chilled. Meanwhile my car was somewhere out there under the waxing crescent moon.

I could've called Kiki, but this was her special evening, and she was busy. Nor would I call Dave, forty-five minutes away. What could he do for me? It would only worry him and the girls. So I took a few steps along the sidewalk, holding my phone like a compass in fifth-grade orienteering. I saw the dot that was me moving farther away from the dot that was my parked car, adjusted my bearings, and set out, determined to move as fast as I safely could. I felt my heartbeat pounding but steady.

Rushing down an embankment to reach the next sidewalk, I cut a corner. Birkenstocks weren't made for damp grass, but my estimated walking time dropped to seventeen minutes. I was vulnerable to animals and people here in the darkness, and I knew it.

When Elizabeth and I lived at the intersection of Lincoln and Grand, a man with a loud shopping cart took up residence outside our window at the bus stop and shouted obscenities that kept us awake. The night that he lit a fire under the bench, we called the cops, who warned him but had nothing better to offer a man with nothing. They left him out there, still yelling, still needing so much more.

But homelessness had another face much closer to mine. Inherited shadows. When she started writing letters to Grandpa Oscar, Grandma Lillie was a teacher who'd lived in other people's houses for years—first to get an education because she had a gift for words, and then fully orphaned, made homeless by her father's widow, who took everything. Though I didn't know the details, generational echoes lived on.

From childhood onward, I followed Grandma Lillie around her garden while she narrated the names of the flowers—*pansies . . . petunias . . . lilacs*. I'd sit beside her on the living room sofa as she clutched a sharp pencil in her gnarled hands. She'd fill in the crosswords with disjointed words based on minimal clues—*elan . . . arid . . . apex*—fully erasing the errant letters. We watched *Wheel of Fortune* together. And, of course, she made those legendary family meatballs. Grandma Lillie hinted at sorrows but didn't share details. When Grandpa Oscar told stories, she acted aggrieved to silence the memories that triggered her.

Lost in the shadows of St. Paul, namesake city to the apostle, I wrestled with that same strange wordy silence that Grandma Lillie maintained. How would I put my displacement to words? That's another reason I didn't call home. I had the autonomy I'd been reaching for. But at what cost? When the time came for me to speak for myself, with no obligation to anybody, what would I say?

The stillness gave me time to absorb that I wasn't without resources. I simply needed to trust myself. Whatever this journey required, I would receive. Here was my miniature Road to Damascus, the last temptation of Amy before I rejoined the world as an author. In this version, I neither heard the voice of Jesus, nor saw the flash of lightning. Mine was chillier, dimmer, guided by street-light haloes and the flicker of my phone screen. It called me to stop displacing myself. Mercifully, my phone battery held up. I was well on my way back to where I started.

On a more challenging level, I'd come face-to-face with a specific fear: I could drive home from St. Paul, but would I find my way back to my beloveds? What if I'd wandered too long? What if, after my book was published, it took me farther away from them?

The last time I saw Grandma Lillie alive, long after I watched Grandpa Oscar gasp his last breath, she stared at me with unseeing blue eyes from a hospital bed. She didn't caress my hand the way she always had on the sofa. She didn't murmur, "You have beautiful hands, so long and slender. If I had hands like yours, I would always wear lotion." She was displaced and she displaced herself, so used to being an outsider that she didn't know how to belong.

That last time I saw her she'd long since run out of words. Afterward, I'd walked down the corridor with Dave and the girls, suppressing tears until I buckled myself into the front seat and burst into sobs. Two-year-old Olivia's clarion voice came from the backseat, much like my young reassuring voice must have sounded to Grandma Lillie. "Don't cry," Olivia said. "Lillian is only sleeping." That afternoon we went out and picked apples under the bright blue autumn sky. And I never returned to see Lillian ever again.

Both of my grandmas died at ninety-four, the age I imagine I'll live to be, but I've always said that I don't want to fade away like Grandma Lillie. Or Aunt Vivian, her vivacious daughter. What if I was already doing that?

And yet, early on in our marriage, I started speaking word spells to Dave, incantations to ward off vast distance, and Dave followed suit. Before one of us left home, the other would say: *Get everywhere and back safely. Promise? Love you.*

The response: *Promise. You stay safe. Love you.*

Or if one of us was already gone, on the way home, the call ended with: *Get home safely. Love you.* And the other responded: *Promise. Love you.*

As our girls became mobile, we extended the practice with sayings that I set to simple tunes to keep them safe: *We don't walk in the parking lot because it's not safe for little girls. So when we go walking in the parking lot, Mommy and Daddy have to carry us.*

And at bedtime: *Love you, love you, always thinking of you,* so that they would never forget. The *love you* was instilled in me during childhood by *my* mom, who as Grandma Lillie's daughter knew that you take every chance you get to invoke love before you part ways, no matter what other emotions you feel. The words carry you forward.

That evening in Como Park, I needed someone's words to carry me forward. That person turned out to be *me.* I was narrating my story that night as I walked it, casting word spells across Como Park. At last I could see the GPS lot, up another hill from the sidewalk, and I ran off course toward it. I was so close that the two dots nearly touched— parked car and I—when a tangled wire fence came into view.

It bordered tall prairie grasses. But I could see my Forester. Diffuse street lights revealed my pale-green car. I made my way along dark wire, until I reached the final post and bolted across the dimly lit parking lot, clicking the remote. My car beeped and headlights flickered on.

I jumped into the car, slammed the door, locked it, and fumbled the key into the ignition. Then I reset the GPS route and started driving, all the way to the border of Como Park.

Only then did I call Dave to relate the barest gist of what had happened to me. In my frightened voice, I heard a lost child asking him to acknowledge my fears. Not from pity, or the inertia of seventeen-year-old vows, but genuine reassurance that I belonged home.

"That sounds really scary." Dave's voice was tender. "Amy, you should probably focus on driving. Can you stay awake?"

"Forty minutes. I will."

"Get home safely. I love you."

"Promise. Love you."

Spoken Word

In a beautiful act of synchronicity, *German Awakening* was going to launch on October 3, 2018. This date was not random. October 3rd had been my original pregnancy due date, before we found out I was carrying twins, when it became my only job to hang on as long as humanly possible, preferably until September, and that's what I did.

More globally, since 1990, October 3rd has been *Tag der Deutschen Einheit*, the Day of German Unity, marking the day the two Germanies reunified. So that was delightful.

But suddenly, there were kids in cages. The news broke as we prepared for publication. Brown-skinned, Spanish-speaking refugee children were being intentionally separated from their parents on arrival at the southern border and locked up. President's orders.

To be clear, the holding pens were already there. Obama put them there to protect people from the sun and heat. But the optics were terrible. How this administration decided to use them was novel and especially cruel. They separated children from parents on purpose, inflicting generations of trauma. In the United States of America.

How could anyone deny the parallels? This was what the Nazi government did. They separated families and created orphans. We're still feeling the repercussions of that trauma on both sides of the Atlantic. As it happened, my book *German Awakening* addressed that history through personal stories. I never expected that convergence, but I added it to my launch party agenda: Address the Kids in Cages.

A studio had practically fallen into my lap thanks to Roseanne, my friend at Wise Ink. It was in an ivy-covered building on a quiet Minneapolis industrial side street, which felt too good to be true.

I couldn't have designed it better. One wall matched the red from my book cover. The adjacent back wall was antique brick with thick grout and bright windows. It could easily have been a reclaimed warehouse in Hamburg or Berlin. The room would be mine for the evening, including bookshelves to display books, and a desk on which to sign them. Those covers deserved to be on full display. There were three finches, black, red, and gold to echo the German flag, plus vibrant green leaves with saturated touches of blue and pink. The pallet of boxes would soon occupy prime garage space.

As the date approached, I spent one whole morning in my bathtub, soaking in epsom salts, where I read aloud from printed pages, water dripping down my arm, smearing ink, making notes on the dissolving paper, too many scenes to unlock all the important-to-me connections in the twenty minutes I planned to speak.

Here's the crux of the challenge, I had recently realized: Story—at heart—is active translation of lived experience into words. It doesn't capture *everything*. That would be too much. Only kaleidoscopic bits. We gather shiny objects that show significant parts, which then point to the whole. Paradoxically, the more fully we ground our stories in specific details, the more other people can relate.

Their telling brings up parallel stories, connected by energetic patterns beyond facts. You can feel it when it arrives. One story leads to other stories, and everyone has a story. Kids locked up in cages, for example, taken away from their parents. *Lord of the Flies*. How could I work with that?

A lightbulb went off in my head. Since I had the studio space, why not stage an exhibit? I started to map out pieces for a gallery display. It would definitely include the Berlin Wall. What if I highlighted personal heroes? Courageous Wordsmiths and Germans? Goosebumps. That's what I would do with my launch—recreate my perspective. I wouldn't have to read it all aloud. Much of it could be on display. I wanted to stage it with my German memorabilia. Better yet, an interactive museum with plenty to look at, and plenty to eat. Food was already ordered: Black Forest Chocolate & Cherry Rounds, plus Open-faced Reubens with Sauerkraut.

Then I had a flash of insight. What if I took the finches from my book cover and printed up bookmarks? I knew exactly how it would look: red on the back with white letters, white on the front with the birds, modeled on a bookmark I brought home from a Mia exhibit.

I was a sign-painter's granddaughter, after all. Grandpa Oscar was always handing out yardsticks, bright yellow wood imprinted in black: Hand Lettering by O. WM. JOHNSON—A-1 DOWNTOWN SIGNS & DISPLAYS—BANNERS & CARDS.

But look what I was doing. This was a classroom. Yes! We'd hang a great big banner from paper rolls that Grandpa left me. Then as people arrived, they could write the names of their personal heroes in colorful markers. And then they could write the name and reason on a Courageous Wordsmith card, tucked into a Courageous Wordsmith envelope to take home with them. The secret—which I would reveal—was that whatever we admire in our heroes is exactly the quality required of us. We have it in us, whether we know it or not.

This process was now bearing fruit. I'd print all the posters professionally and laminate them, complete with description placards—all of which I could carry, store, and display in a special portfolio book.

Plus Kiki made me a playlist, from "The Lonely Goatherd" to "99 Luftballons." Elizabeth was bringing—well, if not ninety-nine red balloons, still a bunch. My neighbor Jen from down the street would take care of water, and people were volunteering for jobs, so that I could be the guest of honor.

There was one missing piece. How, specifically, would I bring up those kids in cages?

I used to show a film when I taught Spanish, about a Mexican boy who crosses the US border to find his undocumented mom after his grandma dies. Once, on the study guide, where it asked students what lesson they had learned from his struggles, a nice Christian girl wrote, "Don't be an illegal immigrant."

She didn't see people working hard to make a good life despite harsh conditions, as I did. She saw crime and natural consequences. I saw my Grandpa Oscar, working at lumber camps at her age, and his widowed immigrant mom. That's my Great-Grandmother Amelia. I'm her namesake.

This girl was taking a principled stand as she saw it. Her parents would back her, 100%. Conservative parents expected me to teach their kids about the Holocaust; Spanish-speaking immigrants were something else again. So I said nothing.

Also, I am a white woman. Not Latina. Not brown-skinned. There was a danger here, a needle I had to thread. Funny thing about storytelling: If you protect your heart too much and focus on fixing other people, or if you don't acknowledge distinctions, burdens that other people have and you have never experienced, it comes across as voyeuristic and condescending.

I definitely experienced this with infant twins, when people told me stories of people they knew who had twins. They presumed to know what that was like. Unless you've had twins, you haven't been there. We all have to stay in our lanes.

So here's the caveat: I'm a middle-class, third-generation American on one side, and who knows how many generations on the other. My family's story wasn't the same as these families down on the border. But I did have a family story.

When Grandpa Oscar was ten, at the height of the flu pandemic, his father got into a truck accident with the town doctor and lingered in the hospital for weeks. But hospitals weren't safe then, and my grandpa didn't get to say goodbye to his dad, who was a master stone mason, a hard-working Swede, building his immigrant wife and their five kids a stone house while they lived in the basement.

Amelia lost the house to pay his medical bills. Her husband's grave had no stone. Her children marked his grave with some seashells.

When government officials came to see my newly widowed Swedish Great-Grandmother Amelia, at one of the hardest moments of her life—in a very hard life—they demanded her kids. She'd already buried infant twins before she came to this country. Now she fought the authorities off with her broken English.

"My children! My children! You cannot take my children," she said.

After Amelia closed the door, she turned and addressed her children in Swedish. "We have no time for sorrow. We must work," she said. And then she said the words that came down to me: "Be it ever so bad, it's good for something."

My mentor Cheri Register died before I published my book, but as I gathered artifacts, I found some notes she'd written to wish me well. At my request, she'd also written that fabled phrase in correct Swedish, based on my Grandpa's retelling: *Bli det aldrig så galet, det är gott för något.* It was there in Cheri's jaunty script. I looked it up and saw that *galet* doesn't mean merely "bad," it means "wrong."

It's wrong that Amelia had no time for sorrows. It's wrong that medical expenses cost them their house, that my grandpa had to drop out of school after the ninth grade to work in lumber camps, and that he had no father past ten. It's wrong that, in the richest country in the world by all objective measures, it isn't a given to have time to heal during illness, and time to grieve in the face of sorrows.

It was Armistice Day, 1918, the day my great-grandfather died, the end of the Great War—a War to End All Wars. Meanwhile, many American women were mourning their war dead. Their children.

That was a one-hundred-year-old story. It's fascinating, the things that haunt us. For example, a framed photo of Amelia, three kids, and her husband, outside. The baby in the stroller is Grandpa Oscar. I liked to tell Amelia that I looked after him too. She was there when he was born; I was there when he died. We're bookends, Amelia and I.

In three generations, her offspring assimilated from poor immigrants into a blend of mainstream white people with means. We speak fluent English, albeit with markers of our Swedish roots, and if I didn't tell you about my family background, or my great-grandmother, you'd never know.

I'd reached the pinnacle of Amelia's American dream. But I still bore the traces, funny telltale signs of that trauma. Like being afraid to draw too much attention to myself. Like hanging on too long in a job where I had "security" but not safety. I had subsidized other people's children's wellbeing at the expense of my own children's needs. Then my shoulder froze, and I got to stay home. I finally had time for generational sorrows.

Did my hypothetical story of how my white, Swedish immigrant great-grandmother *could have* lost her children—*BUT DIDN'T*—pass muster? Or was I one more privileged woman, weighing in where I had no business?

I couldn't be sure. Luckily, Saadiah came to stay with us for the launch. My life coach training partner happened to be a brown-skinned immigrant from Australia. She sat on my sofa, helping me streamline my talk. I asked her about Amelia.

"Yeah," Saadiah said. "It's really not a bad thing to be Swedish, is it?"

"We are the prestigious kind of Europeans." I laughed. "But that's just it. Immigrants like us get welcomed. Her kids weren't taken away. What do I say about brown-skinned, Spanish-speaking kids in cages? It's related, but how?" I could see the gears turning in Saadiah's head.

"It's what you've got," she said. "But it's not really about being Swedish. Maybe they were discriminated against because they were immigrants. Probably it was mostly because they were poor. And didn't speak English. I'd go with it."

"Better than saying nothing?"

"Exactly."

"And if it had been so great in the Old Country, they would have stayed there."

"Exactly."

Saadiah went on to explain that historically, immigrant parents, legal or not, have to make hard decisions because they don't have other options. And then there's a pattern of poor people losing their children, which perpetuates poverty across generations.

The complexity does exist. Because she's right that, while these ancestors of mine suffered a loss, Nordic immigrants were never super discriminated against. We weren't redlined out of nice and safe places to live, which made the leap easier. And I'd grown attached to that safety as some kind of virtue, when really it gave me the responsibility to speak truth to power.

On October 3, I awoke to a beautiful sight on Facebook. My book designer, Patrick, happened to be in Berlin that day, so he packed a copy of my book and carried it to the Brandenburg Gate, epicenter and symbol of German Reunification. It used to be walled off. Until it wasn't. I'd written about that.

On that morning, Patrick was able to get close enough that he could hold up my book—no people in sight—and take a picture of *German Awakening*, framed by the gate with its four horses, blue sky, and the sun shining through.

People were here for me. It was almost too much to bear. Every person should be so fortunate.

Author-ity

Launching the book was only the first step in becoming an author. There were so many moving parts to integrate into Courageous Wordsmith, the brand meant to showcase my work as an author and book writing mentor. My business model wasn't yet clear, though there were signs of my basic foundations, such as the logo on my bookmark. Beyond that, I had my second book to write and ideas for a podcast. All I knew for sure was that I wanted to help people to write their own books.

I never wanted to be an entrepreneur until I was one. But now that I was in business, I hungered for guidance. That's why, when I was driving and heard about a free forum for creative entrepreneurs hosted by Minnesota Public Radio, I pulled over to register on the spot. The night of the event, I arrived with pen and notebook in hand. As a prolific notetaker, I wouldn't have left home without them. Just in case, I'd double-checked that there were bookmarks in my purse for networking.

Sometimes I don't even know the real reason something grabs my attention, which I call *shiny objects*. Unlike many folks, I don't dismiss shiny objects as a distraction. I pay attention and take copious notes as a creative practice.

That's often when everything conspires to move me, so crystal clear that I can feel it pulse in my veins. A moment propels me forward, not of my own volition, but because it's what wants to happen. It's not even a single moment, but a whole choreography. Had I not taken so many notes, so caught up in what the speakers were saying, nobody would have noticed me sitting there. Then they wouldn't have spoken to me until I ended up talking with the co-founder of the company, whose business model enthralled me. She and her husband had established themselves as professional artists in New York City but returned to the Twin Cities, specifically because we needed more representation from people of color.

I felt awestruck as she stepped forward, and I handed her a bookmark to mask my shyness. "I'm an author," I said to justify why I was there. "I've written a memoir about Germany." In the presence of this woman who had established a genuine up-and-running business, and an admirable one, I let the bookmark speak for me.

She smiled and greeted me warmly. "I worked in Germany too." That connection disarmed me. I felt the overwhelming pull to let her in on my secret mission.

"I'm writing a second book about parallels between twentieth-century Germany and what's happening in America now. Sins that were always here, but I just didn't see them because of how I was raised." As I spoke, I realized what a big statement that was, perhaps too bold, and so I looked away. "Except who am I as a white woman, really, to be telling this story?"

Then she hit me. Her open palm struck the sleeve of my winter jacket that softened the blow. She meant business, this tiny empowered Black woman who forced me to look directly at her.

"Please tell your story," she said. "Please. Tell it to YOUR people. Because we're tired. You have to start telling the truth." And then she turned away.

She called my bluff, if that's what it was. I wasn't informing her, I was asking permission. This wasn't the first time someone had asked me to take on this cause, only one of the most direct times. This was the call I deferred, that was mine, not hers. It wasn't her job to solve my white-lady reluctance. And so I felt chagrined and grateful, both for her initial warm hospitality, and for her candor before I walked outside into the frozen city.

The following morning, I returned to Minneapolis. When I walked into Open Book, Katherine had already scored a pair of the good tables with four chairs next to the radiators and floor-to-ceiling windows. She'd unpacked her laptop and was typing but sensed my arrival. "Hey!" She looked up and smiled.

I set my overfull tote bag down in the wooden chair across from her. "Let me buy my breakfast, and then we'll talk." I pulled out my small purse and unzipped the pocket where I usually kept my wallet. It was empty. A jolt of panic shot through me. After a lifetime with what I now recognize as neurodivergence, largely thanks to reading Katherine's words on the subject, I know on an intellectual level that something like this shouldn't throw me. It happens enough that I've built redundancies into my system, double-checking for phone, keys, and wallet every time I leave a location. So I went through all the zipped pockets and open flaps. Nada.

"Oh no!" I blurted louder than I meant to. "I'm missing my wallet."

Katherine brushed her fingers through her blond bob, ever calm. "When's the last time you had it?"

I sat down, closed my eyes, and took a breath. I'd paid my bills right before I left for the forum the evening before, and I hadn't needed a credit card for parking or entrance. Even the food afterward was free.

Which meant, when I thought about it, that I'd gone to the forum without a wallet. For two days running, I'd driven to Minneapolis without my license or even one cent. And people at both places welcomed me unquestioningly.

The guy behind the Open Book register overheard. "You OK, Amy? Don't worry about it. Breakfast is on us." With that, he entered an order for my very specific specialty breakfast: eggs and cheese between sliced Roma tomatoes because I try to eat gluten-free. Among themselves, they called it "The Amy" but never added it to the menu because the assembly was too much work for the kitchen staff. He waved away my offer to repay them the next time and set about making my large mango green tea latte. I thanked him profusely and sat down, taking a moment to track down in my mind where I might find the wallet back home.

"You OK?" Katherine asked.

"Oh Katherine," I said, shaking my head no. Then I told her about the conversation I'd had with the forum speaker the previous night.

"Oh Amy," she said. She paused, blue eyes framed behind tortoise-shell glasses, making sure I was paying attention. "I think you have to be honest. Yes, you've struggled with your family, as a mom, and in your career. Absolutely. But you have to admit that you're privileged. Many people don't have the advantages that you do. You get a lot of support." She nodded at the table. "Look at your breakfast."

This is something I love about Katherine. Whether I've landed a piece of writing, or one single sentence, she tells me so, but she doesn't praise all of my writing as beautiful. Instead, she points to morsels I've missed so sweetly that it seldom pisses me off. Katherine's not from Minnesota. She's Texan. And she's usually spot on.

She watched me from across the table, head tipped, while I mulled this over, then pressed her point. "Don't you see you have privilege?"

I rolled my eyes. "I don't want to tell people I'm an asshole."

"Me neither," she said earnestly. "But we have to."

At this, we laughed quite a while. Then we wrote this fabulous bit of dialogue down for posterity. It was oversimplification, of course. Name calling misses the mark, and we both knew it. But that's why it was funny to us.

Also, I had to confess the broader truth of her statement. We weren't saying that people who have advantages are assholes, or at least that's not a given. We were saying that as writers, if we want credibility with our audience, we have to present a full picture of ourselves—certainly not the most private parts, but also not only the good parts. Katherine isn't just a neuropsychologist, she's a mom and a human being. And I'm not just a humbled person, I've been lifted up. As Katherine said, we have to be honest. With you, our dear readers. I can only do that if I acknowledge the parts that I'm not confessing. Not even privately, to myself.

I studied German (I now understand) to make sense of generational trauma in my own family. We're Scandinavian, but German gave me the context I needed. I'll likely always bear poverty's faint mark despite my relative privilege, two generations after my orphaned immigrant grandparents found each other and did their best to heal their pain. Looking at me, you can't suss out that background.

There's also the pedigreed side. The side where someone Black and Indigenous passed as white several generations back—not that long ago. And I always suspected as much because Grandma Doris's family came up through the South, so what are the odds that *nobody* passed? I honor that lineage too. In theory, if the "one-drop rule" truly applied, I would count as non-white. But we all know that's not how it works. I'm lily white, just look at me. Whiteness is a construct, true, but people in our society whose skin is visibly darker can't opt out of that construct at will, whereas I can sidestep it. I can mask my differences because I look like the dominant culture, surrounded by people whose skin looks like mine.

I'm well versed in the ways that I can hide if I choose. Germany brought that to my attention. My brain doesn't work like everyone else's, both a fast and slow processor at the same time. It shows up as awkwardness when I feel put on the spot, and as spot-on pronouncements when I feel safe—but you might not notice this by looking at me. So I can be larger than life, and I can also play small so that people don't comment on my obvious quirks. It took me years to put a name on these traits before I self-diagnosed as neurodivergent.

For that, I thank Katherine. My gift from her is the blessing of artifice dropped. Those beautiful note-taking skills and powers of observation that she so admires, even when she sometimes can't track where I'm going? That's how my brain works. I make snap connections and leap ahead where other folks don't. Not only that, but I often achieve perfect timing and meet the exact perfect people.

And yet to get myself out the door, I repeat a verbal list of basic tasks out loud: *deodorant, hair, teeth, eyes, socks . . .* As I manage one item, I drop it off the list and add another: *hair, teeth, eyes, socks, keys . . .* and so on. Seldom have I left home without my wallet as I did those two days running. But that's by careful design; you only know because I told you so. Because I've learned fierce boundaries. Because I've come to love how my brain works.

There are stories I let myself tell, and then there's the real story. I've suffered, and I've enjoyed great privilege in my life. Both things can be true. When I quit teaching, I got to lay so many burdens down. There were personal sorrows and the sorrows of generations accumulated in my body, crying out for release.

My privilege is as follows:

1. I got to keep my house.
2. I got to raise my kids with a man I love and trust.

3. I got to write books that I've wanted to write my whole life.
4. I got to reconsider who I thought I was and see what I was missing.
5. Or let me restate that. I get to educate myself and use my voice for good.

I don't want to leave it at that. I know that I'm not alone among well-meaning white people. So let me tell you what my friend Stephanie, a brilliant Black woman, has told me when we've talked about inherited white privilege: "Don't beat yourself up. Don't apologize. Be grateful for what that gift makes possible, and where it allows you to be. Claim your abundance, but *show compassion*. Do the work to make abundance possible for the rest of us too."

Sometimes, when I get really quiet, the questions are really simple:

Who am I to tell my story? Who wants to hear it? Do I want to entrust people with my full (or partial) truth? You know, the ordinary tale of someone with so much potential, who received many blessings, still never arrived, and lived on?

I feel lost. Often. Who wants to hear that?

Sometimes a story is there for a reason—it wants to come up, to be acknowledged, to be healed, to be released into the world. Maybe dissolved, maybe get published. Not to get stuck in victimhood stories, but to show patterns. To sort out, if *this* isn't for you, what else do you want? To expose old beliefs to make room for the new, first and foremost for myself, then for my readers. I was living through a midlife revival. That's the exact perfect book for right now.

I've written infinite books in my mind. The book that landed in these pages is the one I retold over and over while I made my way out the door and beyond. Stories tangle in and out, where I've held myself captive. And where I've set myself free.

ReVision

I was an imperfect messenger—the great-granddaughter of six immigrants but also entitled, if I so chose, to join the Daughters of the American Revolution. Even if I denied that part of my history.

Part of me felt deeply unworthy to share my story, knowing that I had relied heavily on Eva's generosity around difficult truths. I'd discovered that memoir is a whole different level of self-revelation, even when you're circumspect in places. If you were an American teen exploring Germany in the eighties, for example, you might think you've revealed yourself at a safe distance. When actually you've immersed yourself in someone else's historical baggage and bypassed your own.

Still I'd launched the book, although I wasn't prepared to talk about those broader implications. If I'd waited until I was ready, I would never have published at all. Fortunately for me, Roseanne kept showing up and pointing out opportunities to showcase my book.

Thanks to one of her leads, I landed two gigs teaching writing in Northfield, one at the Arts Guild, one at the senior center, where we raised such questions in service to narrative craft. If I didn't yet feel like a real author, I happily welcomed back my teaching authority as second nature.

Then Roseanne issued a more significant invitation, something special to her, without knowing my personal connection to the venue. She had arranged for me to speak at the Arts Center in Grandma Doris's city. My scheduled appearance, five months after publication on a Saturday in March, fell through due to a freak late-spring snowstorm. By that Monday, when I drove Olivia to school, the snow had melted. All the way home, a rainbow dominated the blue sky directly over Grandma's assisted-living enclave, which I took to be a sign.

On my alternative date in September, when the weather was nice, the city closed the neighborhood roads for a community fun run. I got the clear sense that Grandma Doris had a different expectation for my book, and indeed my rescheduled author talk landed on my book's first birthday. Grandma always did like birthday parties.

I felt relieved by the previous two cancellations because I was coming to realize that my book addressed forces much bigger than me, much bigger than the limited scope I had given myself permission to acknowledge. Such things, unspoken, don't go away.

I felt it was only fair to let the Arts Center know that I needed to talk politics. That's the Minnesota Nice girl in me. So I arranged to go over to the site beforehand and meet with the coordinator to apprise her of my topic. While I was there, I wanted to check out the gallery space.

Although I'd seen the Arts Center many times from the freeway, I'd never visited the building, so I programmed my phone's navigation. When I got close, the map on the dashboard rerouted me through the parking lot of the saltbox church, in one end and out the other. I recognized the path immediately.

You could chalk it up to the church's proximity to the art gallery, I suppose, except that GPS has never guided me through a church parking lot before or since. So I pulled into a spot and parked for a moment. Studying the familiar beloved building, I thought about what this detour could possibly mean, since these were anything but neutral grounds.

"What do you want me to say?" I said aloud.

I sat behind the steering wheel, watching.

This was the parking lot where Mom had dropped me off for summer camp right before we quit going there. As the bus doors closed, I'd rushed forward in tears. "Don't make me go!" I cried. "I don't know anyone."

Mom had run to the door and hugged me tight. For a moment, I thought she'd give in, and we could go home. She would have conceded, too, had my counselor not raced to the door in my wake and pulled me back onto the bus. The doors had closed quickly, we'd driven off, and she'd escorted me to my seat, where we sat together. Once my tears subsided, she introduced two cabin mates to me and asked them to sit beside me.

While I made some acquaintances, it bothered me even at ten that I never felt their cheerful certainty about the Good News at camp. When a fireside story in the darkness brought my fellow ten-year-old campers to tears en masse, overcome that Jesus had died *just for them*, I'd been as dry as a bone. Swedish camp had felt far more like a religious experience to me than this Christian camp. In the years to come, I would learn to celebrate that God spoke to me through different channels than strictly Christian ones.

When I'd abandoned the saltbox church again as an adult, I'd decided to slip away and email my former friends only once I'd landed at one of the very progressive churches they most feared. Afterward they'd called and written, hoping to bring me back "home." But I'd excommunicated myself. I didn't want to be saved. Not that way. The problem was me, knowing what the church was and expecting otherwise.

However, there had been a banner. It had hung there on opening day in 1978, and it had been in the same place when I'd returned in 1995. Those Congregationalists weren't big on banners, which is why this one had drawn my attention hanging beside the Meetinghouse doors. More Light Yet to Break, the banner proclaimed.

Whatever disagreements I'd had with Grandma's church, they taught me reverence, and they taught me the fallacy of muting my voice, and they even taught me about belonging in places where I didn't seem to fit. Deep down, I always wanted to believe that the prophesy would come to pass. More light would break open, God willing, and I'd finally feel the spirit that everyone else claimed to sense. Indeed, I realized that God had been speaking to me all along—through shiny objects and stories, a glimmer and its unfolding.

That felt like an answer, as subtle as it was. I had no idea who would attend the talk, nor could I control what they believed. But I could let that part be. It was never my job to feel the spirit for anyone else. It was my job to show up for myself. That meant honoring where—and who—I came from.

Grandma Doris was a force of nature, and she kept impeccable minutes. When she retired from City Hall, they hired three people to replace her. She dedicated years of service to making elections run smoothly and fairly. In the years after her career, her genealogical work was her way of seeking more light yet to break.

She dedicated herself to making sure that I knew who I was, even if she didn't always express her love as I wanted. Even if we were often at odds. Even if her efforts were not entirely altruistic. She lavished love on me in so many ways.

Sometimes—often—she really did see me. Grandma believed I could be an author before I did, as evidenced by the ditto-paper manuscript I once destroyed as a teen and the cassette tape of me reading when I turned five, recorded for posterity. I had carried on her legacy, albeit in a different way than she'd envisioned.

So if I was going to speak at an Author's Forum in her community, she would want me to remember that as a child, I'd gone to high school concerts and movie theaters there. That my cousin Ellen and I once shared a bedroom. That I first heard about the settlement in our hometown teachers' strike while watching TV in her room over the garage, surrounded by surplus office supplies and a hidden stockpile of notes that we wrote. Grandma squirreled them away for us. For me.

By my own choosing, I'd worked at a bookstore ten minutes from her house, a half-an-hour drive from mine, where I met my husband. Grandma would want me to acknowledge that I was baptized there as a baby, and that I marched through the town with a burgundy hymnal. And once upon a time, I'd played on the City Hall floor while she typed.

Grandma never, ever skimped on the agenda. Nor on all those years of cards she sent, sometimes including a poem. *Love you dearly,* she always wrote. And she meant it. She wouldn't want me to skimp on my lineage. My blind spot of omission in this case was a lie. Grandma Doris would want me to acknowledge who she was, too, publicly, and with love.

I could decline the DAR and stand my own sacred ground without denying Grandma. In fact, I really had to because she was a part of me. As my step-cousin said, I was the one most like her—committed, fierce, devoted. Sometimes scared of change, sometimes playing small, sometimes judgmental, but often courageous. And I wasn't protecting Grandma by being circumspect, I was protecting myself. In so doing, I was keeping myself from her best trait: unfettered joy.

A song stirred in my head. *This little light of mine, I'm gonna let it shine.* Another Black spiritual borrowed—like so many songs from my lifetime. I hummed the tune for a bit. Old lyrics morphed into new:

I know what I know. I'm gonna let it shine.
I'm guided by my voice. I'm gonna let it shine.
With gratitude, for abundance is mine.
Let it shine, let it shine, let it shine.

I took this to mean that my story was my inheritance—meant for me—and I could trust myself to tell it correctly. I sang all the way to the Arts Center, for which, unsurprisingly, my phone now gave a direct route.

So here's what happened the day of my talk. People showed up. They heard me share my religious foundations. They received my story of how I, as a seventeen-year-old exchange student, requested that my German host mom (and child of the war) drive me to Dacchau, a concentration camp. Mami fed me, drove me to school, kept me safe, and cared for me in every way while working full time—but flat out refused to take me to the most painful place she could go. She was no Holocaust denier. She planned a family road trip to show me Bavaria, Germany's pride, and I asked for a detour. Mami rightly said no.

In her refusal, Mami gave me an immeasurably better and truly priceless gift—that of her childhood story told without embellishment, which I'd faithfully recorded in my book, and now read for this assembled congregation. She'd been a displaced child who'd wandered lost with siblings through a desolate, destroyed nation, not allowed to return to her hometown of Königsberg, which became Kaliningrad. So she built a life near the opposite border of West Germany in the Black Forest.

I shared how as a child I'd often felt like an outsider, hemmed in by stories passed down by people who wanted to shield me, and themselves, from shadows. Thanks to Mami and her daughter Eva, I began to rethink the idea of freedom.

I said that my exchange sister, Eva, once told me, "You know an awful lot about our history. Perhaps you should learn more about your own." I shared the story of standing with Eva on the curb at the White House, and recent run-ins with politics (despite my best efforts to steer clear) and my German/American take on the forty-fifth president, with the caveat that it came from my perspective and expertise. And I talked about the museum, where I was kindly educated by two Black women about Emmett Till. How I hadn't known his name, and the women said, "Now you do."

Several people during Q & A quoted me back to myself and said how my stories sparked theirs. It turns out that many people with German heritage held equally strong feelings about this topic. They likewise found the parallels glaring, and they appreciated me giving it voice.

However, one elderly white man in the front row, who appeared to listen intently, asked a strange question. "When you finally did visit a concentration camp, though, which one did you visit?" I thought I'd been clear.

"I haven't," I said. "I honored Holocaust victims by educating myself and my students in other ways." I had, in fact, detailed exactly what I'd taught my students, including a Nazi Propaganda film that we'd analyzed, and that I had described that very day. Did you know that the Nuremberg rally shown in the film looked just like any religious ceremony? It did. I taught Holocaust lessons from primary sources for seventeen years.

It was like Eva said: I was better served by visiting the American equivalent than by entertaining my readers with German guilt. The Holocaust was abhorrent. And it was time for me to shine a bright light closer to home.

We can all honor people's trauma without the need to go to faraway places. We'll find examples right in our own backyards if we're paying attention. I really think this man was captivated by the idea of German concentration camps and American saviors. But he wasn't curious in any helpful way.

Afterward, he and his silent wife waited in the signing line. He told me that he hadn't bought the book. This was fine by me. I want my books to be read by people who choose to read them.

He leaned in to school me. "You ruined a beautiful presentation by bringing in politics." He sighed. "It was like dumping water over the whole thing." He trotted out some tired statistics about *how good the Blacks and Mexicans had it these days, never better.* "The economy is doing well," he said. "If you'd only give our president a chance." (You could say the same thing about Hitler: The economy got better, by certain metrics, before it got undeniably worse. Things looked pretty good for a while. On the surface at least, for Germans not of Jewish descent. If you wanted to believe. That was the point of the propaganda film I spoke about at length. And Mami's story. And mine.)

"Do you watch Fox News?" the man asked.

I breathed in and smiled politely. "Hell no."

"Excuse me?" His face registered shock.

"Hell no." I put on my stern teacher face. "I draw the line at children in cages, separated from their parents on arrival." It threw him off guard. Nevertheless, he persisted.

"You're brainwashed." He shook his head and tried to convince me of my error. Said I didn't understand and was being misled.

I thought of a German play on words. *Erklären* means to explain. *Herr* means man. Put them together and you get *Herrklären*: to mansplain. I was a daughter raised in the patriarchy. His was the centered male voice of the trolls I disdained: *Young lady, be nice. See it my way. Be reasonable. There's a good girl.*

When I stood my sacred ground it felt, well, grounding. "Thank you for coming," I said, not unkindly. "With all due respect, we disagree. And I have other people who want to talk with me. Have a nice day." I didn't exclude him from hearing the telling. He was free to interpret it as he liked. But I honored my wisdom. My boundaries. The sacred stories entrusted to me.

Even telling you this, the nice Minnesota girl inside me worries that you're going to turn on me. I can imagine you thinking that I'm a shrill bitch. You'll ask me who I think I am. But I've spent a lot of time wandering in the shadows, learning that what I know matters. We can't afford to play small with our God-given gifts. Too much is at stake for us. And so I resumed conversations with guests who'd purchased my book, people who wanted to hear what I said, who had ideas to add. It was delightful.

Translator

Brilliance

The week that COVID shut down Minnesota, I finished recording my *German Awakening* audiobook in a home basement studio three suburbs over. On the drive back, I grocery shopped for quarantine food, especially soup and vegetables. Because I was no longer a teacher, I was able to prepare before my family's three schools inevitably shut down. They joined me at home from mid March on.

We would never eat the frozen bags of Brussels sprouts or kale that I bought in a panic, nor the giant tub of peanut butter; otherwise I chose fairly well. To this day, we possess a jumbo unopened package of toilet paper that we keep in reserve. Dave has proclaimed that we always will.

Because I was already living an isolated life and already using Zoom to teach writing classes and record podcasts, this lockdown didn't floor me the way it did so many, if social media was to be believed. For once, my learning curve was gentle.

I steeped tea in mugs for my family each morning, and made dinner each evening with a motherly reverence I'd never displayed before.

I saw this as my chance to resolve lingering motherhood gaps. Like many families in lockdown, we streamed movies daily and ate copious amounts of ice cream. Virtual school posed the potential for disaster, but we carved out solitary spaces and settled for mixed blessings.

I knew this was all temporary. Eventually, our daughters would leave home. They were both supposed to go on European trips through school like I did at their age, but that didn't happen. We made the best of a bad situation; in the absence of certainty, we were grateful for security, health, and each other in our family bubble.

And then George Floyd was killed by a policeman on Memorial Day. And I knew that corner personally—Thirty-Eighth and Chicago. Pre-COVID, I'd turned onto Chicago Avenue there every week when Katherine and I met to write. It's part of a vibrant, multicultural neighborhood.

We all saw what happened. Captured on video by a Black girl the age of my daughters and shared to the entire world, Floyd lay facedown on the pavement, Chauvin's knee to his neck for nine and a half minutes. We all saw it. All for a fraudulent twenty-dollar bill at CUP Foods, a convenience store in South Minneapolis.

It definitely wouldn't have happened to me. When a snow-white girl like me shows up without transportation in a diverse neighborhood, people offer me rides to other parts of the city. I'm really not kidding. It happened in Chicago in my mid-twenties, and it's happened since then in Minneapolis. White people look out for a white girl like me, and I'd even say people of color consider my safety.

During winter break from college my junior year, I landed an overnight temp job in a call center half a mile from my grandparents' first-ring suburban condo. In theory, we took orders for infomercial sandwich grills.

"Hey, Sally Jesse!" a young man called out on my first day because I wore red glasses like the talk show host Sally Jesse Raphael. "Come sit over here." His friends cleared me a station. "We'll teach you to talk like a Brother," he said, playfully yet insistent. And then he and his friends launched into surprisingly earnest lessons on how Black dialect works. They talked and I listened.

Dozens of us operators were standing by to answer the phones, but nobody called all night long. Calls only started trickling in around dawn, which meant we had plenty of time for my coworkers to talk, and they educated me—not just on Black semantics, but they offered a primer on Black Minneapolis culture as well.

One word stands out from their lessons, common back then: *dis*, short for "disrespect." As in, *Do not disrespect me as a human being.* Everything else arose from that concept, and what respect looked like to them.

We laughed often and went deep into details. They gently chided me to keep up. It felt as if we had both all the time in the world and no time at all. One evening, I locked my keys in my parents' Dodge Caravan—which I noticed as it happened—and one of the men volunteered the exact tool from his trunk to slide down into the window and jimmy my lock. The whole interaction took less than ten minutes and opened up a whole new, revelatory thread.

He kept the slim jim not because he was a criminal but because—in a similar situation to mine—he would never consider calling the cops. The system isn't broken. It works as designed, which doesn't bode well for men like him. His friends made sure that I saw the discrepancies, plain as day, sending me out each morning with their promises to return to our conversation at nightfall. The temporary call-in assignment lasted a week before supervisors dismissed us en masse. I returned to college, and we never saw each other again.

George Floyd could have been any of them. His death proved what my long-ago coworkers had taught me during our educational vigil. My Minneapolis looked like theirs, but it wasn't the same.

My rockstar friend, and our violin teacher, Jillian—a white woman—lived down the street from what was quickly dubbed George Floyd Square. At her house on Chicago Avenue, a portal into another, more creative realm, Jillian and I talked shop. She let me practice life coaching on her, and we recorded podcasts in her living room. I drove to see Jillian, at a minimum, two afternoons a month. On violin lesson days, kiddo and I circumnavigated parks, lakes, and Minnehaha Creek on regular Starbucks detours when we got there too early. So I knew those surrounding streets very well, albeit as a visitor.

Jillian's social media feed was the first place I learned the name of George Floyd, whose death she decried in focused fury. In the coming days, Jillian would describe life in a war zone, with helicopters hovering at all hours.

Never mind the pandemic. People of every skin color and ethnicity, LGBTQ+ and straight, masked up and marched. Cops fired rubber bullets and tear gas, derailing and detaining medics who tended the wounded in tents. Looters looted and vandals vandalized.

Mind you, residents weren't destroying their own neighborhoods, though that was one line of thought out there. Cameras captured white male agitators who came from out of town to set fires and foment chaos. And parts of Minneapolis burned, but not George Floyd Square, where they gathered to pray.

And me? I stayed home and scoured the web. The morning after the first fires, my friend Lisa, a multiracial Minneapolis author and businesswoman, was out with her team. They were busy clearing debris on Lake Street and transporting supplies in what had become a food desert.

Wanting to be in the city I love, I masked up and drove in to visit Kiki, in theory to deliver two pots of yellow begonias, but really I wanted to talk about what I could write. I needed—my panicked brain screamed—to raise awareness RIGHT NOW about racism in Minnesota. It had taken me fifty years to slow-walk myself into this Black Lives Matter cause, but now I wanted to bypass this pivotal moment, jump into solutions, and feel better fast.

Kiki—who is also white—actually lives in South Minneapolis, not in immediate danger, but still. Normally she's my biggest cheerleader and creative collaborator, and when I come over, she makes sure I have a steaming cup and a hearty snack, like Grandma Doris would. She eagerly listens to everything I have to say. Usually. But not this time. As I outlined the stories that I had in mind, Kiki fixed her blue eyes with a withering stare.

"Amy, stop." She looked up from her perfectly appointed sofa. "Right now, listening to you, I'm so incredibly angry. Unless you're willing to go into the street, and pour milk on your face for the tear gas, go home. Nobody wants to listen to middle-aged white women today."

I stammered some words to make things right, to quell the discomfort, but Kiki cut me off.

"Yes, I still love you, but go home. The time will come when you need to step up. Go home, read up, and listen."

It's a really good friend who tells you the hard truths instead of letting you go make an ass of yourself. Kiki was right, and I knew it. Still, as I drove home through Grandma Doris's lily-white adjacent suburb, I felt the potent sting of my friend's words and the everlasting shame of a four-year-old girl sent away because she said the wrong thing. What made things worse was that on the same day that Derek Chauvin killed George Floyd, a white woman named Amy Cooper tried to sic the cops on another Black man in New York City, in Central Park.

His name was Chris Cooper. He was birding while Black. He'd spoken to Amy Cooper (no relation) when her dog was running off-leash, as prohibited by posted signs. He'd filmed the woman who cried *African-American Man* on her 9-1-1 call, and in so doing, probably saved his own life. They shared the same last name as each other.

She shared her first name with me. She said she's not racist—not a bone of it. But what else shall we call it? He, too, could have died that day.

Thanks to COVID, everyone was home alone, together, forced to pay attention to patterns. Such things happen in New York, and they happen here. But I'm not that Amy. Am I? I'm a progressive white woman of the Greater Twin Cities.

Parts of Minneapolis and its twin, St. Paul, were burning. I knew people with homes in both places, who lived near the frontlines while we faced the truth of red-lined racism laid bare—and wasn't our hometown shame already laid bare with Philando Castile, two years prior? He was an elementary school lunchroom supervisor shot point-blank in front of his child. And this was just Minnesota.

None of these deaths were OK. As I drove, my emotions reached a magnitude I hadn't felt since I quit my career. I saw no option but to listen to that keening child inside.

"Nobody wants to listen to me." The words burned my face; I called my mom from the road. Mom was busy and hung up fast. I drove on. "Nobody wants to listen to me," four-year-old Amy repeated. It was a scream in my brain, raging and bouncing. At last, defeated, the voice got unusually quiet. "Nobody wants to listen to me."

I felt the release of cleansing tears, and I heard myself answer. "I do. What's going on?" In fact, I had to listen to myself; while I was not at the center of this tragic maelstrom, I was close enough, and therefore involved.

"I'm sad," young Amy said. "And I want to help." I assured her we could. But first we had to do our own work.

I was mourning the death of George Floyd, whom I had never met, along with the waning illusion that Minnesota Nice institutions were designed to keep us all safe, secure, and in relative good health. Measured against my personal failures, I now knew it just wasn't so.

I'd already learned in my career that nobody wins, not really, when people serve systems instead of the other way 'round.

But I could no more expect to solve ingrained, multilayered Minnesota racism than I could fix education as one lonely teacher. Shortcomings that had derailed my career were laid bare for everyone with the advent of COVID. No way would I turn back, but I had no defined public sphere in which to process. So now what?

I felt entirely isolated, despite the cars on the road. My chosen route took me past Grandma's church. I flashed back to a summer picnic at a neighboring park before we moved into the saltbox building. After lunch I'd wandered off and decided it was a good idea to wade into the drainage pond, shoes on, to wash off wet concrete I'd stepped in from the construction. The bottom dropped off fast and my feet sank, deeper and deeper into the unstable silt.

I pulled at reeds that unearthed themselves and floated gently on the surface, delicate and useless to save me from quicksand. I didn't dare to abandon those shoes. I cried out, "Help me!" my voice disappearing on the wind, my body sinking down, flailing. Mom finally heard me and rushed to find me, calling my name. She quickly assessed the situation. "Lean back," she said. "Float in the water." My shoes released into the pond with my feet still inside them. Mom reached out to grab my hands and pulled me to shore.

The current crisis felt like that kind of sinking, like there was no bottom to this bad situation, no way to ground myself in this Minneapolis muck, but actually there was. I needed to lean back and let myself float.

12.2 TRANSLATOR

Twin Cities

My calling was in front of me and all around me. As a Twin Cities native, I knew both cities well, and I had reliable friends on the ground from many life stages. During the uprising, I amplified their trusted voices.

Police got aggressive with journalists. WCCO, the local CBS station I'd trusted since childhood, unflinchingly aired the footage. Anchors I'd known since early adulthood leveled with us. The images were visceral. I watched the National Guard in their riot gear march past the church where I'd married Dave and baptized our children and sang in the choir. Further north, they corralled protesters at the gas station where I filled my tank when I drove home from writing. By night, city-dwelling friends kept watch with neighbors to guard their homes and alleys from anarchists in out-of-state cars. By day, street artists painted murals and turned the boarded-up windows into an open-air museum.

During those days of crisis, I was in the right place to do what life had prepared me for all along, which was simply to watch, read, and

319

listen for context. People did want to listen to me. And I wanted to listen to other people before I spoke.

I already knew my ground rules by heart:

1. When you come as a guest to someone else's significant moment, you remain on the periphery to show respect for those closer in. You don't press in on the inner circle with your backstory. They can invite you closer—or not.
2. Be that as it may, your stories will come up. Let that guide your awareness.
3. Some powerful things that arise won't make sense in the moment, but they'll resonate deeply. Take note and let them be what they are.

I'd been thinking of the two Black teachers who'd met me over the phone all those years earlier for my multicultural studies project at the University of St. Thomas, along with the Indigenous professor who'd assigned the interview project. Theirs became a legacy of blessings bestowed in lingering questions. At the time I had merely wondered how I would ever complete the assignment. I now realized how essential that moment was to my education, pivotal and preparatory to the one that was happening now. All three women told me to read more books by people of color. Now I finally dove in, along with all the other well-meaning white people. It turned out that I'd learned more since college than I'd thought.

Inevitably social media channels proclaimed that this author or that one had "issues," and that we should disregard books that don't get racism quite right. But I could let neither imperfection, nor bypass derail me. Certainly I ruled out voices who claimed that systemic racism no longer exists—if it ever did—or that racism was reversed. I was already familiar with those refrains.

Black Lives Matter, the rallying cry, means exactly that. Patterns show that Black lives haven't mattered enough to everyone by default, or we wouldn't need to say so. In that vein, I had no time to humor white people who insisted on saying, "ALL lives matter." Yes, we were ALL up against oppressive forces. Was it ALL our work to put out the blaze? Absolutely. And did God love us ALL? Definitely. But I refused to split pious hairs, or cling to *Love, Light, Thoughts, and Prayers.* My best entry points were authentic stories, in which I looked for the frames. Every story has one.

I attended teach-in calls hosted by women of color in my circle, including my friend Lisa, who invited white people to listen, but we were not the focus. These were gracious offers, in which we were welcome to witness Black requests of us, without us asking for anything in return. Black people owed us white people nothing. They'd already given too much. They were asking us to step up, finally.

And again, I didn't have to look very far. One woman looked out into the Zoom room, largely a sea of white faces. "I'm so angry," she said. "If you want me to speak for all Black people so you can feel better, I'm not interested." This echoed the conversations from my Catholic university in St. Paul. "If you want to get to know me and the good parts of my culture, then I'm Stephanie. Reach out."

Here was the invitation I had been looking for all those years earlier. By now, I had the language to contact her and propose that we start a friendship, specifically centered on exploring our parallel American cultures. I modeled that vision on my friendship with Eva. In turn, Stephanie would become a dear friend.

Within a week of the uprising, I had three writing classes to lead—already scheduled with groups of mostly white, conscientious women like me. I offered up the space to process. We teach what we're finally ready to learn.

One month after George Floyd's murder, Dave and I drove into town, passing the burnt-out buildings and parking in Jillian's alley. Due to COVID, we sat on lawn chairs six feet apart in the backyard, while she and her husband, Eric, caught us up on their local perspective as insiders living close to ground zero.

When we understood the lay of the land, Dave and I walked down Chicago Avenue to George Floyd Square, indefinitely blocked off from traffic. On the pavement as we approached, a litany of painted names greeted us like a bloody red carpet. Ambassadors at the borders welcomed us in with squirts of hand sanitizer. At the corner, we stood beside the place where George Floyd's body expired, outlined in white, and we quickly moved aside. Meanwhile, Black mourners sang, prayed, and marched in processions. One teen skateboarded straight down those names.

On Jillian's advice, we walked a few blocks over to an art installation on a grassy clearing. Rows upon rows of tombstones commemorated the names of Black lives, shamefully wasted, who hadn't mattered nearly enough to the powers that be. SAY THEIR NAMES, block letters insisted, on the opposite berm. We stood on the grassy knoll and breathed in the humanity, reclaimed. Their names were a painful deluge. Their names were a prayer.

"Twenty dollars," I said under my breath.

"Yeah," Dave said under his. "Twenty dollars." Two flimsy words that echoed forever. On our walk back, I considered their relative value.

Twenty dollars signify so many promises made and dishonored. During Obama's presidency, Harriet Tubman was supposed to take her place on the twenty-dollar bill. By 2020 we hadn't replaced Andrew Jackson. I've heard that Harriet Tubman bought her mother out of slavery in the South for twenty dollars. George Floyd's life was ransomed in Minneapolis for the same price. I've paid more for museum tickets. As we passed along familiar streets, a thought arose: *I am not a tourist here.*

My mind carried me northward, toward the Mississippi River. Three miles down Chicago Avenue stands the formerly Episcopal hospital, now part of a major medical center, where I entered the world. Dave was born a few years later at another hospital you pass on the way. Four miles away from George Floyd Square, a converted warehouse birthed me as an author.

A mile and a half away on the parallel Park Avenue, my paternal great-grandpa and my step-great-grandma, Cora, lived across from the American Swedish Institute.

Less than three miles away, on Nicollet Avenue, stands the Congregational church that we claimed as our home.

Three miles away, on Eleventh and Nicollet, my Grandpa Oscar rented his small storefront, A-1 Downtown Signs & Displays. The Twin Cities are full of my ancestral and personal markers.

And yet. None of my great-grandparents came from here. My ancestors traveled far for me to arrive here. They were seeking the promise of a good life, and surely didn't concern themselves with what Black people needed. And now here we are. Nevertheless, people—known and unknown—invested dearly in me, and my children, with no guarantee of a return.

Less than five miles away from George Floyd Square, the Hennepin Avenue Bridge rises up beside an iconic neon sign, a giant silver bottle cap with large white words: Grain Belt Beer, it says, on a diamond of red. At eighteen, Eva and I watched fireworks from that bridge, blocked off from traffic. The sign's letters would have shone through the night, but I'd have barely noticed. From that vantage point, the current flowed, steady and calm. I certainly wouldn't have imagined myself—this present version—here and now, contemplating the relative value of American Black Lives.

For someone who's mostly lived in Minnesota, with few German ancestors to speak of, Germany certainly plays a strangely prominent role in my history. But perhaps it's not so odd. We find it easier to step beyond our natural bounds, seeking truths from others, before we're willing to see for ourselves. Immersing myself in German taught me to recognize generational patterns.

What happened ages ago is often present today. Whether we name the patterns or not, our origins will remain. I am from Minneapolis, City of Lakes, astride the Mississippi. And I'm the product of my German-Catholic hometown in the Minnesota River Valley, built on Dakota ancestral land where I still live. All these things are true.

As we arrived back at Jillian's alley, these disparate pieces of me washed into each other. The situation on display was not exclusively a Minneapolis thing. It exists in plain sight everywhere, including the suburbs.

The veil of American racism—Minnesota style—was lifted. What that lifting revealed is not pretty. But at least we white people were finally talking about it. The irony didn't escape me that the spark ignited here. Not in the South, below the Mason-Dixon line. Not New York City, Chicago, St. Louis, or any of the usual urban suspects. Nice, pleasant, hot-and-cold Minnesota had to get everybody's attention. How else would anyone know that we white people mean it this time?

And I pray that we do.

Dearly Beloved

Let me tell you how I find guidance these days.

On April 21, 2016, three months after I quit my job, I drove mid-morning to my daughters' middle school to drop something off, interrupting a less-than-satisfying writing session. As I left home, I turned on a Minnesota Public Radio station known as The Current and heard breaking news: Prince—the music legend—had died at Paisley Park, his local studio where he also lived.

Then they played Prince's "Let's Go Crazy." I listened until the end and turned the radio off as I pulled up to the school—formerly my own high school. It was the perfect eulogy. I've never owned an extensive collection of music, but I did have Prince's *Purple Rain* and *1999*. We all knew his music in high school.

I can't remember what else was happening, only that the song transported me to an ethereal place, and that the familiar title gave me the solution to the chapter I'd struggled to land: Go crazy.

And so I wrote about my own craziness, and it landed. Prince was right. We all want that permission not to be normal, even if normal keeps us safe. Secretly we want permission to thrive as creative people. Prince did that while living quietly in Minnesota. We knew him as ours. Even his signature color was Minnesotan. Our football team's jerseys are purple, and we're politically purple too.

The sky was all purple, Prince sings in "1999," and that evening the Twin Cities sky really was purple, including over my house in the Minneapolis suburbs. Crowds of Minnesotans gathered at the lit-up First Avenue, the concert venue where he got his start. They stood in the streets, crying and singing his songs. A mighty spirit had been released, and the energy was palpable. We all felt it. I wore a purple jacket to Open Book the next day. I didn't choose it consciously, but everywhere I stopped, someone asked me about it. We traded favorite Prince stories. I'm not a fangirl, but everyone has a Prince story.

A few days later, I had to drop Mira off at a Catholic school and church near Lake Minnetonka, where her best friend was putting on a play, after which Mira would sleep overnight. On our way, I saw a sign for a townhome development where Vivian had bought a unit following her divorce. I knew the name well because my parents had taken the property off of Vivian's hands so that she could move to Florida instead. We painted and wallpapered it a few times for incoming rental tenants, until my parents finally sold it.

I remember after Vivian signed the lease, how she said that the bedrooms were small. Sam was with me at Grandma Doris's house in the small bedroom I shared with Ellen, the one time I remember Sam being there. Sam and I agreed, small bedrooms were cozy. I hadn't realized where the townhome was relative to anywhere else, like so many details I hadn't yet placed. It's within a mile of Ellen's childhood home, where her parents still live. Somehow this detail felt important.

Once we got to the drop-off spot, Mira and I sat for a long time in the empty parking lot, surrounded by trees, wondering if we'd gotten it wrong. At last we realized that this was the wrong door, but it also dawned on us at the same time that we needed money. This was a fund-raiser for the school, and Mira's friend hadn't offered a ticket. This brought up anxiety for both of us because money . . . well, we worried a lot about money. Mira didn't want to arrive late, but more importantly, neither of us wanted her to appear cheap or less able to contribute. This friend's mom had treated Mira too many times.

GPS showed me a bank. Out we went, turning right out of the com-plex, back the way we'd come, past Vivian's rejected townhome, past my aunt and uncle's longtime neighborhood, to the bank. And then of course, we returned the same way, meaning I drove past each property three times. The kicker: There was a much closer ATM, which I saw as we returned. We wouldn't have needed to go all that way. Also signifi-cant: Mira arrived exactly on time. I brought her in and said goodbye. Leaving the church once again, I turned left at the exit and took a dif-ferent path altogether.

Once something repeats itself in my awareness three times, I pose a question. For example, what would Vivian want me to know? I was seeking additional clues. I'd know when I saw one. The Current was playing Prince, A to Z, and I trusted myself to find my way home along the winding, tree-lined road. This happens to me sometimes. There are messages for me.

I have an acronym for the process of unpacking the answers: Pose questions. Observe clues. Play freely. Simple steps. POPS for short. Then live into the answers. Here's what that looks like in practice:

After I dropped my daughter off at the Catholic church, as I drove that winding road through the trees, it occurred to me that Vivian almost settled for a good-enough life, but she didn't. It wasn't her dream. Against her family's better advice, Vivian moved to Florida, where the bedrooms were small and cozy, but she had the entire out-doors to inhabit.

She lived her dream. I figured that was the message. I didn't want to move to Florida or sell dresses—those were Vivian's dreams. But what did mine look like? Here in Minnesota? Being a mom, an aspiring author, maybe a life coach? Then something interesting happened. I arrived at a familiar intersection. I turned eastbound onto Highway Five, and traffic slowed to a crawl.

I realized that I was in line to pass by Paisley Park, where people were paying respects. It's a small white complex that wouldn't grab your attention if you didn't know what it was. I'd driven past there for years, but that day I couldn't miss it. People were streaming from parked cars like ants in Lake Ann Park on the north side of the highway. They filed into the underpass tunnel and emerged alongside the fence. They carried flowers and handmade signs to place there. Traffic had slowed so significantly that I had a moment to pay my respects.

In 1993, the same year I dropped out of graduate school, Prince abruptly changed his name to an unpronounceable symbol. It was a mashup of the male and female signs. If we needed a verbal name, we could call him "The Artist formerly known as Prince."

Eventually, the recording contract ran out and Prince reclaimed his name. And that's what I saw in Prince: a man who organized his life around his creative process, who grew up in Minneapolis and stayed in Minnesota because he chose to, who nurtured brilliance. Prince could pull a song out of thin air, given a few ingredients, whatever he had. Starfish and coffee. Raspberry berets.

That's what I needed to see. I don't know what everyone else admired, but I know that this slender, gender-ambiguous, lyrical, quietly religious, intensely mysterious Black man revealed glimpses of his authentic self as our local rockstar. We loved him.

Paradoxically, the more fully you ground yourself in the truest circumstances of your life, the more clearly people can see themselves in you. In this way, your life inspires them without your ever needing to know it. Without even needing to try. Without needing any person to be just like us. We all get to define ourselves. We all get to create from our own lives.

And even though it would take years to sort out my particular details, that was my first inkling of the life that I wanted to lead, in Minnesota, the day I knew that I wanted to be a wordsmith who created sanctuary spaces and opportunities for kindred writers. Together and individually, we would translate our lives into language that heals our burdens and changes our world.

The Veil Grows Thin

A college friend and I walked through the cemetery, six feet apart due to COVID. It was November 2020. Along our route, a flock of turkeys flew up into a towering oak, magnificent creatures like brown, dappled peacocks. Each perched on its own crooked branch, outlined against the steely blue heavens as if to confirm beloved spirits nearby, carried on lake breezes that wafted off Bde Maka Ska.

Vivian would be eighty, Grandma Doris would be 103, and I was fifty, each a product of our times. And also: Humans evolve, hope against hope. God willing, I'll show Vivian's granddaughters the aunt that I knew, my great spiritual teacher. And I'll carry forward my grandma's devotion.

The day early voting opened in Minnesota, Mom and I masked up, and I drove us to City Hall. Everything—forms, machines, pens, even the moistening bottles to hygienically seal envelopes—reminded me of Grandma, who reverently ran elections those many years. She would have done her level best to make sure that all of the ballots were counted properly. Any insinuations to the contrary would have offended her honor.

Grandma never would have voted for Joe Biden or any Black woman candidate, to be honest. But my mom and I did. Nevertheless, Grandma taught me the sacred covenant of the vote.

That same evening, near sunset on the High Holy Day of Rosh Hashanah, Ruth Bader Ginsburg, Supreme Court justice, passed on. Grandma turned sixteen the year RBG was born. It occurred to me that both women shared a tireless work ethic. Both listened intently and pored over words, getting them just right by burning the midnight oil after evening events. They were public servants, widows and wives, grandmas and mothers, separated by one generation. Grandma got to retire and RBG never would.

One beautiful thing that happens when our beloveds die—if we're lucky—is the way we look back, review stories, and follow the dots. When the veil of space and time lifts, we see how connected we are. In this sense, their memories truly offer a blessing.

From here, I see a progression that I never noticed before. In 1962, the year that Vivian married at twenty-two and started to put her first husband through school, Grandma became a primary breadwinner at forty-five with clerical work. That year, Ruth Bader Ginsburg, newly graduated at the top of her class from her second Ivy League law school, couldn't get a job in America, so she went to Sweden and saw how society could be better for women. In 1964, Kamala Harris was born.

Justice Ginsburg started her revolution—landmark cases with which she ushered in new ideas—in 1970, the year I was born. Her work changed the world. I wouldn't learn her name until the summer I left St. Louis, when she received her lifetime appointment to the Supreme Court. Because of RBG, I had options.

I chose to be a teacher. And a mom. I choose to publish my stories under my own name. My grandmother grew up in a whole different America. There but for the grace of Ruth Bader Ginsburg go I.

Grandma believed she'd been born at the greatest of times, and it would only get worse. She tried to make me a lady of her generation, and I was trying to make her a woman of mine. We left so much unresolved, so much unspoken. And in the end, the only thing we knew for certain that we agreed upon was love. She felt sorry for later generations. Perhaps she was right, if you value unquestioned white Christian male hegemony. That perspective loomed unbelievably large.

There's not enough mercy to change the past. I can't undo privilege received, nor sorrows endured. That's an impossible frame. I don't know what my ancestors went through. I'm not here to feel ashamed of them or judge them or glorify them. I can only tell truth as it reveals itself now. I can acknowledge what got me here, and repurpose those gifts in the present. It's my job to gather artifacts, and ponder their meaning for me, in this context. And create fresh meaning from there.

So I'll never join the Daughters of the American Revolution, nor another Christian Church. But I am from the Protestant, DAR tradition. I'll never be an impoverished child of immigrants, nor a starving artist. I do come from homeless immigrants who learned not to starve, who still believed in a greater good. I'll forever bear the markers of this inheritance. And there's this: Though I'm no longer a language teacher, I still teach through words.

There comes a moment when you know that life won't turn out as you expected, but you'll count the blessings in roles you once played.

> *Blessed be the Mentor, for she envisioned a life.*
> *Blessed be the Innocent Child, for she observed everything.*
> *Blessed be the Wild Woman, for she forged new patterns.*
> *Blessed be the Empress Mother, for she honored the past.*
> *Blessed be the Student, for she planted seeds for the future.*
> *Blessed be the Seeker, for she found other pathways to God.*
> *Blessed be the Puppet, for she gained wisdom from pain.*
> *Blessed be the Muse, for she will discover her voice.*

*Blessed be the Fool, for she believes with her whole heart that
we are all—each of us—infinitely more than one thing.
Blessed be the Witness, for she will question the lies.
Blessed be the Advocate, for she inspires remembrance.
Blessed be the Translator, for she knows connection remains.*

She ponders all that she's lived through and poses an open question: What does this make possible now?

This is what I do as a writer. I set out my shiny objects on the edges of bookshelves and ask for signs. They're only breadcrumbs, but I can make a full meal of them when taken together.

There comes a moment when one tiny artifact reveals everything. Remember when Dad felled the dollhouse at my request, how I found a miniature drawer with a gold-toned handle the shape of infinity on the freshly swept garage floor?

I would all but complete my first draft of a manuscript in progress, nine months after my chaos-and-fractals revelation, four months after I quit my career, before I had any inkling of what it meant. One early May morning in 2016, I sat at my computer typing when Dave opened the door and peeked in. He wore his standard Saturday T-shirt, jeans, and Big Sky cap.

"I'm going to help your parents pick up furniture for your brother."

"I'm going with you." The words were news to me as I spoke them.

He meant a dresser set, the only pieces remaining in a formerly vibrant family hub, Grandma Doris and Grandpa Hubert's condo, bought together and shared for two decades. When they moved out, I hadn't gone over, as a mother of premature twins who barely left home lest my girls catch a virus.

Then we had the real-estate crash. The condo became a rental investment and finally an empty shell, vacant but for a few staged pieces, now also gone. Mom had mentioned that it was finally sold, and only the dresser set for my brother's wife—or possibly his daughter—remained. Who knew what I expected to find? Regardless, I felt called to go.

When my parents pulled up in their dark-red station wagon hauling an open trailer on loan from their next-door neighbors, I pulled on my tennis shoes and hopped in the backseat. When we arrived at the condo building, Hubert's youngest granddaughter let us in at the back stairway door.

The hallways radiated the same faint chlorine smell as ever. The front door knocker echoed against hollow wood. Nothing lingered inside the unit, not even the persistent smell of dish soap. Only brass knobs. I took stock of leaf-shaped cabinet pulls and towel rings. I touched nothing, wandering from room to room, taking in blank white walls.

Dave and Dad walked back to the bedroom. I followed in my reverie. They hoisted the dresser and carried it out. Mom took away one nightstand. I grabbed the other when our husbands returned for the mirror. On the next trip upstairs, I picked up two drawers. And stopped. This moment filled me so fully, I can close my eyes, and I'm forever there.

I survey these full-sized duplicates of a much smaller drawer perched on the edge of my bookshelf back home, and I know why I came: yes, to retrieve this gift for my brother and his wife. And also, Grandma wanted me to know that this job matters, safeguarding family treasures. But she and I both misunderstood. We each must interpret these gifts for ourselves, according to our own path, according to our spirit's calling. That's how each individual contributes to the greater good of the collective.

It's not for me to know why my brother wants this, nor what it means to his family. Only what I make it mean. What you make of my story isn't my business. I'm the delivery person. That's all. I walk down the stairs and place the drawers in the trailer, then return to the empty apartment and gently pick up two tempered-glass nightstand tops, without fear of dropping them.

And I begin to sing in a deep, soft voice:

May the circle be unbroken. By and by, Lord, by and by.
There's a better world awaiting in the sky, Lord, in the sky.

I may have lost my religion. But I've kept the faith.

Live into Answers

For the longest time after I quit my profession in a highly public and traumatic way, kind people would ask how I was. After a while, people started to ask two specific questions, and they clearly wanted to hear fuller answers. That's how I knew that I was finally ready to write this book.

The first question felt like academic curiosity on their part: How did I get from there—a former German teacher—to here, a creative nonfiction author, podcaster, and book writing mentor? They weren't asking about my work per se, but rather how I healed the tremendous schism in my life to forge a different path. Which may have been personal to them, now that I reflect on it.

This led to the second question, more about them than me, I suspect: How does one write a book about one's own life? As an indirect answer, I've woven hints into this book's structure. There are twelve sections centered on a progression of archetypes, which are recurring symbolic roles that people play, specifically ones that I see in my life.

Within each archetype, four chapter titles introduce aspects of story-craft that can help you to trace your own narrative path. For this final translator section, I broke that pattern with five chapters. Sometimes we need to let go of our frameworks and see what happens.

Let me tell you a secret: There is no one right way to write a book, except to begin.

I've been writing to heal myself and my lineage for more than twelve years. Soon this second book will join *German Awakening* out in the world. These twin stories come from two different places on the same narrative arc. One book—an origin story—arose out of wandering mourning. One book—this one—comes from renewal of purpose. I'm sharing my lived experiences *and* I'm teaching people how to revision their lives through writing. Nobody has to do it alone, and nobody does it alone.

It's been seven years since I walked away from the classroom. The question of who I am—a constant companion—doesn't bother me so much anymore. And when it does, I now know how to listen. It's opened so many doors.

I've mourned and celebrated in equal measure, over the long term. My deepest, darkest fears—lack of language, loneliness, and uncertainty—turned out to be my deliverance and my education. Wisdom is not what your head thinks—so smug, so certain—but what your curious heart knows. This is a kaleidoscope world, where stories echo facets of truth. Over the last twelve years, I've designed my writing room where I go on retreat and work at this life every day.

This past fall, I moved everything around so that my desk would occupy center stage, rather than the cramped corner where I'd been hiding inside what resembled a makeshift cave. With Dad's help, I added gauzy aqua curtains and a paper pendant light by the book-shelves. I let Grandma Doris's velvet chair hold court in the corner, but after the novelty wore off, I felt constrained.

"OK, Grandma," I said. "Let's compromise." I emptied a mostly empty desk cabinet in the hallway. Dave helped me carry it down-stairs so that I could give it away. I brought my inherited chair out to the newly vacated space, and placed it beside a hollow aqua ottoman that houses copies of my first memoir. Atop that, I set a pewter stained-glass lamp to light my late-night reading. "Look at that," I told Grandma, sure that she could hear me. "It's our own tiny altar."

Where the desk once stood, I rest on the daybed and ponder ideas beneath the floral banner that I painted, and ruined, and restored, after a strange and wonderful encounter with Grandma. People see it on Zoom calls. When they comment on it, I talk about the messes I've made. I'm neither good nor bad in this story, I'm still learning. But I am already whole.

For the foreseeable future, Dave and I stay on here, happy together, happy that our daughters happily come and go from their colleges in the Twin Cities.

It can feel super scary out there. But when the fear-mongers spout their othering venom—not-so-innocuous strictures and shoulda-woulda-couldas—that's when courageous tender words, even in tiny doses, become a soothing balm. Our hard stories can be beautiful when we let them unfold.

Those trolls in our heads and out in the world? They're counting on our silence. Or frazzled drama. Maybe they don't mean to harm us. Maybe they even mean to help. It doesn't matter. Beyond their grasp, muses still shine a light. Our calm and centered voices? Powerful. Radical. Love prisms through us. And we'll locate places where we belong, learning the lessons that matter the most.

On writing days, life feels expansive. Messages reveal themselves as if planted for me: I walk in the shelter of birch trees and oak. Monarchs dance. Breezes whisper. I practically trip over signs. Milkweed pods breaking open. A delicate robin's egg shell. What else is possible? Witness an acorn. Hear a dove's cry.

That's the creative process that found me in that liminal twilight where I wandered, seemingly aimless, but never quite lost. When I dropped all pretenses (well, many of them) I started to say things nobody said in my circles: *I'm lonely. This isn't working for me. I'm ready to embody my gifts. I'm tired of status quo.*

Then, in countless quiet conversations, I discovered that many other someones were feeling it too. *I hear you,* they said. *I want to be courageous too. Let me share my version.* We've all walked close to the veil, some with eyes more open than others.

We don't need permission to love, to feel fully, to gather up stories like stones. Or seashells. To give them beautiful names and release them with joy. Let the echoes ripple around us. We are (and were) never alone.

The veil grows thin; a portal opens.

Enter. Welcome home.

Acknowledgments

To Dave and our daughters, this makes two books that I've written you into. Thanks for letting me. Love you, love you, love you.

To Eva, thanks for witnessing decades of history with me, for sharing your honest perspectives, and for being yourself.

With creative nonfiction, we write a composite of our lived experiences, including real people. To my friends and family members who appear in these pages, whether I used your real name, a pseudonym, or a nameless reference—or you were there to cheer me on, I'm grateful for your presence in my life. Thank you.

Thanks especially to the following people:

To Roseanne Cheng, you've opened so many doors for me. Profound thanks for being my books' fairy godmother.

To Saadiah Freeman, thanks for being a reliable compass whenever I've needed to sort out my thinking, find my words, or see the humor.

To Lisa Harris, thank you not only for affirming that I could use stories to teach, but also for showing me *why* that matters so much.

Acknowledgments

To Elizabeth Lorenz-Meyer, thank you for being my emotional support cat and beloved gracious hostess. You always bring the perfect finishing touch to a book launch, this time the house.

To Keri Mangis, thank you for your wise counsel as a fellow writer, and for helping me to get clear on what this book wanted to be.

To Paul Nylander of Illustrada Book Design & Craft, you've created a truly beautiful book that embodies the spirit of *Tiny Altars*. Thank you.

To Katherine Quie, thanks for being the writing partner and friend who's shown up week after week, month after month, year after year.

To Susan P. Thomas, you added the theological grounding that this story required. Thanks for showing up at exactly the right time to offer your patient reading and astute observations.

To Stephanie Walton, the conversations I've shared with you have helped me to know my sacred ground. Thank you for being my friend.

To Jennifer Hopeman Wood, I've always admired your writing. I'm so thankful that you were here to advocate for this book and for me personally as I navigated challenging themes.

To the writers who took the time to review my book and discuss it in podcasts, thanks for being my creative peers. It's my honor to include your comments and voices.

And finally, to Christina "Kiki" Kelley, my dear friend and this book's editor, you are Beatrice. Words cannot capture the dedication and love that you've brought to this project. Thank you for choosing to be the guardian for *Tiny Altars*, and for making this book's final journey to publication into a grand adventure.

With love, Amy Hallberg
January 2023